BOOGORAMA

Selected Articles, Speeches, Screeds, and Letters of Dennis "Boog" Highberger, from 1983 through 2018

with a foreword by Pat Kehde

@RtH*Le Press
Lawrence, Kansas, USA
2020

first edition, second printing

ISBN 978-1-7346381-0-3

Please address all inquiries to:

@RtH*Le Press
PO Box 1313
Lawrence, KS 66044
mrboog@att.net

Contents

“Although the Bible says Ye shall know them by their fruits, are the things we scrawl onto paper, whether written or printed, our fruits?”

–Johann Wolfgang von Goethe

“A life’s work held up to the light & no one will see it with the same reverence the author licks his fingers with.”

–mIEKAL aND, *Samsara Congeries*

This book is dedicated to...

my family and friends, for their inspiration and for letting me print their letters and tell their stories, and to Lawrence, Kansas, wherever you are...

Acknowledgments

Thanks to Donna Eades, without whom this book would not have happened, for inspiration, gentle editing, and French translation; to Tim Brown for digital magic and whipping this puppy into shape, not to mention Zoorafa and back cover photography; to Pat Wittry for faithfully translating my bad Spanish; to Tim Miller, for Stephen Gaskin quote research; to Craig Patterson, Mike Yoder, Richard Gwin, Shelby Schellenger, and Kathy Lafferty for photo hunting; to Tom King for an early review of the manuscript and wise advice; and to Beki Dickherber, Brenda Frankenfeld, Brendy Latare, Bob Cutler, Sue Ashline, Julie Green, Bonnie Blosser, and Teri Canfield for helping me make connections.

foreword

I have been lucky to have known Boog for almost forty years. We met when he came to work at the Information Center at the University of Kansas in 1983, where I worked too. I wasn't part of his circle of close friends, but we kept in touch. And we always had a lot to talk about when we bumped into each other on the streets in downtown Lawrence, or at the Community Mercantile, or at The Raven Bookstore, or at rallies and meetings. I got to be part of his successful political campaigns. The first one was for Lawrence City Commissioner and then as a representative for the 46th district of the Kansas Legislature. During all these years, Boog has always been a kind and attentive friend. I have watched him be a compassionate advocate and an insightful, smart, and well-read spokesperson for a variety of issues. And he is also quietly funny.

Boog shares his thoughtful, original, and exuberant writings in this book. He describes himself as a "gentle anarchist" and a "pragmatic radical" during his college years, he introduces the reader to the wild careers of Frank Harris and Ron Kuby, two KU attendees, and in a speech made to a rally for gun sense laws, he analyzes what the Second Amendment really guarantees for all citizens.

The last part of the book contains his letters to friends and family. The letters are delightfully surprising. His introduction to this section contains a beautiful ode to the pleasures of writing and receiving actual letters that are delivered at your door, in an envelope with a beautiful stamp. Letters, he says, are objects that can be re-opened again and again. Now we have this book, to open again and again.

Pat Kehde

preface

I'm still not quite sure what to call this thing. Scrolling through the list of "Subjects & Genres" offered by the program that assigns International Standard Book Numbers, I selected "Curiosities and Wonders" as the "First Genre" and "Literature Collections" as the second. "Mishmash of vaguely related scribblings" was not an option, nor were "Half-baked pseudo-literary collage" or "Narcissistic potpourri." ("What's a potpourri?" asked the Hudson Brothers of my youth on their short-lived Saturday morning children's TV comedy show. "Why don't you wait and see?")

This project started out as a collection of the few old articles and speeches that people have asked me about from time to time. It soon became clear that there wasn't enough material for a decent-sized book, so I got the perhaps misguided idea of fleshing it out with some of the hundreds of letters to friends that I have written and copied over the years. And so here we are.

This book is not intended as an autobiography, but I suppose it can't help being somewhat autobiographical. The real subject of this volume, though, at least in my mind, is Lawrence, Kansas—described elsewhere herein as "my dream, my burden, my home"—and all the wild and wonderful people that live here and have passed through here. I thank them all for teaching me things and keeping me entertained over these many years, and for letting me tell their stories.

To be honest, I think that including the letters in this book is a good thing for several reasons. First, they are contemporaneous with a lot of the other writings and help put them in context. Second, they are a reminder, for me at least, of how great it was to get real letters—physical things, with handwriting and drawings and aromas and unusual stamps—objects with histories, that were touched by people you knew and that came from faraway places that you hadn't been to yet but that you might someday—objects that you could put in a folder or a box and open up and read thirty years later, long after all your e-mails and text messages have evaporated into digital purgatory. And lastly they are full of quotes from inspiring and amusing books that I have read over the years that might inspire and amuse you as well, and they contain occasional words like "jazzetarian," "juxtapositionism," "uglyplex," and "nuck" that you might not have seen elsewhere before.

Narcissistic mishmash or not, I hope you enjoy this collection of scribblings, and I hope it inspires you to write some letters and make some speeches of your own.

I'll see you in the mailbox and on the street...

the Costume Party

The Costume Party was conceived on the couch on the front porch of the house at 1614 Kentucky Street, now the Olive House, in the fall of 1983. A group of us, some of whom lived in the informal cooperative house that was there at the time, had been doing political street theater on campus. One of us got the bright idea of taking that to the upcoming Student Senate election. I filed to run for president, with Carla Vogel as my running mate. About a dozen of us from a variety of backgrounds and orientations filed for Student Senate seats.

Although some of us were nontraditional-looking and we occasionally did show up in costumes, we were actually fairly serious. Among other things, we argued for changing the name of the Office of Foreign Students to the Office of International Students, shutting down the campus nuclear reactor, and ending the Endowment Association's investments in companies that profited off the racist regime in South Africa. We pushed for making the student government more inclusive—one of our posters was printed in twelve languages—and for giving the student government more real power over issues that affected students.

We ended up in third place when the votes were counted, twenty-some votes behind the winning coalition, which was fine with us. The second-place coalition, however, filed a complaint alleging irregularities in the election. The University Senate investigated, found that the election was "fraught with inconsistencies and ambiguities" (meaning that the people who were used to running things stuffed the ballot boxes), and voided the election results. To make a point about hierarchy (and just to keep people guessing) Carla and I switched places on the ticket for the rematch, and much to our surprise, we won.

Unfortunately, the format here doesn't really allow for reproducing our campaign posters. One of my favorites was issued in response to some folks who were calling us Marxists. (A few of us happily self-identified as anarchists, but our detractors didn't seem to appreciate the difference.) Anyway, the poster was titled "Are the Costume Party Marxists?", and it featured images of Karl Marx, Groucho Marx, and myself and a couple of my fellow Costume Partiers in a Woolworth's photobooth photo, all speaking in cartoon balloons. Groucho quoted Karl, saying "The ideas of the ruling class are in every era the ruling ideas... The class which has the means of material production at its disposal, has control at the same time over the means of mental production." Karl quoted Groucho, saying "You go Uruguay, I'll go mine." I quoted German anarchist Gustav Landauer: "The Marxists' materialist interpretation of life and history stands in the way of a new, better society." And finally, my colleagues concluded by admitting that "Of course we're Marxists—we've seen A Day at the Races twelve times." At the bottom of the poster is the Costume Party mantra: "After all, isn't this what higher education is really all about?"

The articles reproduced here both appeared as guest columns in the *University Daily Kansan*. The first, published before the 1983 Student Senate election, was our first opportunity to use free election publicity to inflict our wild-eyed idealism on a large number of KU students. The second, an article about the South Africa divestment movement from 1984, is more of a fact-based call to take action for social justice. Together, I think they provide a good outline of the Costume Party's pragmatic radicalism.

The Office of Foreign Students was eventually changed to the Office of International Students, and the campus nuclear reactor was eventually shut down, although I'm not sure either had anything to do with us. The Endowment Association eventually made some gestures toward divestment, and the South African apartheid regime eventually crumbled, although how much of a role the divestment movement played in that is still a subject of some debate. However, our legacy endures. The last time I inquired, the KU Student Senate was still using the hand gestures I introduced for communicating with the chair during meetings, about making motions and getting on the speaking list—so let no one say that the Costume Party did not make an enduring contribution to student life and governance at KU.

Process is important to the Costume Party (1983)

"An insurrection of clowns and gurus, in behalf of their strange, beautiful and transcendent sanity—that would be a revolution to match the need for our time." Words from Theodore Roszak.

Hello. My name is Boog. I'm a member of the Costume Party. So are you, if you want to be. Some of us are running for positions in KU student government. My name will be on the ballot as the Costume Party's candidate for president, but that's just because it was my idea that we run. We really don't have a president—we don't have any leaders at all. I believe that a just and humane society must be organized on the basis of freedom and equality. It must be built on the foundation of relationships based on mutual love, trust and respect. To me, this means that we must do without power and authority, without leaders and judges.

The Costume Party is an association of free and equal individuals of all different colors, sizes and shapes. Nobody gives anyone else orders, and when we make decisions, each person's voice carries equal weight. For us, consensus is not just another catchy name—it's a way of life. I realize that sounds utopian and idealistic, and it is, but it is still very practical. We do it. It works.

I'm not trying to imply that we all agree on everything—of course not. There is conflict sometimes, but that conflict is necessary for the growth we must go through to reach acceptable solutions to our problems. We have taken definite stands on what we believe to be important issues, but our "platform" is really the way we deal with each other and the way we reach our decisions. The process is as important as the product—our means will define our goals. We can't make progress toward a better university and a better society with a campaign based on power games and empty slogans.

We aren't running for student offices because we want power and authority -we want instead to learn and to grow and to understand. Authority is a zero-sum game, but understanding isn't.

Nonetheless, we do want to get more votes than the other candidates, and I think there is a good possibility that we will. However, I don't think that getting the most votes is the same thing as winning. If we compromise our values or moderate our desires to obtain this short-term goal, we will have lost no matter how many votes we get.

To see this diverse assortment of men and women, hippies and punks, Americans and people from other countries working together and finding their commonality and treating each other with love and respect, to see all of this has filled me with joy and a renewed hope for our future. We are all brothers and sisters. Together we can make it work.

The Costume Party invites you to join us as we work to be free.

South African apartheid thrives (1984)

I did not invent the boycott of South Africa. Organized resistance to brutally racist policies in South Africa dates from at least 1893 when Mohandas Gandhi began to fight for the desegregation of South Africa's railway system.

Nor is the fight against apartheid new to the University of Kansas. At commencement in 1979 a man was arrested for carrying a banner asking the KU Endowment Association to divest from South Africa. In a related incident the next year, this man had his wrist broken by KU police. Twelve others were arrested.

So why are people so upset about South Africa? Perhaps some background information will be helpful:

• All political power in South Africa is in the hands of the white minority, who comprise only 16 percent of the population. The other 84 percent—Africans, Indians, and "coloureds," or persons of mixed ancestry—are subject to the system of racial discrimination known as apartheid. Apartheid demands strict racial segregation. There are separate schools for blacks and whites, separate beaches, separate buses and trains, separate ambulances. There are even separate countries; by law black people are denied citizenship in white South Africa and are given citizenship in "bantustans," tribal "homelands" which most of their citizens have never seen. The bantustans comprise only 13 percent of the land in South Africa and are the most barren areas of the country.

• Black Africans make up 71 percent of South Africa's workforce, but receive only 29 percent of all wages paid. Organizing a black trade union can legally be punished by death. Written or verbal criticism of apartheid also constitutes a capital offense.

• Sixty percent of black households in urban areas are living—if you can call it living—on below subsistence level incomes. An estimated 2.9 million black children under 15 suffer from malnutrition. Per capita expenditures on education are eight times higher for whites than for blacks.

This litany of suffering and despair could go on and on, but it all boils down to this: Black South Africans are being brutally oppressed and the government of South Africa has expressed its intention to continue that oppression indefinitely.

So how does that affect you and me?

U.S. investment and U.S. corporations are crucial to the economic survival of the Republic of South Africa. The *University Daily Kansan* editorial of July 13 stated that "it is South Africa's economic growth that is breaking the back of apartheid." That is absolutely false—apartheid's back is not being broken. The wage gap between black and white workers is increasing, and real wages for blacks are decreasing. South Africa's economic growth is serving merely to increase the strength of the white South African regime. This will only lengthen the long struggle that is coming. Anything you and I can do to decrease U.S. involvement in South Africa will be beneficial to the people there who are fighting for their freedom.

All black South Africans must carry an identity pass in order to travel outside of their bantustans. Enforcement of these pass laws is made possible by the use of computers supplied by IBM. American companies sell 70 percent of the computers purchased in South Africa.

South Africa must import nearly all of its oil—U.S. companies supply 40 percent of it. U.S. corporations and educational institutions have almost single-handedly supplied South Africa with its nuclear power capability. Two billion dollars in U.S. loans bailed South Africa out of a debt crisis in 1974.

In an interview before his death at the hands of South African police, black freedom fighter Steve Biko said this: "The argument is often made that the loss of foreign investments would hurt blacks the most. It would undoubtedly hurt blacks in the short run because many of them would stand to lose their jobs. But it should be understood in Europe and America that foreign investment supports the present economic system of political injustice… If Washington is really interested in contributing to the development of a just society in South Africa, it would discourage investment in South Africa. We blacks are perfectly willing to suffer the consequences! We are accustomed to suffering."

But U.S. corporations aren't interested in social justice—they're interested in profits. According to Milton Friedman, the guru of capitalism, "Few trends could so undermine the very foundations of our free society as the acceptance by corporate officials of a social responsibility other than making as much money for their stockholders as possible." Let's not kid ourselves with any nonsense about free market economics—exploitation in South Africa is maintained not with an invisible hand but with an iron fist. And U.S. corporations help make it all possible.

It seems clear to me that the only way to justice in South Africa is through the immediate end to white minority rule. The *Kansan* editorial board recommends "evolutionary rather than revolutionary change." Things in South Africa have been "evolving" for almost a hundred years—are you asking the people of South Africa to wait another hundred years for their freedom? The Student Senate cannot end the suffering of the oppressed people of South Africa, but we can help. Thousands and thousands of South Africans have shown their willingness to suffer and die for their freedom. All they ask from us is that we refuse to share in the blood money, the profits wrung from their bodies, hearts and souls by their oppressors. All that they ask is that we no longer support the people that keep them enslaved. Is that really too high a price for us to pay?

the gentle anarchist

Because of its critical attitude toward capitalism, the title of *the gentle anarchist* was generally written in lower case. At least 15 issues of the magazine were published in Lawrence between 1984 and the fall of 1987. I was writing for and helping publish the magazine by the time the issue labeled "Vol. 2, No. 3" appeared in the fall of 1985.

"What is Money?" appeared in the last issue of *the gentle anarchist*, No. 15, which was co-published in the fall of 1987 with another local publishing project titled *Project 1313.* During the city commission election of 2003, someone found and circulated a copy of this article that someone else had posted on the internet. My impression was that most people who actually read it found it rational and reasonably well-written, and I think that electorally it helped me more than it hurt.

"Technology" was printed in *the gentle anarchist* No. 11. It was part of a series titled "Notes Toward a Statement of Principles," which was intended to summarize our positions on specific topics to be fleshed out in more detail later. As you might have guessed, that didn't ever happen. This article was directed in part toward the primitivist wing of the anarchist movement of the time, who argued that mankind's troubles ultimately stemmed from literacy and numeracy. To put it politely, even if that was correct it didn't seem like a viable basis for a progressive political program.

What Is Money? (1987)

Thinking about money in this society is like being a fish wondering about the nature of water. We build our lives around money, we live money, we breathe money, we swim in it like fish in the sea.

Millions of people spend (so to speak) 40 hours a week, 50 weeks a year doing nothing but playing with money—printing it, minting it, counting it, recounting it, taking it from here, sending it there, juggling it, smuggling it... sitting in offices in huge buildings making phone calls and shuffling bits of paper, adding & re-adding endless columns of numbers to make sure that they come out exactly the same... yeah, but...

What Is MONEY?

"I don't know what money is today, and I don't think anybody at the Fed does either."

- Richard Pratt,
Chairman of the Board of the
Federal Home Loan Bank, 1982

Money Is Inevitable

Money is not an accident. Neither was it the "invention" of some particularly progressive culture or clever individual. Money in various forms has arisen independently, in different ages and on every continent, wherever the local economy has evolved beyond the level of subsistence.

Wherever there is surplus, trade inevitably follows, and primitive barter economies progress almost inevitably to money economies, as certain articles of recognized usefulness slowly come to symbolize wealth and are accepted at a fixed value. In an area where cattle are the common form of wealth, money is born when a cow comes to have the value of <u>1 cow</u>, regardless of its size, weight, health, or other physical characteristics.

From there the process of abstraction continues: cattle come to be represented by tokens bearing pictures of cattle, the tokens evolve into coins symbolizing value in general, and on down to our own day where value is symbolized by marks on paper and the magnetic configurations of silicon wafers.

And the inevitability of money is clear even in the present day. Wherever national governments have attempted to impose worthless currencies as the means of exchange, black markets dealing in "hard" currencies have arisen. This phenomenon perhaps reached the peak of absurdity in the 1970s in Communist Laos, where the official money of the country was the "kip," but the only money accepted by the Laotian government was the US dollar.

The Soviet Union is the only country in the world where counterfeiting is a capital offense (so to speak).

Money Is Inequality

John Locke thought that money arose before society, and that <u>by its use people have consented to class society</u>: "it is plain, that Men have agreed to disproportionate and unequal Possession of the Earth, they having *by a tacit and voluntary consent* found out a way, how a man may fairly possess more land than he himself can use the product of, by receiving in exchange for the overplus, Gold and Silver, which may be hoarded up without injury to any one, these metalls not spoiling or decaying in the hands of the possessor. This partage of things, in an inequality of private possessions, men have made practicable *out of the bounds of Societie, and without compact,* only by putting a value on gold and silver and *tacitly agreeing in the use of Money* [emphasis added]."

Georg Simmel, writing two hundred years later, was not nearly so naive about the nature of money and society. Simmel recognized that money is "entirely a social institution," and said that "When barter is replaced by money transactions, a third factor is introduced between the two parties: the community as a whole, which provides a real value corresponding to money." Those who become "rich" are those who manage to monopolize big chunks of the social wealth for their own ends. Far from being a tacit agreement, this is done despite the sometimes violent resistance of those whose share of the social wealth is being taken away.

The division of labor in society depends on a money economy. And so does capitalism. It's very hard to extract surplus value in a system based on barter exchange. The growth of the state has gone hand in hand with the growth of the money economy—the emerging nation-states imposed taxes payable only in money, replacing taxes payable in kind and driving more and more people into alienated labor and the money economy. Like S. Herbert Frankel says, "a trustworthy, disciplined monetary system is indispensable for the free unfolding of the extended division of labor on which the growth of world economies depends... A reliable standard in which long-term debts can be expressed is indispensable for the growth of capital."

So capitalists didn't invent money... but perhaps we can say that money invented capitalism. For once money has been born into the world it quickly begins to recreate the world in its own image.

Chrematophobia: Fear of Money.

Money Is Midas

Like King Midas, money turns everything it touches to gold, or at least into <u>commodities</u> that can be exchanged for gold. Unique living beings become standardized <u>things</u>.

"Trade is the reduction and quantification of the world to commodity equivalents, the leveller of quality, skill, and concrete labor to numerical units that can be measured by time and money, clocks and gold..."

– Murray Bookchin

And as money itself becomes more abstract and divorced from concrete reality, so do the society and people that use it. As Simmel puts it, "The increasing replacement of metal money by paper money and the various forms of credit unavoidably react upon the character of money—in roughly the same way as in personal relations when somebody allows himself to be represented by others, so that finally he receives no greater esteem than is accorded his representatives... The idea that life is essentially based on intellect, and that intellect is accepted in practical life as the most valuable of our mental energies, goes hand in hand with the growth of a money economy."

Money Is What Money Does

Featured on the back of the Swiss 1000-franc note, the highest valued item of currency in regular circulation in the world, is a figure of the Grim Reaper.

Money Is the Secret Name of All Things

In many ancient cultures, to know the name of something was to control it, to have power over it. In the Christian Bible, Adam is given authority over the animals of the world when God allows him to name them. In the underworld of the ancient Egyptians, the dead had to pass through a series of gates to reach the Kingdom of Osiris, the Land of the Blessed. The key to passing through each gate was to know the secret name of the gate and the secret name of the gatekeeper. Today everyone and everything has the same secret name: MONEY.

Money Is White Sugar

> "What we call the primitive is a mature system with deep capacities for stability and protection built into it. In fact it seems to be able to withstand everything except white sugar and the money economy trading relationship; and alcohol, kerosene, nails, and matches."
>
> – Gary Snyder

Money is electricity: power stripped from its context and refined to its purest form. We have created elaborate networks for its circulation. We have devised ingenious instruments and mechanisms to let it do our work for us. It jumps through hoops at our command but it is no longer clear who is the master...

Money Is a Pyramid Scheme

It's highly appropriate that there's a picture of a pyramid on the back of the US dollar bill, because money is the original pyramid scheme.

Here's how it works: You go to work to help make something for the boss. At the end of the week you get a few pieces of paper that are a promise that somebody else will give you some stuff you want. So you worked all week for the promise of a promise.

But where did the boss get the money to pay you? Well, either he sold the stuff that you had already made for him (and pocketed his share), or he "borrowed" it. And where did this "borrowed" money come from? From a bank. And where did the bank get it? From somebody like you, who had some money to save, who wanted to wait a while to cash in their promises. So the bank gives the money to the boss, who gives it back to you. And all this works just fine, most of the time. The only problem is when everyone wants to cash in their promises all at once and they find out there are more promises than stuff. Every pyramid scheme eventually crashes, and when a pyramid scheme crashes somebody always gets burned. Guess who?

Money Is Shit

Freudian psychoanalysts equate money and feces. Ernest Bornemann says that "according to ancient Babylonian doctrine, gold was referred to as the 'feces of hell,' and Theodor Reik mentions that the Aztecs used to call gold the 'feces of the gods.'" Freudians also make a connection between money and guilt. Again according to Bornemann, "capital accumulation and indebtedness are as closely related as feces accumulation and feelings of guilt." Unfortunately Bornemann uses this sound base of symbolic insight as a jumping off point for some painfully goofy flights of imagination, as when he speculates that "there is no reason to assume that a desire for the private ownership of the means of production would have to persist in a socialist society with appropriate weaning and toilet training."

"Money is like muck, not good except it be spread."
- Francis Bacon

The phrase "money doesn't smell" was coined by the Roman Emperor Vespasian who had taxed the collection of urine because the ammonia it contained was used by the Romans to do their laundry. The Roman Emperor Tiberius feared that he was made of feces, and forbade Romans to enter public toilets with rings or gold coins showing his portrait.

Money Is A Disease

A 1972 report in the Journal of the American Medical Association found 21 different disease-causing microorganisms living on samples of paper money. 42% of the bills tested carried one or more of the pathogens.

In medieval Russia, there existed silver coins so small that it was impossible to take them by hand from a table. When transactions took place, the buyer emptied his purse on the table, the amount to be paid was separated out, and both parties then picked up their share of the coins with their tongues and spat them into their respective purses.

Money Is Freedom, Money Is Slavery;
Money Is Community, Money Is Alienation

Yeah, and money is a paradox...What money gives on one level it takes away on another. Money frees us to realize our wildest desires—money is pure choice—but at the same time it binds us to a system of wage slavery in which we have to sell our time to survive. Money strengthens our connections to our fellow human by tying us into a system of production that makes us all mutually dependent... but at the same time it cheapens and destroys even the most intimate of our interpersonal relations by reducing them to the level of commodity exchanges.

Locke celebrated the fact that "money... replaced the utter dependence on nature by a new dependence, a dependence on other individuals and on society." Locke looked forward to the promise of such freedom with an optimism that seems naive from our jaded 20th century perspective. As Frankel explains it: "Today we have more freedom but are unable to enjoy it properly; money makes it possible to buy ourselves not only out of bonds with others but even out of bonds with our possessions. We develop a rootless search for ever *new* things because money is our only nexus with them. Money's abstract power to command *anything* ultimately seems to command *nothing*."

And again with the paradoxes: while money as an institution may threaten our freedom and our sanity, in the short run certain forms of money work greatly in our favor. In particular, banknotes and metal money are a protection against the people who want to monitor our every motion. Consider this serious proposal from a lawyer who had a friend whose wallet had just been ripped off:

ABOLISH PAPER MONEY AND ELIMINATE MOST CRIME

Paper currency is the lifeblood of crime and corruption in the United States. Without paper money it would be virtually impossible for criminals and corrupt officials to profit from illegal activities. If all substantial transfers of money were recorded in bank transactions, nobody could conduct profitable illegal activities without creating highly visible permanent evidence of the illegal activities or of income tax evasion or both. With the chances of profit from illegal activities so slim, it is difficult to visualize large numbers of persons running the risks of imprisonment. Crime would be reduced dramatically to the point where today's police forces could effectively control it. Fortunately, technology has advanced to the point that today there is a substitute for paper money: a 'payment card' system keyed to bank accounts.

Each person wishing to spend money other than coins, which would remain in circulation, would be required to have a bank account. The bank or federal government would issue to each depositor a U.S. payment card similar to plastic credit cards. In addition to the necessary codings, each card would contain the photograph and fingerprint of the depositor... Every business establishment, including taxicabs, would be equipped with a terminal in which the payment card could be inserted... (and) make a visual display of the charge so that the customer could see the exact amount being deducted from his bank account... In the event the customer did not have the amount in his account the terminal would so indicate...

O Brave New World that has such people in it!

Money Is Faith, Money Is Power

Non aes sed fides: not by iron but by faith. This inscription formerly found on Maltese coins sums up a very important truth about money: that the value of every kind of money, including metal money, rests on trust. Money cannot be enforced, and money is accepted only when people can exchange it for a certain amount of real stuff at some point in the future.

This is perhaps an important point to remember in times of impending economic crises. In the face of short term economic upheaval, conservatives are correct to insist on accepting only gold and silver as "real" money, since they are relatively rare and can't be manufactured out of common materials by the government. But ultimately the value of gold and silver as money rests on faith and trust in the future, just like paper currency does. When the real crunch finally comes, it may be useful to remember that there are more calories in paper than in silver or gold.

And here we come to yet another of the paradoxes of money: while money depends on trust at the personal level, that trust ultimately depends on the power of the issuing authority. Our currency is backed not by the gold in Fort Knox but by the guns in Fort Knox. The value of money, whether gold or paper, ultimately rests on faith, and the value of the US dollar rests on the faith that the US domination of the world economy is backed by the US Army, Air Force, and Marines.

For several hundred years economists have recognized that our money has value "to the extent of our faith in a viable tomorrow." Thus it seems surprising that no economist has drawn a connection between the dawn of the nuclear era and the chronic inflation that has characterized the post-war economies of the industrial nations. Perhaps this can also help explain the willingness of both liberals and conservatives in this country to rack up huge federal deficits—what's so bad about stealing from tomorrow when there's not going to be a tomorrow?

MONEY

Money, get away
Get a good job with more pay and you're O.K.
Money it's a gas
Grab that cash with both hands and make a stash
New car, caviar, four star daydream,
Think I'll buy me a football team

Money get back
I'm all right Jack keep your hands off my stack
Money it's a hit
Don't give me that do goody bullshit
I'm in the hi-fidelity first class travelling set
And I think I need a Lear jet

Money it's a crime
Share it fairly but don't take a slice of my pie
Money so they say
Is the root of all evil today
But if you ask for a rise it's no surprise that they're
giving none away

– Pink Floyd, "Money," from *Dark Side of the Moon*

Money Is Information

Money is information—the only problem is that it's not very much information. Money talks, but it doesn't say much. In the wonderful world of capitalism, everything—and everyone—has a price, and that price is the only information that matters in the marketplace. For the marketplace to work, reality has to be simplified and standardized. As our everyday life becomes more and more characterized by exchanges, by buying and selling, many of the facts and observations about the objects in our lives become irrelevant and are no longer valued. Commodities have no history. There are no tenses in the language of money—prices are always now.

Interest rates, stock prices, and commodity index futures all provide information about the economy and provide clues as to how to most efficiently organize society's resources. But as with prices, lots of information is lost in the translation of daily life into economic indicators. Countless facts about millions of people doing millions of different things get reduced to a few bits of data which are interpreted by economists like Chinese mystics prophesying from the pattern of I Ching sticks—all economics is voodoo economics. Through their interpretation of the magic signs, the best allocation of economic resources is determined—but best for who? Priests who prophesy against their masters usually don't have much job security...

This development is an inevitable consequence of the increasing abstraction of money. When money becomes intellectualized, intellectuals control money and the economy. And, as always, the intellectuals are controlled by the governments and corporations that sign their paychecks.

And thus the productive forces of a society are organized to maintain the existing power relations of that society. Simmel again: "Money is thus one of the great cultural elements whose function it is to assemble great forces at a single point and so to overcome the passive and active opposition... by this concentration of energies. We should think of the machine in this context."

Welcome to the machine...

Money Never Sleeps

The speed of electricity approaches that of the speed of light, and today the speed of money is the speed of electricity. Every day billions of "dollars" race the sun around the globe. As one financial market closes, the dollars rush on to the next so that not a moment is wasted.

"Knowledge - Zzzzzp! Money - Zzzzzp! - Power!
That's the cycle democracy is built on!"
- Tennessee Williams

What Can I Do?

Raoul Vaneigem says that "a truly new reality can only be based on the principle of the gift." And many anarchists have argued the need for the abolition of money. But history has shown that money cannot be abolished before people's need for money has been abolished. Until we have created a society of the gift that is no longer built on a system of commodity exchanges, money will be necessary or perhaps even desirable. So what we need are some practical short term strategies that will move us in the direction of the type of society we want to see, and at the same time we need to create new monetary institutions that will reduce some of the more destructive effects of money in the meantime.

Burning money is always good theater, but until we have provided ourselves with a permanent non-money means of sustenance, doing very much of it will be counterproductive. Removing as much of our daily lives from the arena of commodity exchange seems important, since that's how the new reality will be created—by individuals consciously removing themselves from the old, destructive system. So freely giving and receiving as much as possible seems like a step in the right direction.

And while money is still with us, we need to place limits on the money we use. Instead of passively accepting ever expanding and accelerating forms of money like they were divinely commanded by some all-powerful god, we need to raise the awareness that money is essentially a social relationship and as such we have the right to collectively determine the nature of that relationship.

Some anarchists in the past have argued for placing time limits on money, such as issuing money that expires and has no value after a certain date. What seems more practical is to create new forms of money that are spatially limited—regional, decentralized currencies only good in a specified area. This may seem impractical, too, but experiments like this have worked in the past, and one such project is in progress right now in the United States.

Part of the benefit of regional or local currency comes from the fact that a banknote essentially represents an interest-free loan to the central government. On the Isle of Man in the early 1800's, citizens there replaced all the English money on the island with their own local currency, invested the English money, and in a few years had earned enough interest to finance the construction of a new public hall.

In the Berkshires area of Massachusetts, the SHARE (Self Help Association for a Regional Economy) program is currently making loans that encourage greater regional self-sufficiency in the production of basic necessities, and plans to soon issue a regional currency called "Berkshares," with a value based on the value of cordwood. Berkshares are designed to meet the criteria for an appropriately scaled currency proposed by Robert Swann of the E.F. Schumacher Society. Swann says that the new local currencies should be: 1) consistent with customary practices (i.e. taking the form of cash and checks and being compatible with common accounting systems); 2) redeemable in some form of real everyday value; 3) based on local production but tied to a universal measure of value; and 4) controlled by the community, perhaps through a non-profit bank. It's too early to evaluate the success of the Berkshares program, but in its first stages it seems to be a short but firm step in the direction of local autonomy.

Closing Benediction and Words of Inspiration

Capitalists understand far better than the rest of us what money does, but with rare exceptions they seem to have little idea about what money is. It's the same with computers—often the best programmers have little idea of how their machines are built. And Beethoven didn't know how to make pianos.

But here is where our opportunity lies. Only those who understand their tools can really control them (what happens to Beethoven when his piano is broken?), and only if we understand the tools that are used to control us can we fight back effectively. So, by coming to understand the reality behind the shell game & light show of the current world economic system, perhaps we can learn to build the hardware for a new way of organizing our productive activities that will build community instead of destroying it and will empower us as individuals rather than enslaving us and reducing us to cogs in an incomprehensible and uncontrollable machine.

"Go out and fight so life shouldn't be printed on dollar bills."
–Clifford Odets

Technology (1986)

To be human is to use tools. To be antitechnology is thus at some level to be antihuman. Although sometimes I, too, wonder if civilization is a good idea, this is mostly just tongue-in-cheek, pseudo-intellectual cynicism. As long as we're living and working in the material world we need to accept the fact of human civilization with all its faults and come to grips with technology.

Technology is not value-free. Although it would be too broad an assertion to say that technology determines social relations, the use of any technology is compatible with only a limited range of social relations. In a given society, the development of a more powerful technology than that currently existing does not inevitably lead to the adoption of the new technology and the displacement of the old. However once social conditions are favorable, the new technology will be adopted and it will alter its social environment to favor its own further development.

The level of technological determinism is affected by the prevailing social and economic relations. In a traditional society with strong social cohesion there is a relatively low level of technological determinism. In a market-oriented society with a money economy there is a high level of technological determinism. Thus the Greeks understood the principles of the steam engine, but treated it as a curiosity and used it only to create magical effects in their temples. Watt's "invention" of the steam engine had a somewhat different effect on 18th century England.

The development of the internal combustion engine has had an even greater impact. Mechanization of agriculture has all but eliminated the self-sufficient farm. The automobile has destroyed the city and the small community, replacing them with endless acres of suburbs filled with strangers alienated from their work, their environment, and each other. Television has effectively destroyed regional cultures. Modern communication and transportation systems are obviously incompatible with community. Like Wes Jackson says, "high energy destroys information."

The response of Amish and Mennonite groups to 20th century technology illustrates this point. The Amish and Mennonites are Christian sects characterized by strong communities and simple living. Most accept modern technologies but only up to seemingly arbitrary limits. Some groups, for instance, allow gasoline engines for powering stationary devices such as washing machines but not for vehicles. Some allow tractors but not cars. Some allow electricity in the barn but not in the house. These restrictions are reminiscent of religious taboos in some cultures, and seem to perform similar functions. These restrictions represent a refusal by these groups to submit to technological determination of their social relations. Amish and Mennonite community relations are far less mediated by money and commodities than those in the surrounding culture. They therefore retain enough community social control to set limits on their technology, and they have, for the most part, been able to maintain thriving communities while community has been eradicated all around them.

Technology that is complex beyond the understanding of the people dependent on it is a threat to freedom. Such technology disenfranchises people by taking away from them the power to make the decisions that affect their lives and placing it in the hands of "experts." Autonomy and self-management demand a technology that is subservient to its users. If you depend on something, you need to know how to fix it.

Technology that demands centralization and vast concentrations of capital similarly are incompatible with autonomy. Consensus and democratic decision-making work only in small groups. Mass organizations such as the modern factory demand hierarchy, coercion, and authority for their functioning. Many existing production technologies are capable of being organized in much smaller units than they are normally found today—from the beginning, centralized factory production was instituted not for economies of scale but to facilitate control of labor. However, some technologies, such as automobile production and nuclear power, by their nature demand big capital and centralized production and are thus inherently authoritarian.

Environmentally destructive technologies are the social equivalent of spending one's capital. If you live only on interest you can do it forever, but if you use up your capital it's gone and there isn't any more. Dependence on such technology means sacrificing the well-being of the planet and of future generations of humans for our own immediate material interests.

Thus an anarchist society must be based on technology that is simple, decentralized, and environmentally sound. In practice, this means that we must change the way we live our lives to end our dependence on coercive & destructive technologies, and we must also organize resistance to such abusive technologies. Examples of such practical anarchy include:

* buying more locally grown foods & organizing marketing co-ops for local organic producers

* riding your bike instead of driving your car & fighting the new highway project

* chopping your own firewood & fighting nuclear power plants

* blowing up your TV and doing street theater

The Luddites were right!

Disorientation

The KU campus magazine *Disorientation* was more or less a cross between similarly-titled publications at the University of California at Berkeley and other universities, and the *People's Yellow Pages* published at KU from the late 1960s to the early 1980s. While it had a definite progressive perspective, the KU *Disorientation* avoided opinion pieces and attempted to provide students with interesting and useful information that they didn't get at orientation, like quirky bits of campus and local history, how to live cheaply, and how to get politically involved on campus.

The first *Disorientation* was photocopied on 8½" x 11" paper and was paid for out of our own pockets; subsequent issues were the same size but were professionally printed and saddle-stitched, and were financed by student activity fees allocated by the Student Senate. The magazine appeared on a somewhat erratic schedule with a similarly erratic numbering scheme:

Disorientation 1	Fall 1985
Disorientation 2	Fall 1986
Disorientation 2½	Spring 1987
Disorientation 3.2	Spring 1988
Disorientation 4.0	undated (probably 1989)
Disorientation mini-zine	undated (probably 1990)
Disorientation 5-O	undated (1990)

Issues of *Disorientation 1-L* were distributed at the KU School of Law by the school's student chapter of the National Lawyer's Guild in fall 1990 and fall 1991, and another group of students published a *Disorientation* in fall 2001.

The magazine met with mixed reviews. In response to one issue, the *University Daily Kansan* said that "Impressionable young people have been given a very irresponsible publication for guidance." According to the *Kansas City Times* it was "a call to insurrection, of sorts." In its review of issue 3.2, the zine review magazine *Factsheet Five* described it as "Definitely not another boring school paper" and said "I wish my university had something like this." Our favorite KU publication, *The Plumber's Friend*, called it "Our favorite K.U. publication."

The last five of the articles reproduced here were from a regular series titled "KU Alumni They Don't Tell You About."

Strategic Shopping Initiative Proposed (1986)

Developers recently unveiled yet another proposal for a shopping mall for Lawrence, this one calling for an orbital shopping area located thousands of miles over the city. This "Strategic Shopping Initiative" (SSI) would rely on an as-yet-untested particle-beam transporter system for moving shoppers from earth to the space mall.

"Nobody wanted a downtown mall, nobody wanted a cornfield mall, nobody wanted a riverfront mall," said the architect of the new proposal, H.T. "Buck" Rogers of the PIO Corporation of Cincinnati. "So we thought, hey, why don't we just put the damn thing in outer space? Sure, it seemed outrageous at first, but so did tearing down half of downtown and building an ugly concrete bunker with a 6-story parking garage, and people still took <u>that</u> seriously."

The plan calls for 250,000 square feet of shopping area anchored by three major department stores. Two major retailers have already verbally committed themselves to the project, Rogers said, and a third has "extended serious feelers."

The mall would be placed in a stationary geosynchronous orbit at an altitude of 22,000 miles, directly over downtown Lawrence. A particle-beam teleporter facility would be built on the ground, probably west of the city along the route of the proposed Lawrence bypass, on land owned by a wealthy local developer. Shoppers would be dematerialized and beamed to the space mall overhead, where the elemental components of their bodies would be reassembled in their original pattern. "Just like in Star Trek," said Rogers. "You know, 'beam me up, Scotty,' and all that."

Rogers admitted that there were still some technical details to be worked out before the project could be completed. "The particle-beam transporter in particular needs further research and development work. We see this as an excellent opportunity for cooperation between the business and university communities. SSI could bring millions of federal research dollars into KU. KU could become a world leader in particle-beam transporter research."

Highly placed sources in the KU administration agreed that the Strategic Shopping Initiative could have great benefits for the university. One official said he thought that an orbital mall would be at least as good at attracting spoiled rich kids to KU as a winning football team, and probably cheaper to build. "Besides attracting more of the best and brightest students to an already overcrowded campus, this project provides an excellent opportunity for the university to use public funds to help line the pockets of wealthy individuals and huge corporations," the official stated. "After all, isn't that what higher education is really all about?"

According to Rogers, the plan avoids several drawbacks of previous mall proposals. "No existing buildings would have to be razed, parking problems would be eliminated, and property taxes would not have to be raised significantly to finance construction. We've already been in contact with people in the Department of Defense and the National Security Council. They are very interested in cooperating with us on this project. If we play our cards right this baby will pay for itself, while at the same time becoming a vital link in the defense of this country against communist adventurism. What real red-blooded American could oppose that?"

Lawrence Chamber of Commerce officials were enthusiastic about the new proposal. "Lawrence will be the only city its size in a 7-state area to have an orbital shopping mall," said Chamber spokesman Jerry Toebone. "Sure, there are some mossbacks and lardbutts who say that real economic development would mean creating meaningful work for people instead of more minimum wage fast food jobs and jobs in factories making Kool-Whip containers. These people seem to think that we should be supporting locally-owned small businesses instead of franchises and big corporations, respecting the earth instead of paving it over with concrete, and building a thriving local culture instead of importing mass-marketed junk from the East or West coast. There are always people who oppose progress. Did you know that there were people who even opposed the Wolf Creek nuclear plant—they said they thought it would be better to try to use a little less electricity instead of poisoning Kansas for the next 20,000 years. There are some people who just don't realize that this kind of thing went out of fashion 20 years ago. If we left things up to people like that we'd still be reading books, growing our own vegetables, and walking. You know, I've heard that some of those people don't even watch TV."

Mike Walnut, a mossback and member of Citizens of Lawrence Against the Mall (CLAM) denied Toebone's accusations. "I've watched TV before, and so have a lot of my friends." Barney Kominsky, a lardbutt and also a CLAM member, said he was glad that the city's "movers and shakers" no longer wanted to demolish downtown Lawrence. He said that CLAM still opposed any mall development because it would hurt locally-owned small businesses. "Besides, there's got to be a catch somewhere. Has Bob Buildings figured out a way to own outer space, or what?"

Meanwhile, in Washington, aides for Senator Robert Dole deny that the senator plans to introduce legislation that would allow private citizens to claim property rights to an altitude equal to half the distance from the earth to the moon. They pointed out that such legislation would conflict with existing UN guidelines on the use of outer space. However, reliable diplomatic sources say that the Soviet Union is also interested in orbital shopping and may be willing to concede changes in the existing agreements in exchange for strategic shopping technology.

Representative Jim Slattery said that he firmly supported any mall proposal that had the proper support in Lawrence. "Through their representatives in the Chamber of Commerce, the people have spoken. Whatever the citizens of Lawrence want to do to their city is OK by me. After all, this is a democracy, isn't it?"

The Turnip Crusade (1990)

One hundred years ago this fall, the People's Party took over the Kansas House of Representatives. In the elections of 1890, Populist candidates were elected to 96 of the 125 House seats, while their candidate for Governor lost to the Republicans by a mere 8,000 votes. At that time, US Senators were elected by state legislatures, and the Populist majority in the House still prevailed over the smaller all-Republican Senate. Longtime US Senator John J. Ingalls was sent packing and was replaced with long-bearded *Kansas Farmer* editor William Peffer. Peffer joined the five People's Party candidates from Kansas elected to the US House as the first Populists in the national legislature. Lame duck Senator Ingalls surveyed the damage and declared himself "the innocent victim of a bloodless revolution—a sort of turnip crusade, as it were."

A Revolution Waiting to Happen

Times were hard for Kansas farmers in the 1870s and 1880s. A six-year depression beginning in 1873 sent crop prices plummeting. A drought and a grasshopper plague the following year compounded the misery. Land prices boomed in the mid-1880s. New settlers flocked to the state and bought land on credit, while old settlers borrowed to expand their acreage. When the land boom went bust in 1887–1888, many farmers were left holding mortgages vastly greater than the value of their land. In the meantime, farm income dwindled to the vanishing point. 1884 to 1887 were years of severe drought; still crop prices fell while railroad freight rates rose. In 1889, corn sold for less than it cost to ship it to market. In place of expensive coal, most of that year's corn crop ended up in Franklin stoves vainly burning against the bitter winter chill and meanwhile, southern Kansas coal miners and their families were going hungry. To plant new crops and to survive through the winter, farmers had to borrow against the coming year's harvest, so that by the time the wheat came in, it all belonged to local merchants.

Many people came to identify the railroads and the banks as the villains behind this state of affairs. The railroads were the biggest landlords in most Kansas counties, having been given enormous land grants in attempts to lure their tracks this way and that. In addition, farmers were entirely at the mercy of the railroads to get their crops to market, and the rates, rather than following any law of supply and demand, always seemed to rise when crop prices were falling.

Banks had an especially tight grip on Kansas farmers because of the scarcity of money. The policy of the Republican governments since the Civil War had been to make war bonds redeemable only in gold—"honest money"—and to withdraw the war-era greenbacks from circulation. The result was a shortage of money and usurious interest rates that kept farmers permanently indebted.

A long series of third parties arose to battle these evils. In turn, the Greenback, Independent-Reform, and Union-Labor parties challenged industrial capitalism and its negative effects on farmers and workers. Each, however, had limited success. Kansas was a leading third-party state, but none of the third parties captured more than 12% of the votes in a statewide election—until 1890.

The Farmers Alliance

The People's Party grew directly out of the organizing work of the National Farmers Alliance and Industrial Union, the Knights of Labor, and other loose strands of the third-party movement. It is unclear how the Farmers Alliance first came to Kansas, but it is widely believed to be the work of the Vincent family of Winfield, publishers of a newspaper called the *Nonconformist* who were regionally notorious for speaking out in defense of the Chicago anarchists framed after the Haymarket massacre in 1886. Two of the Vincent brothers went to Texas sometime in 1888, saw firsthand the cooperatives created by the Texas Alliance, and brought the Alliance message back to Kansas.

The Alliance marketing and purchasing cooperatives were designed to break the hold of the bankers and furnishing merchants on the small farmer. Alliance lecturers crisscrossed the state, organizing local chapters, explaining the currency problem, condemning the railroad monopolies, and organizing Alliance encampments, to which the farmers streamed by the thousands to show their solidarity. As the Alliance swept across Kansas like a prairie fire, plans were made for a political party that would fight to implement Alliance demands. Members of the Farmers Alliance, the Grange, and the Knights of Labor met in Topeka in June of 1890. They adopted the platform of the national Alliance—which included the abolition of national banks, issuance of legal tender notes, and an end to grain futures speculation, reclaiming unused land from corporations and railroads, and nationalizing "communication and transportation"—and vowed to field a full slate of People's Party candidates for the upcoming state elections.

Although labeled by the Republican press as "anarchists," "communists," "misfits," "loafers," "calamity howlers," and "dastardly villains," the Populists won 96 of the 125 state House elections, five of seven seats in the US Congress, and would soon elect one of their own as a United States Senator.

The new state House of Representatives set right to work passing a host of banking and railroad regulations, and mandated an eight-hour workday for all government employees. The party leadership prepared for "the great conflict of 1892," when the People's Party would organize nationally and field its first presidential candidate. That would also be the year that Kansas would elect "the first People's Party government on earth."

Iridescent Dreams

The Populists were as radical a bunch as ever participated in Kansas politics. Congressman Jerry Botkin declared himself a Christian socialist. Lecturer Mary Elizabeth Lease toured the state urging farmers to "raise less corn and more hell." Frank Doster, Chief Justice of the Kansas Supreme Court from 1897 to 1903, caused a ruckus in 1891 by asserting that "the rights of the user are paramount to the rights of the owner of capital." Soon after becoming Chief Justice he announced that he did not believe in "hell fire, nor human slavery, nor high tariffs, nor the gold standard, nor in millionaires, nor in the wage system"—most of which were things dear to the hearts of Kansan Republicans of that time. Congressman John Otis said that Populism "takes for its guide the golden rule and not the rule of gold" and "holds the earth to be a common heritage of the people... Every person born into the world is entitled equally with all others, to a place to live and an opportunity to earn a living."

"Sockless" Jerry Simpson, Congressman from 1891–1895 and 1897–1899, argued that the existing land system was "robbery," and said that "Man must have access to the earth or he becomes a slave." But land was not just a political issue for Simpson: "The magic in a kernel, the witchcraft in a seed; the desire to put something in the ground and see it grow and reproduce its kind. That's why I came to Kansas." Governor Lorenzo Lewelling, at his inaugural in 1893, announced that "the 'survival of the fittest' (or the strongest) is the government of brutes and reptiles, and such philosophy must give place to a government which recognizes human brotherhood."

Brotherhood, however, was a scarce commodity in Kansas politics in 1893. In the bitterly-fought election of 1892, Populists won the governorship and took control of the state Senate. Both sides alleged voter fraud in a number of state House races, and the control of the House hung in the balance. Just prior to the elections of 1890, Senator Ingalls had infuriated Populists by declaring in a widely circulated interview with the *New York World* that "The purification of politics is an iridescent dream. Government is force. Politics is a battle for supremacy. Parties are the armies... To defeat the antagonist and expel the party in power is the purpose... In war it is lawful to deceive the adversary, to hire hessians, to purchase mercenaries, to mutilate, to destroy." The Populists learned this lesson the hard way in January of 1893, when the struggle for control of the Kansas House of Representatives nearly erupted into bloodshed.

The Legislative War of 1893

"Is the Kansas Trouble the Incipiency of a National Anarchist Uprising?" So asked a headline in the *Kansas City Gazette*. But Kansas was suffering from too many governments rather than too few. For several months two separate groups claiming to be the real Kansas House of Representatives met, debated, passed bills, and eventually prepared to shoot at each other.

Populists and Republicans each suspected vote fraud in a number of state representative elections. Both sides came to Topeka determined that the winners of the elections they questioned not be seated. The Populists wanted to bar the challenged legislators from taking their seats until an investigation conducted by the House, which, without the challenged legislators, would be controlled by the Populists. The Republicans wanted to seat all candidates holding certificates of election and then begin the investigations—with a Republican-controlled House. The day before the House session began, the dispute still was not resolved. That night Jerry Simpson told assembled Populist representatives that "you must take charge of the government. You must organize the legislature in this Hall tomorrow, and I wouldn't let all the technicalities of the law stand in the way. Call it revolution if you will... but see to it that you organize the legislature here tomorrow."

The next day, after being called to order by the secretary of state, both sides elected speakers. Two separate houses began to conduct business simultaneously in the legislative hall. Neither side dared to adjourn for fear of being locked out by the other side, so both sides camped out in the legislative hall through the long, cold night. The next day they agreed on a truce, and set up a schedule for taking turns using the hall. Populist Governor Lewelling accorded recognition of the Populist House, but the Republicans persisted because they expected the matter to be resolved in their favor by the Republican members of the Supreme Court.

The Republicans forced the situation on February 14 by ordering the arrest of the clerk of the Populist House. The next day, the Populists rescued their clerk, barricaded themselves inside the hall, and posted armed guards at the doors. The Republicans, led by future governor Ed Hoch, marched to the hall, battered down the door with a sledgehammer belonging to the Atchison, Topeka & Santa Fe Railroad, and chased the Populists out. Nearly a thousand armed Republican sergeants-at-arms and sheriff's deputies surrounded the hall, and the state militia set up their Gatling guns on the Capitol lawn.

A violent confrontation seemed imminent. Republicans refused to leave the hall. Governor Lewelling ordered the militia to clear the building, but the Republican militia commander refused. At this point Lewelling gave in. The Populists agreed to let the Supreme Court decide the disputed elections and to no one's surprise they were resolved in favor of the Republicans. Only eleven days remained of the legislative session, and nothing of substance was accomplished except the passing of a law guaranteeing secret ballots. The Republican press managed to fix the blame for the debacle on the Populists, and this was a major factor in their serious setbacks in the elections of 1894.

What's the Matter with William Allen White?

William Allen White built his national reputation on Populist-bashing. His 1896 editorial "What's the Matter with Kansas?" was widely reprinted all over the country and launched him into national prominence. In this tirade, White made it clear what Republicans, the decent people of Kansas, thought of the People's Party: "Whoop it up for the ragged trousers; put the lazy greasy fizzle who can't pay his debts on an altar and worship him. Let the State ideal be high. What we need is not the respect of our fellow man, but a chance to get something for nothing." White described State Senator John Leedy, the Populist candidate for Governor, as "an old moss-back Jacksonian who snorts and howls because there is a bathtub in the statehouse." Of one of the Populist congressional candidates he said that "we have raked the ash heaps of failure in the state and found an old hoop skirt of a man." Frank Doster, soon to be elected Chief Justice of the Kansas Supreme Court, was "a shabby wild-eyed rattle-brained fanatic."

Ten years later, the Sage of Emporia had changed his tune. Doster was now "a perfectly honest gentleman of unusual legal ability," and White attempted to explain his mistake: "Those were paleozoic times; how far the world has moved since then. This paper was wrong in those days and Judge Doster was right; but he was too early in his season, and his views got frostbitten. This is a funny world. About all we can do is to move with it."

And move the Republicans did, laughing all the way to the statehouse. As Doster noted in 1910, by that time the self-styled "insurgent" or "progressive" Republicans had adopted all the positions, other than railroad nationalization and the details of the currency reform proposal, that the Populists had campaigned for in the 1890s.

Forgotten But Not Gone

The People's Party vanished from the political stage almost as quickly as it appeared. The People's Party was the most successful third-party movement since the Civil War and was the last mass attempt to stop the corporate industrial transformation of America, but it has mostly faded from the public memory. Although Populism has been forgotten, it is not completely gone.

A few scattered individuals still claim to be Populists today—most of them are ultraconservative southern racists who have no connection to the historical People's Party and share none of its progressive goals. Still, these self-proclaimed Populists have helped spread the idea that the original Populists were similarly conservative and racist. This is simply not true. Although the Populist movement was indeed conservative in that it attempted to maintain a way of life that was being destroyed by industrial "progress," its solutions looked to the future rather than the past. This can be seen in the anti-capitalist and socialist ideas of many prominent Populists, and also in the Populists' attempts to work with the emerging labor organizations of the time. By today's standards, many of the members of the Populist movement were indeed racists, but the People's Party as a whole was probably less racist than its Republican and especially Democratic opponents. A number of Populist leaders were in the forefront of the campaign for women's suffrage in Kansas, although others opposed it bitterly. The Kansas Populists fielded black and women candidates for state office when the other tickets were all male and lily white. In this respect, the Populists were far ahead of many of the bigots who attempt to usurp the name today.

We're Off to See the Wizard

What may be Populism's strangest legacy has also proved to be its most enduring. One historian has argued that *The Wizard of Oz* by L. Frank Baum can be read as an allegory of the Populist movement. Baum lived on the dusty drought-stricken plains of South Dakota during the Alliance days and so experienced the Populist uprising firsthand. Perhaps it's not unreasonable to believe that Baum used the current events of his day as the seeds of his iridescent flights of fantasy.

Dorothy, the theory goes, represents the people, naive and innocent and just looking for a way back home, back to the simple life she used to know. The Scarecrow, of course, represents farmers, and the Tin Woodsman represents Eastern industrial labor. The yellow brick road is the gold standard of the Republicans, which in the book leads Dorothy and her friends to an Emerald City of false prosperity and broken promises—in Baum's book the city isn't really green and sparkling, it just looks that way because of the green glasses everyone is forced to wear there. In the book Dorothy's slippers are silver, and this represents the free coinage of silver demanded by the Populists. Perhaps the weak point in the allegorical theory is the identification of the Cowardly Lion as William Jennings Bryan, the Democratic candidate for president endorsed by the Populists in 1896. In any event, Dorothy's silver slippers and the Populists' silver coinage got them to the same place—right back where they started. Dorothy, though, had a home to come back to, and the Populists had only an industrializing corporate America in which they really had no place. When the Populists returned from Oz, their farms had been repossessed by the bank, Auntie Em was in the poor farm, and Uncle Henry had a job with the railroad. The Populists were among the first Americans to learn that there's a darker meaning to the old assurance that "There's no place like home."

The REAL Dollar (2001)

Welcome to the only city in the world where you can buy a locally brewed oatmeal stout with a three-dollar bill and get enough change back for a good tip.

Lawrence, Kansas, is one of growing number of communities around the US and the world with its own local currency. Lawrence's local currency, called the REAL dollar, is issued by a nonprofit community organization called the Lawrence Trade Organization (LTO), and is accepted by close to 100 local businesses. The LTO has issued bills in denominations of one, three, and ten REAL dollars, which can be used not just to buy beer but also to rent a movie, get a massage, or buy a sandwich, a light bulb, a pair of pants, a futon, or a bag of kitty litter—just about all the necessities of modern-day life.

The goals of the REAL dollar system are to encourage people to spend money locally, to defend Lawrence's unique local identity in the face of increasing cultural uniformity, to help provide economic opportunities to people left out of the recent economic boom, and to encourage people to think about what money is and how it works.

The REAL dollar system is modeled partly on a scheme that was used successfully on the Isle of Man in the early 1800s. The good Manx citizens wanted to build a community hall, but they couldn't afford it. Someone came up with the idea of replacing all the English pounds circulating on the island with Isle of Man notes issued by the community. While the new local currency circulated on the island, the English pounds were taken to London and invested. Within a few years the invested money had earned enough interest to pay for a community hall, and then the original English pounds were exchanged back for the local currency.

This plan takes advantage of the fact that every currency represents an interest-free loan to the issuing authority, and appropriates that advantage for the community rather than for the central government. Another way to look at it is that money can serve either as a store of value or a circulating medium, but the Isle of Man plan essentially splits the same money into two, so that it serves both functions at once. This is essentially the same as what happens when you write a check. From the time you write a check until the time it clears at your bank, the same money exists in your checking account AND in the account of the business that accepted your check. So every time you write a check you temporarily create money. Similarly, every time the LTO sells a REAL dollar, it creates money, but that money stays in existence for as long as the REAL dollar stays in circulation.

The LTO takes the US currency that it gets from the sale of REAL dollars and deposits that money in a local financial institution. Just as with the Isle of Man plan, the LTO's deposited money provides backing for the REAL dollars in circulation, and the interest on that money is used to pay the LTO's operating expenses.

The LTO can also create money through its no-interest REAL dollar loan program. The way it works is that the LTO makes small business start-up or business improvement loans in REAL dollars. The LTO works with the borrower to make connections with local suppliers who will accept REAL dollars and to sell REAL dollars to supporters, to cover expenses that can only be paid in US money. The borrower agrees to accept REAL dollars for his or her goods or services, and uses those REAL dollars to pay off the loan. These are loans that would not be made by a bank because they would be considered too risky or not sufficiently profitable.

Another less tangible benefit of a local currency is that it can turn an everyday anonymous transaction into something a little more personal. And every REAL dollar is a miniature local history lesson. The three-REAL-dollar bill features a portrait of Beat author and long-time Lawrence resident William S. Burroughs, with images of his house and his cat Ginger on the back. The one-REAL-dollar bill shows a drawing of Pelathe, the Native American man who made a valiant attempt to warn the citizens of Lawrence about Quantrill's raiders during the US Civil War. A portrait of poet Langston Hughes is featured on the ten-REAL-dollar bill, with the back of the bill showing a photo of Lawrence's Pinckney Elementary School from the time when Hughes was a student there.

You can get REAL dollars at the Liberty Hall box office (642 Massachusetts), at the Free State Credit Union at the Community Mercantile (901 Iowa), or from any store with the red REAL dollar sticker in the window.

Frank Harris (1986)

Attended KU: Fall 1874
Degree: None

H.G. Wells once spoke of him as "the best editor in England." William Allen White wrote that "the English language does not seem to contain the nicely tailored word to fit his character. Scoundrel is inadequate for it carries a content of courage. Scalawag won't exactly do. Its edges have been worn off. Bounder, which approaches slang, has a gusto and robustness that he did not carry with him in Kansas. To characterize him properly, I should have to tread the primrose path of etymological dalliance and pick up the word stinker for him." George Bernard Shaw called him "the Homer of Anarchism." Kate Stephens, one of Harris's Lawrence acquaintances (and, incidentally, the first woman to attain a professorship in Greek and Latin at an American university, which she did at KU in 1878), later described him as "a chimpanzee pretending to personal intimacy with Bernard of Clairvaux."

As editor of *Pearson's Magazine* and the *Saturday Review*, Frank Harris helped launch the literary careers of Oscar Wilde, H.G. Wells, and George Bernard Shaw. Harris is probably best remembered, however, for his autobiography, *My Life and Loves,* which has been described as "one of the most enduring works of pornography in the English language." After its release in 1925 it was immediately banned in this country and many copies of it were burned. Speaking from the bench, US Supreme Court Justice Levy denounced the book as "obviously and unquestionably obscene, lewd, lascivious, and indecent" and "disgusting and utterly revolting." Upton Sinclair, a friend of Harris, declared that "it is the vilest book I have ever laid eyes on." But that, of course, was 1925. Although such taboo subjects as VD, adultery, and premarital sex are discussed very openly and frankly, there is very little graphic description of sexual activity. While there is a healthy amount of heavy breathing and some fondling of breasts, anything beyond is left to the imagination. Today, a movie version of the book would probably earn a rating of PG-13.

Harris came to the United States in 1869 at age 14, after growing up in Ireland and spending several years in a boarding school in Wales. He worked for a month in the underwater caissons used in the construction of the Brooklyn Bridge, then moved on to Chicago, where he spent a few months as a hotel manager. Before settling down in Lawrence, he spent a year as a cowboy, driving cattle from Texas to Chicago. His last visit to Chicago coincided with the Great Chicago Fire of 1871, and *My Life and Loves* contains a vivid description of that event.

In Lawrence, Harris quickly made the acquaintance of Byron Caldwell Smith, Professor of Greek Language and literature. Smith introduced Harris to the works of Karl Marx, and fired his interest in modern English literature as well as the Greek classics. Harris later attributed the course of his subsequent intellectual development to his acquaintance with Professor Smith of KU.

But Frank Harris did more than study in Lawrence. His brother Willie, also living in Lawrence at the time, lost most of Frank's money in real estate scams that collapsed in the wake of the Great Depression of 1873. After that Frank had to go to work, first as a waiter at the Eldridge House. Later he held a job guarding money for the keeper of a "gambling saloon" (whose wife he seduced on a regular basis) and also made money by renting billboards and booking lectures and other entertainments at Liberty Hall.

Harris's enchantment with Lawrence faded after the departure of Professor Smith, who moved to Philadelphia in 1874 for health reasons. Harris reports that soon after Smith's departure, the University instituted mandatory chapel, which violated a provision in the University charter against religious teaching of any kind. When the professors holding the first chapel session refused to halt the service. Harris walked out, breaking down the chapel door on the way. The next day, "by unanimous vote of the Faculty," he was expelled from KU.

According to Kate Stephens, though, that story and many others in *My Life and Loves* are simply not true. Kate Stephens was Byron Caldwell Smith's lover during Harris's stay in Lawrence, and rates several favorable mentions in the book. Stephens declined to marry after Smith's death in 1877, and after the publication of *My Life and Loves* in 1925 she launched a campaign to dissociate the memory of her long lost lover from Frank Harris the pornographer. Stephens spent most of the last years of her life in this crusade and in 1929 published a book titled *Lies and Libels of Frank Harris*.

Harris spent the last years of his life in Nice, France, where he became close friends with exiled anarchists Emma Goldman and Alexander Berkman. He died on August 26, 1931, and was buried two days later. Nine people attended his funeral.

A copy of *My Life and Loves* can be found at Watson Library.

Don Henry (1986)

Attended KU: 1935–1937
Degree: None

Don Henry used to be a nice boy. Then he came to KU and got his head filled with all sorts of dangerous ideas.

Don Henry grew up in Dodge City where he was a "religious boy with a normal outlook," and "a Boy Scout 'interested in patriotic and religious activities,' with no Communist tendencies."

As might be expected, Don was exposed to ideas at KU that he hadn't been back home. He "grew solicitous for the lower classes," joined the YMCA and then the Young Communist League.

In 1936 Fascist General Francisco Franco led a military revolt against the Republican government of Spain. During the 1936–37 school year the *Kansan* ran numerous editorials endorsing the Loyalist anti-Fascist cause. Don Henry became interested in the struggle and left KU to go to Spain to fight the Fascists.

In Spain Henry served as a first-aid man in the Abraham Lincoln Brigade. He was wounded on the Aragon front on Sept. 2, 1937, and died the next day.

The Spanish Loyalists included large numbers of communists and anarchists. Henry's death touched off a red scare that shook the university and eventually the entire state.

Committees of the state legislature, the Board of Regents, and the university faculty all scrutinized the university for its potential for subverting the youth of Kansas. In a statement released in 1938, Dean Paul Lawson of the College of Liberal Arts and Sciences denied that KU had a subversive effect on young Henry, saying that "no official of the University is in the least bit communistically inclined, nor had any more to do with Don Henry's going to Spain than they had to do with his birth."

By 1940, however, the storm had blown over, since the university was "now making an outstanding contribution to the national defense effort" and KU students now showed "a wholesome attitude toward the principles of Americanism." The university would soon send hundreds of its students to die in World War II.

Harry Kemp (1986)

Attended KU: 1906–1911
Degree: Nope

During his days in Lawrence. Harry Kemp was known as the "Vagabond Poet" and the "Poet of the Open Road." Like Frank Harris, Harry Kemp came to KU after several years of worldly adventures, which for Kemp included a few years traveling around the world and a short stay in Elbert Hubbard's utopian colony in East Aurora, New York. Finally feeling the need for a more formal education, Kemp was drawn to KU after reading a German textbook written by KU's Professor William Herbert Carruth.

Kemp was enrolled at KU from January of 1906 through 1911. Although he completed the equivalent of a full course of study, he remained a "special" student throughout his stay at KU and did not receive a degree. In his words, he pursued his studies in "an intense but haphazard way. Doctor's degrees and graduation certificates did not interest me. I meditated no career in which such credentials would stand me in stead. But the meat and substance of what the world had achieved, written, thought—it was this that I sought to know." He spent endless hours in the stacks at the library, reading the books that looked interesting. That's how he discovered Paracelsus, "who whispered to me that wisdom was to be found more in the vagabond bye-ways of life than in the ordered and respected highways. That the true knowledge was to be garnered from knocking about with vagrants, gipsies, carriers... from corners in wayside inns where travelers discoursed."

Kemp's presence in Lawrence livened up the sleepy college town somewhat. Soon after his arrival in Lawrence he made a well-publicized walking pilgrimage to Emporia to visit William Allen White. On the way he encountered a howling rainstorm, and spent the rest of the night in a leaky outhouse, reading Keats by candlelight until dawn. Kemp claimed to be "a Socialist of the violent, fiery type—with a strong cast toward the anarchism of Emma Goldman," and during Emma's visit to Lawrence in April of 1911, he set up an afternoon tea for her at one of KU's fraternity houses ("The boys liked her," Harry later reported). Frequently Kemp indulged in bootleg beer with members of the same fraternity, and on one drunken evening in the country Harry and the boys ripped up a good portion of an unlucky farmer's cornfield before they realized what they were doing. Harry spent at least one summer living naked on an island in the Kansas River, and spent at least one semester as a fully-clothed model for painting classes (because "the farmers throughout the state were not yet prepared" for nude models).

Harry moved on to greener pastures in 1911 and achieved some recognition in literary circles for his poetry and drama. His most lasting claim to fame, however, is his dramatic elopement with Upton Sinclair's wife Meta later that year. She left him after a few months.

William Brevda, author of a recent biography of Kemp, says that Kemp's philosophy of spiritual development through the "Adequate Life" of the senses soon led to excess, and "Kemp began to need more and more wine to sustain the reality of his obsessive dream of immortal fame... Kemp ended as a failed writer who published his own books in Providence, Massachusetts." He died in 1960 at the age of 77.

Bernofsky of America (1988)

Sure, they tell you about Don Johnson, but they <u>don't</u> tell you about Gene Bernofsky.

KU Days

Eugene Victor Debs Bernofsky was born in Brooklyn in 1941. His mother was a "streetfighter, organizer, and soapboxer." His father was a "theoretician, scholar of Marxist literature, and musician" who taught at the progressive Jefferson School. He came to KU in the fall of 1959 with great expectations.

"I expected a place where I could do some serious studying," Bernofsky says. But it didn't work out that way. "Anybody with my kind of imagination had no place in the university—I found that out as a freshman... The universities in this country are more or less a sham. They are deadly places for young people who have any desire for improvement in society."

But there was a lot more going on in Lawrence than just studying. There were great paintings to be created. There were beans to be liberated. And there were flaming mattresses to be dragged through the streets. Also, Bernofsky says, "I spent a lot of time at the dish machine" while working at the Kansas Union.

Despite all that, Bernofsky received a BA in Psychology in 1964. After four years at KU, Gene and his wife Jo Ann set out "looking for a place to build a reasonable civilization." They went to Africa. After months of searching there, they returned to the US. In the spring of 1965 they founded Drop City outside Trinidad, Colorado.

Drop City

Peter Rabbit lied. Peter Rabbit's 1971 book *Drop City* told the tale of the life and death of what it described as "the first hippie commune," but according to Bernofsky, Rabbit doesn't quite get all the facts straight: "Peter Rabbit is full of shit."

Geodesic domes began to sprout out of the desert soon after the Bernofskys arrived in 1965. The walls of the domes were made from old car tops, which the Droppers chopped with axes out of wrecked cars in nearby junkyards. But Droppers couldn't live by car tops alone, and they learned to salvage all sorts of other useful things from other people's garbage. "We were living in a very poor area of Colorado... Everything had been scrounged over in that area... but we were the scroungers of the scroungers and we scrounged from the scroungers and carefully put together—we didn't have a cent—materials from all kinds of sources and that was part of our work." Buckminster Fuller awarded the Droppers his Dymaxion Award in 1965, and sent the Droppers $500.

Peter Rabbit came to Drop City after the Droppers had already been scrounging there for a whole year. His publicity efforts attracted lots of losers, seekers, and hangers-on. "Peter had no idea of what we were trying to achieve with the place," Bernofsky says. "He made it very public, while we were trying to live quietly and busy ourselves making things." Things started to fall apart as Drop City became famous. "We just lost control and it went in a totally screwy direction. There was too much anarchy and too much toilet paper... Whenever anybody wanted to take a crap they dug some hole somewhere and did it. And after a few years the place was literally covered with shit."

The Bernofskys left Drop City after the "Joy Festival" organized by Peter Rabbit in the summer of 1967, which Bernofsky describes as a "complete farce." They returned eventually to Lawrence where Gene received a BS in Education (in 1971), worked at the Post Office, and made movies.

Films for the Blind

"This is one filmmaker I can recommend for the blind." That's what Bucky Fuller has to say about Gene Bernofsky's movies. Many other people seem to agree, even if they don't know what it means.

Bernofsky himself would be the first to agree that his films aren't strictly conventional. "Whatever film is, it hasn't been explored yet... We're not talking Hollywood."

Many of Bernofsky's films were produced in Lawrence, including *1993*, *Postmaster*, and *Lawrence of America*. The latter two were among the films shown at the River City Reunion in September 1987.

Bernofsky's current project is a documentary called *The Big Open* and is being sponsored by the Rocky Mountain Film Institute of Missoula. "The Big Open" is an 11-million-acre area of eastern Montana (approximately the size of Belgium) with a population of only 4,000 people. The movie is part of a bigger plan to repopulate the area with wildlife and save it from the people at the Pentagon who want to add to the hundreds of Minuteman missiles already in the state. "We want to have the entire state of Montana become a park: Nation-Park-Montana... Others could be next."

Postslave

But film making isn't putting food on the table yet, so off and on for the past 25 years, Bernofsky has been working for the Post Office. He began as a clerk in San Francisco in 1962 (during a short break from KU), and later worked as a letter carrier there. In 1982, he began working at the Post Office in Lawrence, where he was not extremely popular with the local postal management. The feeling seems to be mutual. Bernofsky is currently co-editor of *The Ringknife,* the newsletter of the Missoula, Montana postal workers. On the cover of each issue is a picture of a strange, snarling animal that Bernofsky claims is the "mythological superhero of the postal worker... the beast comes in to slit the throats of postal managers... rips them right down to the jugular." He doesn't have much use for the national postal workers unions, either. "They dress the same, they have the same environment... they're in bed with management." Despite some occasional red-baiting (some fellow workers "will call you a communist to your face... people want to fight over it") Bernofsky says it's the local union rank and file that has enabled him to survive the post office all these years.

Onwards

From founding a commune, to making movies, to working in the local union, the common thread that seems to run through all of Gene Bernofsky's work is the emphasis on group efforts toward building a better society. "Positive group efforts may be the most satisfying types of involvement possible for human beings because things can be accomplished... it's a much more satisfying existence to get beyond lives of individual selfishness... The power structure likes and encourages lives of individual selfishness—that's why there are television sets in everybody's house."

Gene and Jo Bernofsky now live and work in Missoula, Montana. Their nine-year-old son Sam is in the 3rd grade, and David, 6, is in kindergarten. They don't have a TV.

Although the Bernofskys haven't lived in Lawrence since 1984, they still maintain close ties to the community. Their daughter May, 22, lives in Lawrence, and the KU Alumni Association still keeps in touch. Every few months a cute and colorful Jayhawk-covered message still arrives in their mailbox, even though neither of them has ever joined the Association. Gene seems to appreciate the efficiency and concern and says he plans to encourage his two sons to attend KU. "The non-influence KU has had on me I'd like to pass on to my kids."

As a concerned alum, Bernofsky has some suggestions. The first priority, he says, should be to open the Hawk's Nest cafeteria on a 24-hour basis. This could be financed by scrapping the football team and replacing it with coed intramural football. Second, KU should institute an "imaginative filmmakers program," which Bernofsky says he is willing to come back to direct, even on a trial basis and with a small budget. The program would help teach people how to use film's great potential to "stimulate and build people's imaginations." And because of that, Bernofsky says, "I can promise them that I will attract a lot of students for them," because that kind of stimulation is missing from most students' experience with the university.

"Life is a wonderful thing we have here and if we want to keep doing it we have to stimulate the imagination."

A Portrait of the Lawyer as a Young Maniac (1989)

As a lawyer practicing in New York City, Ron Kuby has learned the enduring value of a KU education. For defending the victims of a recent police riot there, Kuby received an anarchist punk record album and a T-shirt that says "WHOSE FUCKING PARK?" The slogan on the shirt refers to Tompkins Square Park in Manhattan, where his clients were arrested after police attacked a demonstration against the gentrification of a working class neighborhood. The record, *1933* by Missing Foundation, is probably one you haven't heard on KJHK, your sound alternative. The title alludes to the band members' belief that America right now bears a lot of resemblance to the Germany of 1933. They have trouble finding places to play because of the sometimes violent response to their music. They're Kuby's clients, too.

On the Road

Ron Kuby was born in Cleveland, Ohio, and lived there until he was 14 years old, when he was expelled from school for publishing an underground paper called *The Raven*. This was in 1971. Taking advantage of his new freedom, young Ron hit the road. He spent six months living in Israel, then came back to the US and kept traveling. "From 14 to 17 I mostly remember taking a lot of drugs," says Kuby. By this time some friends had started an alternative high school. He attended for a few months and they gave him a diploma.

On the basis of such impeccable credentials he enrolled in college in Cleveland in 1973. He quit a year later and hit the road again, this time ending up in the Virgin Islands, where he got a job working on a tugboat in St. Croix. While he was there, Kuby says, he developed "a serious interest in medicinal plants and ethnobotany." This is not just a cute way of saying he like to get stoned and watch the tourists. Kuby's interest in the way the local people used plants for health and healing would eventually become the subject of his senior thesis in anthropology at the University of Kansas.

Dancing Lessons

"Peculiar travel suggestions are dancing lessons from God." So says the wise man Bokonon in Kurt Vonnegut's novel *Cat's Cradle*. It must have been God talking when a friend of Ron's suggested that he and his girlfriend move to Kansas. Ron was back in New York, and was thinking about going back to school. His friend had just passed through Lawrence, and thought it seemed like a nice place. So Ron and his girlfriend packed their bags, went out to the highway, stuck out their thumbs, and waltzed right to Lawrence. He worked odd jobs to save a little money and started school in the spring of 1976, majoring in history and cultural anthropology. He was serious about school this time, getting straight As and writing a senior honors thesis inspired by his stay in the Virgin Islands. In 1979 he won the Bruce Merwin Award, an annual award given to the top anthropology undergraduate at KU.

"Ron always performed at the very top of the class, even in classes with graduate students," says Professor Don Stull, Kuby's adviser and thesis supervisor. "He's a model I think it would be good for many students to emulate."

"...the best of what a college education is about."

But Ron Kuby did more than just study at KU. Like any good student he was politically aware, but unlike most he acted on his beliefs. Stull appreciated Kuby's political involvement, and says that in no way did it interfere with his studies. On the contrary, his concern with social issues provided an important balance to his academic pursuits, and for Stull that made Kuby's time here "an example of the best of what a college education is about."

Kuby got a chance to put his beliefs into practice in April 1978, when former Israeli Prime Minister Yitzhak Rabin was invited to speak on campus. The invitation to Rabin angered Palestinian students who along with their friends and families had suffered at the hands of the Israeli government for many years. Throughout the day of the speech Palestinian students and their supporters, about 200 in all, demonstrated against Rabin's appearance. In the afternoon there appeared a lone counterdemonstrator—Ron Kuby, waving an Israeli flag he had made the night before. According to the *UDK,* Kuby said that he was there "to show solidarity with the Israeli people and to reflect a general American disgust with terrorism." After demonstrating for two hours, he was joined by almost 50 other students. In retrospect, Kuby is embarrassed that he opposed the Palestinian students, and he says that "if I was at KU now I'd be marching with them."

In contrast, Kuby remains proud of his participation in the anti-apartheid movement. KU had one of the largest groups in the country at the time, Kuby says. "We were able to draw three, four, five hundred people to rallies, which was phenomenal for 1979."

But the anti-apartheid organizers had unexpected help from unexpected quarters. Archie Dykes was KU's chancellor then, and according to Kuby, Dykes really helped galvanize folks on campus. "He could always be counted on to do the wrong thing in an exceedingly bumbling manner... Dykes was just crazy."

During Dykes's tenure challenges to freedom of expression on campus were frequent. A prohibition against distributing literature on campus was issued, and Professor of Religious Studies Tim Miller challenged this ban by handing out copies of the Bill of Rights in Strong Hall. He was not arrested. Around this time the administration "uninvited" educator Jonathan Kozol to speak at KU, apparently fearing that the wrong people would be offended by some of his controversial ideas.

This was the sort of intellectual climate prevailing when the KU Committee on South Africa (KUSA) arrived at Commencement 1979 with a big banner reading "US Out of South Africa." There was a swastika in place of the "S" in "South Africa," referring to the racist policies of that country's government. The KU administration was not amused. After Kuby unfurled the banner in the stadium during graduation ("my graduation," he says emphatically), he was arrested by KU police.

Not many people get arrested at their own college graduation, but for Kuby "it was better than walking ovine-like behind my fellow classmates." In an attempt to stir up more interest in the South Africa issue, KUSA sent out invitations to Kuby's trial that read, "You are cordially invited to witness the prosecution of Ron Kuby." Ron stayed on in Lawrence to be prosecuted and to work for Professor of Social Welfare Norm Forer, who had become involved as a mediator in the first Iranian hostage crisis.

So Ron was still in Lawrence for Commencement in 1980, where KUSA was out in force. They brought the big banner back this time, plus another one specially prepared for the occasion that said, "Help! We're Being Arrested!" And they got to use it, too. This time twelve people were busted, but Ron Kuby wasn't one of them—the KU police broke his wrist instead. "Orders were given that I was not to be arrested," according to Kuby. After everyone else had been taken away, he was left holding the big banner. "They could have gotten it away from me by tickling me but instead they broke my wrist," Kuby says. "The whole thing was handled very badly... the KU police were quite brutal." Chancellor Dykes was credited with encouraging the violent behavior of the cops, and members of KUSA immediately called for his resignation. Much to everyone's surprise, Chancellor Dykes announced his resignation the next week.

Kuby's differences of opinion with the KU administration eventually led him to a major change in career plans. Even though there wasn't much professional future in anthropology at the time, according to Don Stull, Kuby applied for a Danforth scholarship to continue his studies in that field. However, he failed to make the cut at KU, even though he was a straight-A student and had produced original research. Later he learned he was rejected because of his "condescending and arrogant attitude." On hearing this, his friend Jim Atkinson, a fellow bartender at the Catfish Bar & Grill (now the Rock Chalk), said, "Maybe you should go to law school—they like people like that there." So he did.

Gee, Toto, I Don't Think We're in Kansas Any More...

Cornell is different than KU, as Ron Kuby found out when he started law school there in the fall of 1980. "Cornell radicalized me a lot more...

I'd never been around rich people before. I'd never known people whose parents owned banks... In Lawrence you feel like you can just push them out of the way but at Cornell you realized that the only way to get rid of them was to shoot them." While in law school he worked as an intern for the well-known radical lawyer William Kunstler and after graduating in 1983 went to work for him full time.

The list of Kunstler and Kuby's clients reads like a Who's Who of this country's left wing, left out, left over, and fucked over. In addition to the Tompkins Square Park riot victims and Missing Foundation, their recent clients include Darrell Cabey (one of the people shot by subway vigilante Bernhard Goetz), the two Native American men who took over a newspaper office in North Carolina last year to bring attention to abuses against Indian people there, various Puerto Rican nationalists, a Japanese Red Army member apprehended with a pipe bomb in New Jersey, and death row inmates all over the country. They have been involved in the attempt to win a new trial for Leonard Peltier, a member of the American Indian Movement who was framed by the FBI and convicted of killing two of their agents in a shootout on the Pine Ridge Reservation in 1975. Kunstler has "represented the Yippies forever, since they were born," and that's why you'll often see Kunstler's and Kuby's names in the "Special Thanks" section of *Overthrow*, the quarterly magazine published by the Youth International Party in New York.

Despite the long list of clients, the staff consists of just Kunstler and Kuby, a secretary, a dog, and three cats. "The Kunstler operation is a lot more anarchistic than people could imagine," says Kuby.

Does it bother him that many of his clients have been accused of acts of violence and would be considered "terrorists" by most Americans? It hasn't yet, Kuby says. "We will always represent people on the left who have been charged with acts of politically motivated violence or other political crimes. There are a lot of attorneys willing to represent people who sit down in front of the South African embassy but not many people willing to represent someone who blew it up." So they push most civil disobedience cases to other lawyers and stick with the people the ACLU wouldn't touch with a ten-foot pole.

But they do have their standards—they recently refused to represent New York's infamous "Pit-Bull Landlord" who's in trouble with the law for siccing dogs on her tenants. On the other hand, one of their clients is an arms dealer indicted in the Iran-contra conspiracy. At first glance, this might seem inconsistent with their principles, but Kuby says they had ulterior motives. Like God is said to do, leftist lawyers work in mysterious ways—and so does the US legal system. And thus, as defense attorneys for the indicted arms dealer, they got to peruse great piles of classified government documents, including diaries kept by former US Attorney General Edwin Meese. For the most part they were pretty boring, but, Kuby says, "it was good to see it in his own handwriting that it was an arms-for-hostages deal."

Although many of Kuby's clients are political radicals and extremists, he seems to feel that he himself has mellowed out somewhat over the last few years. "Being a lawyer is a very reformist activity," Kuby points out. "In many ways I'm much less of a revolutionary now than I used to be." But this reformist still gets to see the law from both sides of the bars. He and Kunstler both managed to have themselves arrested again recently, while representing the Rev. Vernon Mason, one of the attorneys for alleged assault victim Tawana Brawley. A fight broke out in the court, they were "attacked by court officers," and they ended up spending most of the night chained to a railing in the jail. Later, after they were in their cells, Ron was asked if he wanted to speak with his lawyer. "I said 'yes,'" Kuby says. "I stuck my head through the bars and yelled, 'Hey Bill!'"—to Kunstler, who was two cells down.

Keeping On

Despite all the long hours and occupational hazards, Ron Kuby is satisfied with his life: "I'm one of the few people I know who's doing what he wanted to do." He plans to keep on doing it—forever, he says. And he still has fond memories of his days at KU, although he's a little bothered that he's remembered mostly as a rabble-rouser and a troublemaker. What most people don't know, Kuby says, is that he was a good student, too. "I worked very hard at KU. I graduated from KU with highest distinction. I had a 4.0 grade point average. I didn't like being treated like shit by the administration. I was one of their best students." Nonetheless he still appreciates the lessons he learned from his extracurricular activities: "Getting attacked by the police at a young age helped make me a better person because that's something that's usually reserved for Blacks and Latinos."

Still, he discourages others from following his example, by his words if not by his deeds. "It bothers me to see creative people go to law school," he says, but he doesn't sound convincing when he says this doesn't apply to him because he's not a creative person. Perhaps his deeper feelings shine through when he tells of a friend of his who paints, sculpts, and builds curraghs (a sort of Irish leather boat)—and has decided to go to law school. "I asked him why... He says, 'So I can do what you're doing.' What do you say to that?"

What, indeed?

Boog Highberger
KU Law School, Class of '92

Kaw Valley Independent

The *Kaw Valley Independent* was a biweekly tabloid published in Lawrence from approximately 1998 through 2000. I still feel very lucky to have been a part of such a great group of local journalists, artists, editors, and organizers.

"I Joyfully Carry My Burden of Dreams" was written for an issue of the paper with the theme "Why We Love Lawrence." I think I was nominated to write this particular piece because I had been in town longer than most of the rest of the staff put together. I finished the article in the middle of the night before an 8:00 a.m. deadline, and in my goofy, sleep-deprived stupor I included a number of suggestions for a possible title, including this one. My favorite, though, was "Lawrence: It's Better Than a Poke in the Eye with a Sharp Stick."

The other article in this section was an installment in a regular column titled "One Eye on the Law," which was a reference to bit of local lore involving the 1970 election for Douglas County sheriff. The story as I understand it goes like this: That year a local hippie ne'er-do-well and future *Boston Herald* sportswriter named George Kimball decided to run against long-time local sheriff Rex Johnson. Johnson was known to have a withered right hand, and Kimball campaigned with the slogan "Douglas County needs a two-fisted sheriff." Kimball, on the other hand, had a glass eye, which he reputedly from time to time dropped in other people's beers for amusement. Johnson's campaign reportedly responded with the slogan "Douglas County needs a sheriff with both eyes on the law." Johnson won.

I Joyfully Carry My Burden of Dreams (1998)

It's easy to get stuck in Lawrence, Kansas, but I'm here by choice. The more I travel, the more I appreciate all the things that make Lawrence the place I want to live.

What I love most about Lawrence is the climate. OK, I'm kidding. "May you live in interesting times" is supposedly an old Chinese curse. "May you live in a place with interesting weather" would probably not be considered a blessing either. Our interesting weather does have one advantage, though: it keeps the population down.

Lawrence will never be crowded, and our rents will always be low compared to balmier places. The climate also seems to have a screening effect on the people who pass through here: The ones that stay and are willing to put up with it seem to be a lot more quirky, creative, and independent than the national average.

And that's what I really love about Lawrence—the people who live here. It makes me smile just to think of them all: my housemates, my good friends, the people who I haven't really met but have come to know through osmosis—from years of walking the same streets, hanging out at the same bars, and going to the same meetings—and all the people who I have just admired from afar. I would like to list them all, but I only have 1500 words.

But, even more than the outstanding qualities of its individual residents, what makes Lawrence really special is the sense of community that we have here. While so much of America is turning into an endless sea of identical strip malls and fast food joints, and our civil society is being replaced by a multitude of Internet chat rooms, Lawrence still has a real, living downtown.

Unlike many other places, this town has not lost its uniqueness, its character, its vibrancy and immediacy. The houses in the old part of town still have front porches, and people actually sit on them and talk to other people who walk by on the sidewalk.

Downtown is a place where people live, not just a place people drive to, and when you walk down the street you meet people you know who smile and say hello.

Lawrence still has home-grown restaurants, some independent bookstores, an independent movie theater, and a locally owned and operated natural foods cooperative, the Community Mercantile.

The fact that the Community Mercantile still exists is a monument to the strength of this community. When a natural foods chain store came to town and tried to drive the Mercantile out of business, this community fought back. Many, many people struggled and made great sacrifices to save our co-op. And although we teetered on the edge of bankruptcy for a long time, we prevailed.

Lawrence is the first and possibly the only community in the country where a local co-op has beaten chain store competition. I am, and I will always be, proud to be a member of such a selfless and dedicated group of people.

This sense of community is not an accident but grows out of Lawrence's long history of dedication to social justice.

Lawrence was founded by people who came to Kansas to work for the end of slavery. The struggle for racial justice continued here in the 1940s and 1950s, and in the 1970s and 1980s KU students and faculty were active in the fight against apartheid.

Lawrence has long had a thriving and active gay community. Relations between people of different races, beliefs, and sexual preferences in Lawrence have probably never lived up to the ideals of its more outspoken citizens, but for most of its history it has been an oasis of tolerance and understanding.

Adlai Stevenson once said that "A free society is one where it is safe to be unpopular," and in that sense Lawrence is one of the freest places I know.

But Lawrence's history isn't only a history of struggle; it's just as much a history of love and laughter, of birth and death and madness and triumph and joy.

Sometimes all that history, public and private, is so thick it feels like soup, and I can almost see it and touch it and taste it as I walk down the street: this is the room where Cypress was born, this is the cemetery where Jakey is buried, this is where Don and Laurie were married with a passing jogger as one of the witnesses, this is where Bob Marley and the Wailers played, this is where B. and I made love the first time, this is the bar where the mayor worked, this is the funky basement kitchen with the giant cast iron stove where we cooked a thousand vegetarian dinners, this is where the first woman dentist in the United States had her office, this is where we used to go skinny-dipping on summer afternoons, this is where William Burroughs bought cat food, this is where we loaded the elevator full of bowling balls, this is where K. swept the floor of Off the Wall Hall after the Tofu Teddy show, reciting Green Eggs and Ham backwards, this was once the Forgotten Empire of Dr. Ling, this is where the Droppers dragged flaming mattresses through the streets, this is where the hill was covered with candles on the night of The Day After, this is where Jon Hermes was hit by a dump truck while riding on his bicycle, this is where Michelle Shocked went to a white bicycles meeting, this is where we used to play in the graffiti-covered concrete shell of the old Theta Chi house, this is where I've lived for twenty years, and this is my home.

Some people say the devil is in the details, but I think that sometimes it's just the opposite. The Lawrence I love is in the details, the nooks and crannies, the fine print.

I love the giant floating pumice rock in the Spooner Museum courtyard, the Birger Sandzen painting on the wall of the Kansas Room of the student union, Comanche (especially now that they're not advertising him as the *only* survivor of the Battle of Little Big Horn), the Icarus statue behind the aerospace building on West Campus (although I'm not sure the engineers think about it very much), the community murals downtown and at the Community Mercantile, the mosaic at the East Lawrence community center, the absolute perfection of the Free State Brewery's oatmeal stout, the big stone sign on the House building downtown that always makes me think of Rene Magritte (this is not a house), the rusting crane sculpture in Watkins Park, the "Love Thy Neighbor" sign my old roommate Pete made from a continuous bicycle chain on the side of our garage.

And as if that wasn't enough, in addition to all the people who live here and all the wild things they've done and all the amazing things they've made, I have come to love this *place*.

A lot of people can't seem to live without mountains or an ocean, but I'll take the prairie any day. Like Wes Jackson says, although these may not be his exact words, "Any fool can appreciate California. To appreciate Kansas you need subtlety and character and attention." Yes, and if you give me just a little attention (quoting loosely again, this time from Diane di Prima), "Baby, I can show you enough to love to break your heart forever."

Sometimes I am so stunned by the beauty of this place that it almost brings me to my knees: the unbelievably lush greens of the vegetation in the spring, the almost unbearably magnificent reds and yellows and browns of the prairie grasses in the fall, the indescribable dancing colors of the sunsets on the river, the humbling majesty of the summer thunderstorms, the power and grace of the eagles fishing in the river, the migrating monarchs, the wood of the Osage orange. I can taste the sweetness of the persimmons from the tree in front of Strong Hall and the banana-custard flavor of the pawpaws from the secret places by the river, the dark allure of the morels and the sour bite of the gooseberries.

I could go on and on: I love Lawrence because of Haskell Indian Nations University, which brings Native Americans from dozens of tribes to this place. I love Lawrence because of the Art Car Parade. I love Lawrence because there are millions of books within a few blocks of my house and because it is the only city in America symbolized by *two* mythical birds. I love Lawrence because all of my families are here or close by. I love Lawrence because it is my dream, my burden, my home.

I'll see you on the street.

Sex, Lies, and Legislative History (1998)

President Clinton, before he is hounded from office and consigned to the trashbin of history, should at least be thanked for all he has done to raise the political consciousness of the average American. Now many more people will keep in mind this handy rule of thumb: ALWAYS ASSUME THE PRESIDENT IS LYING. It was even a good reminder for a cynical guy like me.

When this Lewinsky business first erupted, I naively assumed that Mr. Bill was telling the truth, at least in a devious, lawyerly sort of way. Because of the definition of "sexual relations" used in the Paula Jones case, his denial that he had ever had sexual relations with Lewinsky sounded plausible. A person engages in "sexual relations," according to that definition, "when the person knowingly engages in or causes... contact with the genitalia, anus, groin, breast, inner thigh, or buttocks of any person with an intent to arouse or gratify the sexual desire of any person[.]"

Assuming that their sexual contact was limited to Monica performing oral sex on Bill, then he could more or less truthfully say that he had not had sexual relations with her. She, on the other hand, had clearly had sexual relations with him. This, as the Starr report notes, is a bit of a paradox, although it reminds me of certain couples I've observed over the years. As far as I can tell, nobody at the deposition asked Bill if Monica had had sexual relations with *him*, but we'll save the topic of legal malpractice for another column.

Of course, all of this legal hair-splitting will do Mr. Clinton no good whatsoever because he has lied like a dog. Or, as the Starr report puts it, "There is substantial and credible evidence that the President's lies about his relationship with Ms. Lewinsky were abundant and calculating."

But I digress. The real purpose of this is not to keep bagging on Mr. Clinton, well though he deserves it after all of his self-righteous finger-wagging, but to provide a clever lead-in to one of my favorite topics: the history of the Kansas sodomy law.

Under Kansas law, "sodomy" is basically any sexual act that does not constitute sexual intercourse. Kansas territorial law did not use the term sodomy, but forbade "the detestable and abominable crime against nature, committed with mankind or with beast." Prior to 1859, the sentence for a violation of this law was "not less than ten years" of hard labor.

Nowadays sodomy is defined as "oral contact or oral penetration of the female genitalia or oral contact of the male genitalia; anal penetration, however slight, of a male or female by any body part or object; or oral or anal copulation or sexual intercourse between a person and an animal." Sodomy is criminal when it occurs between persons of the same sex, between a person and an animal, with a child less than 16 years of age, or with any person without their consent.

So, for example, the acts of oral sex documented in the Starr report would be considered sodomy under Kansas law, but they would not constitute criminal sodomy. The cigar trick, however, would be sexual intercourse, which is defined as "any penetration of the female sex organ by a finger, the male sex organ, or any object." Any penetration, "however slight," is sufficient to constitute sexual intercourse.

Even without the cigar trick, Monica and Bill have committed adultery as it is defined in Kansas. Adultery is still a crime in this state and it is defined as "engaging in sexual intercourse or sodomy with a person who is not married to the offender," where the "offender" is married or is not married and knows that the other person is married to someone else.

Prior to 1983, the definition of adultery did not include acts of sodomy. So, if President Clinton had carried on his affair with Monica Lewinsky in Kansas before 1983, and if he had not fondled her genitalia or inserted objects in her vagina, then he could truthfully say that he had not committed adultery. Under the law in Kansas prior to 1969, an unmarried person could not commit adultery, and a married person committed adultery only if they "openly and notoriously" lived with someone who was not their spouse. In the good old days, Bill and Monica would both be off the hook.

Fortunately for you, dear reader, Bill did not go down on Monica, and so I will spare you the history of the Kansas legislature's clumsy attempts to fit cunnilingus into the definition of sodomy, amusing as that history is. My purpose here has not been mere titillation or amusement, although I hope you've had a little of both.

Instead I have intended to suggest that the standards of acceptable sexual behavior have varied wildly in different times and places. While some people still insist that the current standards are divinely ordained, history suggests otherwise.

Lying to people in one's own social group, on the other hand, has been almost universally condemned. That will be the real problem for Mr. Clinton when Congress reconvenes for impeachment hearings.

speeches

In my estimation, a speech is successful if one person remembers one thing you said one year later. I know that a couple of the speeches reproduced here have met that standard; about the rest I'm no so sure. I will take the fact that nobody remembers them as a good excuse for reprinting them here, although I understand that one could make a good argument for the opposite. The speeches that are included here were selected not because they were particularly earthshaking, but because they have a good line or two or because they provide a perspective on some bit of local history.

The 1984 convocation speech was given in Hoch Auditorium, in what is now KU's Budig Hall. In the absence of a photo, I should probably note that at the time I probably had more hair than all of the other men on the stage put together. The mayoral acceptance speech took place in the city commission room of the Lawrence City Hall, right after outgoing Mayor Mike Rundle's remarks in which he officially came out of the closet. The site of the KU Honors Program commencement address was the Crafton-Preyer Theatre in Murphy Hall on the KU campus.

I was honored to be part of the delegation that attended the 750th anniversary celebration of Eutin, Germany, one of Lawrence's sister cities, and to be able to offer the words reprinted here on behalf of the city at the Church of St. Michael in Eutin. The presentation to the Douglas County Democrats took place during my 2014 Kansas House primary race, and "Berning Man" was a rally at the Granada Theater in support of Bernie Sanders during the 2016 presidential primary season.

The March for Our Lives was a rally organized mostly by young people who were sick of gun violence and drew what looked like around 2,000 people to the South Park gazebo for a few remarks before a march down Massachusetts Street.

Convocation, University of Kansas (1984)

As you probably noticed, my name isn't on today's program. Although for the last several years the student body president has spoken at convocation, this year we were left off until I said something about it, and then we were told that they FORGOT to ask us to speak.

Well... we may look a little funky but we <u>are</u> the elected representatives of KU's student body and we expect to be treated with the respect due that position.

After we had been granted a place on the program, I started to realize what I'd gotten myself into, started freaking out a little bit, started thinking "Oh No!... now I have to get up in front of 2,000 people and say something that makes sense." If you really think about it, it's a pretty awesome responsibility... it seems like if you've got the attention of 2,000 people all at once, you'd better be saying something pretty damned important.

The first time I sat down to write, this speech came out quite a bit different, because I was thinking "Oh boy! This is the chance I've been waiting for for years. I can write a great fiery speech about the evils of capitalism and US imperialism, and I could tell everybody about the beautiful nonviolent anarchist revolution...," but then I changed my mind.

I thought back to the one lesson I learned in my four years at the engineering school here—they said it over and over and over so I'll never forget it, and what they said was KEEP IT SIMPLE, STUPID. So I threw away my first draft and started over.

In the traditions of the Hopi people there's a wise woman called the Spider Grandmother. Spider Grandmother sums up all of her advice on living into just two sentences, and what she says is this: First, she says, try to be good to each other, and second, try to understand things. That's about as simple as you can get.

I think it's important to notice what she doesn't say. She doesn't say try to get a college degree, or try to get a good job, or try to have lots of friends, or don't take any drugs, or be sure to look both ways before you cross the street...

She says just two things:

Try to be good to each other, and
Try to understand things.

I think the next five or ten years are going to be crucial in determining the future of this planet. I think that if we make the right decisions and make the right changes—and we here at the university are going to be at the forefront of those decisions and those changes—if we make the right choices then we may have a chance to survive; if we don't, we may not.

I think if we listen to the words of the Spider Grandmother and take them to heart and act on them, then we will make it.

Try to be good to each other, and
Try to understand things.

Welcome to KU.

Mayoral Acceptance, City of Lawrence, Kansas (2005)

Pardon me for quoting the Grateful Dead on an occasion like this, but what a long strange trip it's been...

There aren't many places in the world where an ex-hippie-anarchist with a physical disability **and** an unusual nickname can get elected mayor, but as we have just demonstrated, such a thing is possible in Lawrence, Kansas, and that's one of the reasons I love this place so much. Lawrence was founded by people who came to Kansas to fight against slavery, and tolerance and diversity have long been very important values here. I am honored to have the opportunity to serve as mayor of a community that has such a long history of fighting for justice, and I am proud to be a citizen of the only place in Kansas that stood up last week and said NO to writing discrimination into our state constitution.

I would like to congratulate my fellow commissioners on their swearing-in. As I've said before, it's better to be sworn in than sworn at—the beauty of this job is that you get both. We have an amazing depth of experience on our current commission—my fellow commissioners have between them 22 years of city commission service, 4 years of service on the county commission, and 4 mayoral terms. I suppose it's not that surprising to have 3 former mayors on the commission—as I've heard Commissioner Dunfield say from time to time, "Throw a rock on Massachusetts Street and you'll hit a former mayor." The first time I heard that I was kind of shocked—I thought, "You mean they keep throwing things at you even **after** you're mayor?" I don't think that's exactly what he meant, and I'm sure that won't be true in his case. David, I would like to thank you for your six years of service on the commission, and for being well-reasoned and articulate so I didn't have to be. We will miss you, but you have certainly earned some time off.

Mike Rundle—What can I say? I really admire your commitment and dedication to this city. You have been a very thoughtful and energetic and responsive mayor, and it will be a hard act to follow.

Sue Hack—Getting to know you has been one of the real pleasures of my first two years on the commission and I look forward to working with you for a few more years. I really appreciate your attention to making sure that people get recognized for a job well done.

Mr. Schauner—we don't agree on *everything,* but I very much appreciate your commitment to Lawrence's neighborhoods, and I'm very glad that you are back to join us.

Mike Amyx—I also admire your longstanding dedication to this community and your willingness to serve on the commission again, even though you have a good idea of what you are getting yourself into. I look forward to having more conversations with you where you're not talking to the back of my head.

Before I go any farther I would like to introduce a few people who are very important in my life. First, the woman without whom none of this would be possible, my mother, Norma Highberger. My sister Deanna Hattemer is here, with her husband Terry Hattemer, and their sons, my nephews, Alex and Travis Hattemer. My uncle Gene Highberger is here. Gene is a county commissioner in Anderson County, the other half of the Highberger political dynasty. I figured if the Kennedys can do it and the Bushes can do it, why not us? And my housemates Brenda Frankenfeld and Mike McKinney and their children Cypress, Estrella, and Oliver. I see quite a few other people out there that I'd like to introduce, but I think we'd all like to get out of here tonight, so I'll stop, but not before thanking John Thompson in advance for providing the accordion music for our reception later tonight.

I try not to make promises I can't keep, but I will promise that it's going to be an interesting year. During my term as mayor, I intend to resolve the question of the South Lawrence Trafficway. I think the outline of a solution to this problem has been clear for a long time—what we need is the will on behalf of all the parties to sit down together and come to an agreement. With the Kansas Department of Transportation getting ready to start construction of a 4-lane US-59 coming into South Lawrence, and with plans for K-10 to be expanded into 6 or even 8 lanes in the east, those who have opposed the trafficway I think will agree that the no-build option is no longer a viable alternative for our future. Conversely, those who support the trafficway need to accept that this road will not be built through the Baker Wetlands or next to Haskell Indian Nations University. In the very near future I will convene a meeting of all the stakeholders to identify a route for a southern connection between US-59 and K-10 that will meet our traffic needs for the next generation over a route that has the least possible environmental and social impacts. Unfortunately, that's the easy part. The real challenge will be to find a way to pay for it. But I am convinced that if we can identify a route that is acceptable to a broad majority of the community that we can find creative and innovative ways to obtain the funding to make it happen.

During my term as mayor we will complete the adoption of our new zoning and subdivision codes, and will move toward adopting new rules that will allow traditional neighborhood development to happen again in

Lawrence. We will continue to take steps to make sure that the city leads the process of growth in our community, rather than just responding to proposals for disconnected strip malls and subdivisions. We will encourage the building of neighborhoods with a sense of place, neighborhoods that are designed to foster a sense of community, neighborhoods with a mix of people of different backgrounds and incomes, neighborhoods where you don't have to drive a car to meet all your daily needs, neighborhoods where your children can safely walk or ride their bicycles to school and to the park, and, last but not least, neighborhoods where we won't have to come back in a few years and install traffic calming devices.

During my term as mayor, I intend to initiate a community visioning process that will bring together people from all parts of this city, to work on healing some of our longstanding divisions, and to identify the values that we share as a community, not just to talk about what we want Lawrence to look like, but what we want Lawrence to be. I see this community visioning as building on a number of efforts that are already underway, such as the civility workshops organized by Leadership Lawrence, and the Community Housing Assessment Team project that will be taking place here in May. My goal is that the process itself will help bring us together as a community, and the outcome will help guide our local decisionmakers as we continue to balance increasingly greater demands for limited resources.

We will also continue the work that the previous commission has started. We will implement the recommendations of Mayor Rundle's Homelessness Task Force and move toward a comprehensive approach to addressing the problem of homelessness in our community. We will implement excise taxes to pay for the cost of new growth as recommended by the Public Improvements Task Force chaired by Commissioner Dunfield. We will implement the recommendations of the Business Retention Task Force chaired by Commissioner Hack. We will move toward identification of a site and approval of plans for an expanded downtown library as championed by Commissioner Schauner. We will continue the process of identifying land for industrial growth and open space preservation as recommended by the ECO2 committee. We will expand our efforts to work with KU and the Chamber of Commerce to create and attract bioscience jobs in Douglas County. We will, I hope, establish a stable long-term funding source for after-school programs in Lawrence. We will address the problem of affordable housing in Lawrence, and will work toward the goal of making it possible for everyone who works in Lawrence to be able to live in Lawrence. We will continue to work on improving the facilities for the Lawrence Farmer's Market and continue work on the Burroughs Creek Rail Trail. We will continue to do our best to provide excellent city services, and to improve our budgeting for the long-term maintenance of city streets and other city facilities. (I'm not sure what we're going to do with our spare time, but I'm sure we'll think of something.)

As you can see, we've got a lot on our plate, but thanks to our hardworking and dedicated city staff we will be able to move forward on all these projects and more. I think that this is an exciting time to be in Lawrence, and again, I am humbled and honored to be your mayor this year. I look forward to working with all of you, and I remain confident that together we can and we will build a city that our grandchildren will love.

Thank you.

Commencement, KU Honors Program (2006)

Thank you, Stan, for that overly detailed introduction. It's an honor to be here today.

Now I generally don't like it when people start out a speech by talking about their speech, and how they didn't know what to say or how bad they are at public speaking, etc.—I usually wish they would just get on with it—but I'm going to do that today anyway. However, I'm going to couch at least part of it in the form of Advice to the Graduates as a lame attempt to make it OK.

It wasn't until after I agreed to do this that Sandra told me that the previous two speakers had been State Senator David Adkins and Board of Regents Executive Director Reggie Robinson. I don't know if any of you have heard David or Reggie speak, but if you have you'll know that I am way out of my league here. I'm not as funny as David Adkins and I'm not as smart as Reggie Robinson, but you're stuck with me today so we'll have to make do.

So here's the advice part: I expect that a lot of you will be going into public service at some point in your life, and I expect that a lot of you aren't any more fond of public speaking than I am. So here's what I advise: if you can't get out of it, try to do a good enough job that you don't completely embarrass yourself, but not so good that they'll invite you back. And that's the window we're shooting for here today...

I would like to congratulate you for completing the honors program. It's a good thing you're smart, because you are going to need to be. Every generation faces challenges, but the way things are shaping up it looks like your generation is going to have a very full plate.

There is growing evidence that world oil production has peaked or is about to peak, at the same time that global demand is rising. You will be faced with the consequences of global warming—but, on a reassuring note, I expect that many of you noticed that this week the House of Representatives took a bold step to protect the public by voting that global warming isn't happening. You will be faced with even further manifestations of what I have taken to calling "Boog's Law" (but please don't quote that, because I may well have inadvertently stolen this from somebody). Anyway, what I call Boog's Law is the observation that any increase in speed or convenience of any form of communication or transportation increases the time we spend engaging in that activity and decreases the quality of the experience. Now, this could be the subject of a whole long lecture, but in case you are having trouble with the concept, just think back to how great e-mail was—for the first week or two. Or think back to your most recent cell phone conversation...

All that aside, I think that one of the most serious challenges facing you is the widening gap in incomes and possibilities between the various segments of our society, and the increasing social polarization that has come with it. I don't know if Thomas Frank was an honors program graduate, but I think his book *What's the Matter with Kansas?* did a good job of analyzing this problem. The polarization we're seeing isn't so much between Republicans and Democrats, rich and poor, right and left, as it is between people who value learning and education and those who mistrust or resent or feel disrespected by educated people.

I'm not sure that it's fair that Kansas has become a poster child for this, because it's happening all over the country. And it isn't necessarily a new phenomenon, as Richard Hofstadter has documented so well in his classic study *Anti-Intellectualism in American Life.* And although this conflict has probably always been with us on some level, the current climate is a dramatic change from the Kansas I grew up in. The great majority of the people in this state used to be willing to make sacrifices to ensure that their children got a good education. My father was a mechanic, and I think on some level he didn't really trust anybody who didn't work with their hands, but at the same time it was taken for granted that my sister and I would go to college. So I still have that tension between idealism and practicality in my head (which probably explains why I ended up in engineering and law), and I suspect that a number of you graduating today have had comparable experiences.

And that's good, because your job—one of your jobs, anyway—will be to bridge that gap, and to help build a society where we're all in it together, where everyone benefits from the education you have received, rather than one where your education just secures you a privileged position in an increasingly polarized world.

Will it be easy? No. Can you do it? Absolutely. It will take more than knowledge—it will take patience and wisdom and compassion and courage and dedication. And a sense of humor, too. But if those of you I have met are a representative sample, then I am sure that you will have the skills to confront the tasks ahead of you, and I am confident that our future is in good hands.

Thank you for having me here today. Good luck with your future endeavors, and I look forward to working with you.

750th Anniversary Celebration, Eutin, Schleswig-Holstein, Germany (2007)

Honorable Bürgomeister Schultz, distinguished members of the city government and gracious citizens of Eutin, it is a great honor to be here today to represent the city of Lawrence, Kansas, as you celebrate the 750th anniversary of the founding of this beautiful city.

In the year 1257, when Eutin was founded, the city of Lawrence was not even a dream. No European had set eyes upon the place by the Kansas River where Lawrence stands today. There were no cities, but the teepees and camps of American Indians. There were no trees or cultivated fields, but a vast ocean of prairie grasses. There were no roads or cars, but herds of millions of buffalo.

Just as Eutin has changed over the last 750 years, so has my city and my state, thanks in large part to citizens of Germany, including many of my ancestors, who have emigrated to America. Today, one fourth of all the people in Kansas have German ancestry.

I cannot express how honored we are that so many of your community leaders and citizens came to Lawrence in 2004 to help us observe the 150th anniversary of our founding. Knowing the importance of 150 years to Lawrence makes us realize what a significant milestone it is for your city to be five times older. I know that all of the members of the delegation who were here in June would like to be here for these ceremonies as well, and they send their deepest regards.

For four decades citizens of Eutin have opened their homes to Kansas University students, and for 17 years we have shared high school student exchanges. Our sincere thanks go out to the citizens of Eutin, the administration and faculty of your high school, and of course to the Friends of Lawrence and the Eutin Volunteer Fire Department, whose visits we welcome. We are also thankful for the ongoing banking internship program that provides real opportunities for outstanding young people, and which has resulted in at least one marriage!

We very much appreciate the friendship of our older and wiser sister and we look forward to strengthening the bonds of friendship between our two cities in the years to come.

Again, it is a great honor and pleasure to be here today. The hospitality that you have shown to me and to Andrea is beyond words. I can sincerely say, paraphrasing our President Kennedy, “Ich bin ein Eutiner.”

Danke schön.

Douglas County Democrats Candidate Forum (2014)

Good morning. My name is Boog Highberger. My mother calls me Dennis... and just for the record, I’m the one with the three-wheeled bicycle, not the one with the shopping cart and mannequin.

For those of you who live in Lawrence, it was an honor to serve as your city commissioner and mayor a few years ago, and now I would appreciate the opportunity to serve as your representative in Topeka—under our new Governor, Paul Davis.

Some of you have heard me say this before, but I was born in Kansas before it was a Southern state. By that I mean no disrespect to anybody here from the South. What I do mean is that the actions of our legislature and governor over the last four years remind me a lot more of Alabama and Mississippi in the 1950s than they do of the Kansas I grew up in. I was born and raised in Kansas, and all of my ancestors have been in Kansas for over 100 years—and this not my Kansas.

In the Kansas where I grew up, people understood the value of education and were willing to make sacrifices to make sure that their children had a better future. In the Kansas of my childhood, people understood the necessity of good infrastructure for prosperity, and they wouldn’t have dreamed of doing something like raiding the highway trust fund to fill a short-term budget gap. In the Kansas of my childhood, people understood that in order to have a just and decent society we have to provide assistance to our fellow citizens who need a little help taking care of themselves—the issue of Medicaid expansion wouldn’t have even been a question.

Kansas has always been conservative—well, not always—120 years ago it was the most progressive place in the country, but that's another story. Anyway, Kansas has been conservative for a long time, but it was never mean, or ignorant, or selfish, or intolerant or short-sighted—but those are the values I see driving Kansas government today. But those aren't Kansas values—the real Kansas values are reason and fairness and equality and compassion—and those are the values I intend to bring to the legislature if I am elected.

As you know there hasn't been a primary in this district for a long time—but I think a primary is a good thing—I am pro-choice, after all. And although I don't really enjoy running in a primary, I wouldn't be here if I didn't think I was a good candidate. Especially with Paul leaving the legislature, I think my skills and experience will be critical for providing good representation for this district.

I have been a resident of the district for over 35 years, and I think I know the district pretty well at this point.

As I noted earlier, I was a city commissioner in Lawrence for six years and mayor for a year, so I have experience governing. I think the legislature has very little understanding of the effect of its actions on local governments, so I think that that experience can be very important.

I worked for the Kansas Department of Health and Environment for almost 20 years, implementing and applying statutes, and occasionally drafting statutes and regulations, so I have an understanding of how state government works at that level.

I have been a practicing attorney for over 20 years. I certainly don't think that every legislator needs to be an attorney, but given that the job of the legislature is to write laws, I think that having at least a few attorneys in the legislature is really important. It is my understanding that after Paul leaves there will only be one attorney left in the Democratic delegation—not even enough to staff the Judiciary Committee.

I have business experience—I served on the board of the Community Mercantile for about 15 years, including some times that were financially challenging, to put it mildly. Since the death of my father in 1997, I have been the president of our small family farm machinery dealership in Garnett, Kansas, and I have managed my downtown law practice for the last two years.

I have been an active and engaged member of my community for a long time. I have served on many local boards and committees, and I am currently a member of the city Sustainability Advisory Board, the

Douglas County Food Policy Council, the city Public Incentives Review Committee, and I serve on the board of the Community Mercantile Education Foundation, which runs school gardens at West Junior High and Sunset Hill and Hillcrest schools.

And last, but not least, I am good listener, which I think is one of the most important skills for any elected official. One great example of someone who does that is my role model as an elected official—State Senator Marci Francisco. As you know, Marci listens, she is everywhere, and she works really hard—and that's what I intend to do if elected to be your representative.

But ultimately this election isn't about me, and it isn't about Abbie—it's about getting the job done for the people in the 46th District and in the state of Kansas. So whoever wins the primary will have my unconditional support—even if it's me. (And for those of you who know me, you know that's saying a lot.)

And no matter what, I look forward to working with every single one of you to bring common sense back to Kansas government and to make sure that a government of the Koch brothers, by the Koch brothers, and for the Koch brothers SHALL perish from the earth.

Thank you.

"Berning Man," Granada Theater, Lawrence, Kansas (2016)

I always wanted to go to Burning Man... but where are all the naked people?

I'd like to congratulate all the runners-up tonight in the Bernie Sanders lookalike contest... But you have to admit it wasn't even close.

My name is Boog Highberger, and if you live in Lawrence east of Iowa Street and north of 19th Street, I am your state representative... but we'll talk more about that later. The primary reason that I am here tonight is the same reason that you are here—because I support Bernie Sanders as the Democratic nominee for president of the United States. I support Bernie because he is the only candidate who is really addressing the fundamental political issue of this generation—the growing gap in wealth and income between rich and poor in this country and the hollowing out of the middle class. There are many other important issues—climate change, growing student loan debt, racial inequality, immigration reform, political polarization—but in the end I think that for all of these other problems their source—or our ability to solve them—comes down to economic inequality.

By some measures, the gap in income between rich and poor in this country is already greater than in France before the French revolution—and we all know what happened that time...

But there are other reasons to vote for Bernie. Anybody here have any student loans? I would like to apologize on behalf of my generation for the amount of debt you have had to take on to get through college. It has foreclosed options for you that we took for granted. And it is important to remember that this change was not inevitable or some accident of history. It was an easily predictable result of deliberate policy changes made in Washington and Topeka—to shift the cost of college to students to finance tax breaks for the wealthiest Americans. Bernie will make better policy choices and will do his best to make college affordable for every young person in America.

Are there any veterans here? Do you know who the 2015 VFW legislator of the year was? Bernie Sanders. Bernie understands that no matter how you feel about political decisions that have involved us in foreign wars, we must respect and honor the sacrifices that people in our armed forces have made, and if they have been injured in the line of duty we have an absolute obligation to make sure that they receive the best care possible.

Bernie has called for a revolution in American politics. But I think we need to remember that not all that long ago Bernie would not have been considered a revolutionary. 50 or 60 years ago he would have been barely to the left of center in the American political spectrum. Because in the meantime another revolution has happened in America—the revolution that happened when I was in college—the Reagan revolution. That's when this country abandoned its understanding that America only prospers when all Americans prosper (and that is in fact a line from the 1956 Republican Party platform) and replaced that understanding with an ideology of radical individualism, selfishness, and greed. Bernie may sound radical today, but the real radicals are the people who are running the US Congress and most of Kansas state government. And they need to go.

It is absolutely critical to remember that we need to do more than elect Bernie. By himself Bernie can't get anything done. He needs allies in Congress. And Bernie can't fix the mess we're in in Kansas—we are going to have to do that ourselves. So after we get through the caucuses, and when it comes time to vote in August and November, please keep on going down the ballot to vote for state candidates like Marci Francisco and Tom Holland and John Wilson and Barbara Ballard and myself so that we can keep fighting for you in Topeka. I have a nominating petition circulating out there that will get me on the ballot for the August primary—if you would like to sign it, please find me later.

This is my campaign shirt... I don't know if you can read the back... but I think it's something that Bernie would be down with. I look forward to working with you and Bernie to be sure that a government of the Koch brothers, by the Koch brothers, and for the Koch brothers SHALL perish from the earth.

March for Our Lives, South Park, Lawrence, Kansas (2018)

Good morning. I'm Boog Highberger, state representative for the 46th district, and it's an honor to be here to talk to you today. And it's exciting, too... I have been following this issue most of my adult life, and this is the first time that it has really felt like the tide is turning back toward reasonable gun safety regulation. And it is thanks to you—high school students and grade school students and your fellow students around the country—that this change is happening, so I would like to say thank you for all your work and I think we all owe you a debt of gratitude.

I would like to start by saying that I am a supporter of the Second Amendment, but I am a supporter of the Second Amendment as interpreted by the US Supreme Court, not as interpreted by the National Rifle Association. I think it's important to remember that none of our constitutional rights are absolute—because at some point my constitutional rights conflict with your constitutional rights, and in our system of government that's when the courts step in and determine the limits of our respective rights. We're all familiar with the idea that the First Amendment doesn't give anybody the right to yell "fire" in a crowded theater. And so, if the legislature were to pass a law prohibiting yelling "fire" in a crowded theater, it wouldn't be infringing on anyone's First Amendment rights. It works the same way with the Second Amendment—the Supreme Court has never held, for instance, that the Second Amendment creates a right to carry concealed firearms in a public place. And that means that the state of Kansas could limit concealed carry in public places or even prohibit it entirely without infringing on anyone's Second Amendment rights. And it also means that when the NRA calls concealed carry "constitutional carry," that is an alternative fact—or in other words, a lie. And it's the same for assault weapons, large magazines, and bump stocks—the Supreme Court has never found that the Second Amendment creates a right to own any of these things, so the states are free to regulate or ban them without violating anybody's Second Amendment rights.

When I point that out in the legislature, what I hear back sometimes is that the right to carry a gun anywhere you want is a god-given right. Well, you know, I've read the Bible and it's not in there, so I can only assume that they're talking about a different religion.

But the NRA doesn't understand constitutional law—or at least they want to make sure that their supporters don't—and they continue to oppose any limitation on gun ownership whatsoever. This year in the Kansas legislature we have seen a bill that would allow anyone with a concealed carry permit from another state to concealed carry in Kansas, even if that person wouldn't be allowed to concealed carry under Kansas law. We have also seen a bill that would lower the concealed carry age in Kansas to 18, and a bill that would require any elementary school in Kansas that wants to teach kids about gun safety to use a course developed by the NRA.

I have opposed all of these bills. I am not opposed to teaching children about gun safety, but I opposed the NRA gun education bill because I think it has nothing to do with keeping our children safe, but instead is just part of an ongoing effort by the NRA to normalize the radical gun culture that they have been promoting for the last 40 years. But the radical gun culture being pushed on us by the NRA isn't normal—it has no precedent in American history and no corollary anywhere else in the world. Occasionally I hear somebody say that we're going back to the Wild West, but we're not going back to the Wild West, because the Wild West was never like this. If you rode into Abilene or Wichita or Dodge City in the 1870s or 1880s you had to leave your guns with the sheriff and you got them back when you left—and there wasn't any whining about the Second Amendment or god-given rights.

So I say it is not normal for guns to permeate every corner of our society. And it's not normal for a large number of the members of our legislature to come to work carrying loaded deadly weapons. It's an open secret around the legislature, but I'm not sure how widely it's known, that on any given day a dozen of my colleagues on the floor of the House of Representatives are armed with deadly weapons—and a couple of years ago it was more like 25 or 30. And if you think that is outrageous as I do, please contact some of my fellow representatives and let them know what you think about that, because I think you will agree with me that there is absolutely no reason for a duly elected representative of the people to come to the people's house armed with deadly weapons.

In my time in the legislature I have learned that gun rights is one area where reason and facts don't matter—it really is a lot like a religion—and for most of my fellow legislators who are strong supporters of gun rights, no amount of argument or information is going to change their minds. Every mass shooting incident for them is just more evidence that there aren't enough guns in our society. So the only way to change the decisions of our legislature is to change our legislators—so that is why it is critical for you to get out and vote for your state representatives this year. Here in Lawrence, most or all of your representatives already agree with you on this issue, so it is also important to talk to your friends around the state and encourage them to vote for representatives who will support reasonable gun safety legislation. Polls consistently show that a majority of Kansans favor reasonable gun safety laws—so we can make this happen—especially with the energy and enthusiasm that I see here today.

The Constitution is on our side, the people are on our side, and I look forward to working with all of you to make our schools and the rest of our society free from the scourge of gun violence. Thank you.

flotsam & jetsam

The items in this section are something of a mixed bag. "Bedtime for Bonzo vs. the Joy of Cooking" was written in January 1987 and was read from the steps of Wescoe Hall during the Impeach Reagan Rally on the KU campus later that month. (See letter of 29 January 1987 to X.) A slightly different version appeared as a wall poster on the KU campus.

"A Juxtapositionist Manifesto" was written in response to a call for art and political manifestos issued by the good folks at Xexoxial Endarchy of Dreamtime Village in Wisconsin. It was reprinted in a zine or two, I believe, and circulated in photocopy form in the anarchist/mail art network, but until now it has not been published in Lawrence. Pretty much the same goes for "Borders, Boundaries, and Desire," a follow-up piece that appeared a few years later.

One of the few prerogatives of the mayor in the mayor-council-manager form of municipal government is the issuance of proclamations. The proclamation of International Dadaism Month (I know, I know, it should have been International Dada Month) was intended as a minor prank to liven up an otherwise short and uneventful end-of-year meeting; I should have known that it was one of those little things that was quirky and trivial enough to get picked up by the wire services and end up in newspapers all around the world. What made the nut was the replica of Zurich Dada artist Hugo Ball's famous Cabaret Voltaire cardboard suit that Eric Farnsworth made and wore to the city commission meeting to accept the proclamation. The number of days and the dates for International Dadaism Month were determined by myself and my teenage housemate Cypress McKinney Frankenfeld by rolling dice and drawing numbers out of a hat.

Bedtime for Bonzo vs. The Joy of Cooking (1987)

The best way to learn to be a good cook
    is to eat your mistakes
Ronald Reagan you are not a good cook
Ronald Reagan you should eat your mistakes

Ronald Reagan eat Bedtime for Bonzo
Ronald Reagan eat Death Valley Days eat Boraxo soap eat the 20 mule
    team

every single one of 'em
Ronald Reagan eat NANCY your second wife 2 months
pregnant when you were married
who knows she might LIKE IT
on the other hand she might JUST SAY NO

Ronald Reagan eat the General Electric Corporation &
Ronald Reagan eat every radio that ever broadcast one of those sleazy
corporate messages you used to do for them

Ronald Reagan eat the House Unamerican Activities Committee &
Ronald Reagan eat the list of every Communist in the Screen Actors
Guild 1949

Ronald Reagan eat the redwood forests of California
"if you've seen one tree, you've seen them all"
farting cows are a major source of air pollution
Ronald Reagan drink the blood of the college students of California
1968, "if it's going to take a bloodbath then let's get it over with"

Ronald Reagan eat Ed Meese I hate Meeses to pieces
Ronald Reagan eat James Watt, Cap Weinberger, George Bush, William
Rehnquist, Antonin Scalia, etcetera, etcetera, etcetera

Ronald Reagan eat ONE TRILLION DOLLARS of deficit spending
more than all 39 other presidents combined one dollar a second
for 30,000 years

Ronald Reagan eat the Strategic Defense Initiative eat the MX missile
eat the B-1 bomber eat the Trident submarine
Ronald Reagan eat every bomb this country has paid to have dropped on
El Salvador
northern El Salvador is being saturation bombed right now Ronald
Reagan
there's a war going on why isn't this in the newspapers?
Ronald Reagan eat all the mines in the harbors of Nicaragua
another Ollie North scheme
another blatant violation of international law

Ronald Reagan eat every shell the US Navy fired on Lebanon,
    yes 243 Marines died but how many Lebanese did we kill first?
Ronald Reagan eat every bullet fired by the US Marines in Grenada,
    oh we conquered the mighty republic of Grenada, America's a man again
Ronald Reagan eat the screams of the children of Libya
    Moammar Khadafy's 2-year-old daughter will never hijack another airplane
Ronald Reagan the world is safe for democracy

Ronald Reagan eat constructive engagement in South Africa
    there are not many calories in constructive engagement so
Ronald Reagan you'd better have some Krugerrands for an afternoon snack,
    your pal Jerry Falwell will be over to join you
And don't forget the ketchup Ronald Reagan,
    we all need our vegetables

William Casey's scrambled brains for breakfast, Ronald Reagan!
Admiral Poindexter soup for dinner, Ronald Reagan!
& how about some Ollie North on rye for supper Ronald Reagan? cause don't forget,
    Ronald Reagan a hero ain't nothin' but a sandwich
Cocktail hour is all the urine specimens of every federal employee in America,
    Ronald Reagan! This Bud's for you!

6 years of your cooking is enough, Ronald Reagan, you just never seem to learn
Ronald Reagan there is blood on your apron
Ronald Reagan your cabinets are empty
Ronald Reagan your pots are all smoking
Ronald Reagan something is burning
Ronald Reagan your eggs are on fire
Ronald Reagan if you can't stand the heat, get out of the kitchen

a juxtapositionist manifesto (1987)

"I want to be everything, everybody, in every place, at the same time."

–Yevgeny Yevtushenko

To make all the possible connections, to turn the kaleidoscope, to be the kaleidoscope, to smash the old fossilized perspectives and rearrange reality in new vibrant living patterns, to dance the wild, exuberant dance of creation—this is the revolution of juxtaposition.

2

"In place of Newton's mechanical interpretation of the universe, Fourier advances his own 'law of passionate attraction'... a concept of the cosmos as a vast organization that is suffused by life and growth. A vibrant vitalism so completely replaces the despiritized matter of conventional physics that even the idea of planets copulating is not implausible."

–Murray Bookchin

Life is inevitable. Matter wants to live. The stuff that makes up the universe has an inherent tendency toward spontaneous self-organization. Forces of mutual attraction are built into the basic particles of matter. The patterns in which matter arranges itself are predetermined by the structure of the elemental units. The self-organization of the universe is continually increasing. This process will continue until the whole universe is alive. As human beings we are matter that has become self-conscious. As such we have the potential to consciously assist the process of self-organization. We can effectively assist this process to the extent that we perceive ourselves as part of the process rather than something separate from it. The revolution of juxtaposition is a revolution of evolution.

3

"The natural dynamics of (self-organizing systems) teaches the optimistic principle of which we tend to despair in the human world—the more freedom in self-organization, the more order!"

–Eric Jantsch

Decay is a sign of life. The coming collapse of industrial civilization is not a disaster but an opportunity.

In this age the forces of life are stronger than the forces of death. The grass always grows through the pavement. We are the great creeping vines growing over the fallen buildings. Our soft tendrils crumble the hard stone. We take it apart and rearrange it until it's all alive.

"The principle of collage is the central principle of all art in the twentieth century in all media."

–Donald Barthelme

Learning is a process of juxtaposition. One comes to understand a new concept primarily through comparison of negative examples. For instance, we learn what constitutes a house not by endless examples of "house" but by seeing a few examples of "house" and lots of examples of "not-a-house." By comparing a picture of a barn, for instance, to our idea of "house" we learn the limits of the concept much more quickly than from seeing dozens of examples of different houses.

Learning is a process of making new connections, of seeing new patterns of interrelationships between things. Our learning becomes a basis for our further evolution when we use it to begin to create new patterns.

The revolution of juxtaposition is a revolution of learning, a revolution of life.

"The essence of Zen is to remember that it's a cut and paste universe."

–Stephen Gaskin

Sexual reproduction is a process of juxtaposition, an endless experiment with new combinations of genes and chromosomes, traits and characteristics. Living things that reproduce by splitting remain identical—individual organisms die but the individual genotype lives on. With sex comes diversity—and death. Now when individual organisms die, their unique pattern of genes is lost to the world.

As animals evolve, they become less and less governed by instinct and physiology. As they become more and more complex, they become more and more adaptable. They become progressively more helpless at birth, and come to approach Locke's notion of the "tabula rasa," the blank slate. Human beings are approaching a stage of evolution where the primary form of reproduction is intellectual reproduction. Cultural information is superseding biological information in defining the human being. Humans, more than any other animal, are determined less by their parents' genes than by cultural information from other individuals all over the planet.

So the revolution of juxtaposition begins to conquer death, as individuals begin to live on after the death of their bodies through the consciousnesses of their intellectual progeny.

6 **"Laughter is a form of angst-relief... a funny situation is one in which apparently contradictory elements are joined... humor is the 'unity of opposites'... for that instant—the spasm of the laugh—we are released from mechanical thinking."**

—Bill Griffith

If we can't laugh, we're not coming to your revolution because the revolution of juxtaposition is a revolution of laughter.

7 JUXTAPOSITION IS THE LANGUAGE OF DREAMS! Messages from our subconscious selves to our conscious minds come through our dreams. They come to light still encoded in the symbolic language of the subconscious—apparently unrelated images are connected in new and sometimes disturbing ways. We learn from our dreams by discovering—or creating—the patterns which help us "make sense" of the juxtaposed images.

The revolution of juxtaposition is a revolution of dreams.

"Panta rhei ('Everything flows')"

—Heraclitus

Juxtaposition is against hierarchy. Making grassroots connections is a process of decentralization, of circumventing centralized control. Making connections between these at the bottom of a chain of command takes away the power of those at the top of the pyramid by taking from them the control of the flow of information and ideas. The goal of the revolution of juxtaposition is to break down all the obstacles to the natural flow of things, to tune into the tao, to facilitate the process of unfolding of life in the universe.

"Sometimes the truth seems paradoxical."
—Lao Tzu

In many Eastern cultures, black is the color of life. Black is the color of all colors at once. Black is the color of anarchy, of order-in-chaos. Black is the color of the revolution of juxtaposition, and the revolution of juxtaposition is a revolution of all colors.

borders, boundaries, and desire (1990)

Limit gives form to the limitless.
-Pythagoras
Without boundaries there is only jello.
—a juxtapositionist manifesto

States are not possible without borders—society is not possible without boundaries. The job of the juxtapositionist is to tear down the walls that make the state possible and to nurture the organic distinctions of living cultures.

Every membrane is a semi-permeable membrane.
—Julian Beck

A boundary that cannot be penetrated is not a membrane but a wall; a boundary that can be crossed with no resistance is nothing at all. Everything in between is a semi-permeable membrane. Furthermore, quantum mechanics tells us that not even a wall is a wall: Schrödinger's equation demonstrates that there is a nonzero possibility for any given particle to be anywhere in the universe at any given instant, all walls notwithstanding. And the Aspect experiment has shown that, if physical reality exists, then every particle in the universe is connected to every other particle in the universe by a faster-than-light field. How can there be a wall when everything on one side is connected to everything on the other side?

There is nothing that can set bounds to licentiousness... The best way of enlarging and multiplying one's desires is to try to limit them.

—the Marquis de Sade

Desire is the motor of history. Economics, the pursuit of objects, is just a dim spark of the real fire that drives men and women onward. We can pursue objects but we can never <u>become</u> those objects. Objects cannot return our desire. The energy that impels humans together is vastly stronger than the desire for objects because of the possibility of <u>breaking on through to the other side</u>...

At the boundary, life blossoms.

—James Gleick

The creative forces of a society live on its margins. Too far into the center and too much joy has been sacrificed for security; too far over the edge and too much energy is required for mere survival. Art requires freedom but it thrives on struggle.

All patterns are defined by their limits.

—György Doczi

Nothing defines perception like an edge.

—William Irwin Thompson

Consciousness itself demands separateness—for perception to take place there must be both a perceiver and a perceived, and a boundary between them. Transcending that boundary is the goal of most spiritual disciplines but the achievement of that goal is <u>the end of consciousness</u>. The full realization of life in this material world means learning to walk on sharp knives.

Zero and infinity are essentially theological concepts.
—Alan Watts

Zero and infinity are the same place, but they are reached by different paths. The way to zero is through dissolving boundaries until there are no boundaries left, no perceiver and no perceived, no inside and no outside, no form and no content: zero. The way to infinity is by the wild proliferation of boundaries and distinctions until the boundaries go on forever and the space between them disappears—and what remains is infinitely many points, points that take up no space and have no inside and no outside, no structure but absolutely interconnected, on and on forever: infinity.

$$0 = 1 = \infty$$

The way to zero is the path of death and the way to infinity is the path of life.

What we desire is to bring into a world founded on discontinuity all the continuity such a world can bear.
—Georges Bataille

Life is unrealized desire—yearning and seeking but not achieving. The goal of love is always union with its object, but the union of love fully realized ultimately brings stasis and death. But with love not fulfilled, with desire unconsummated, there is motion and life. So love & desire destroy the conditions that make them possible—but like Lao Tzu says, sometimes the truth seems paradoxical...

I know the idea is odious and alien to our culture thatone would deliberately impose restrictions on movement and freedom of the body, but mankind throughout history has always done this. The lessons that can be learned and the life that can be ledby doing this far transcend what can be learned by being comfortable. Being comfortable isn't necessarily leading a good life—that's the myth, but it's not true. Living an uncomfortable life is sometimes more satisfactory than a placid, bovine existence.

—Fakir Musafar

International Dadaism Month Proclamation (2005)

Office of the Mayor
Proclamation
Lawrence, Kansas

WHEREAS: Dadaism is an international tendency in art that seeks to change conventional attitudes and practices in aesthetics, society, and morality; and

WHEREAS: Dadaism may or may not have come into being in the summer of 1916 at the Cabaret Voltaire at 1 Spiegelgasse in Zürich, Switzerland, with the participation of Hugo Ball, Tristan Tzara, Emmy Hennings, Marcel and Georges Janco, Jean Arp, and Richard Heulsenbeck; and

WHEREAS: The central message of Dada is the realization that reason and anti-reason, sense and nonsense, design and chance, consciousness and unconsciousness, belong together as necessary parts of a whole; and

WHEREAS: Dada is a virgin microbe which penetrates with the insistence of air into all those spaces that reason has failed to fill with words and conventions; and

WHEREAS: zimzim urallala zimzim urallala zimzim zanzibar zimzalla zam;

NOW, THEREFORE, I, Dennis "Boog" Highberger, Mayor of the City of Lawrence, Kansas, do hereby proclaim the days of February 4, April 1, March 28, July 15, August 2, August 7, August 16, August 26, September 18, September 22, October 1, October 17, and October 26, 2006, as

"INTERNATIONAL DADAISM MONTH"

and I encourage all citizens.

Dennis "Boog" Highberger
Mayor
December 27, 2005

letters

As you can probably tell, I used to really like to write letters. At some point in the mid-1980s I started copying my letters rather than rewriting a lot of the contents into the journal I was keeping at the time. At some point the journal stopped, and the letters became a substitute for the journal. The letters reprinted here were selected from over 500 of which I located in various boxes, filing cabinets, and hard drives.

We quickly abandoned any attempt to reproduce the feel of the actual letters. Over the years they evolved from handwritten to typed to printed in a crappy font on a dot-matrix printer to an embarrassment of colors, fonts, and inserted graphics after the advent of the cheap inkjet printer. Many were embellished with doodles and drawings. Some of them were 11" x 17" pages jammed full of what looks like 10-point type; toward the end they were mostly 5½" x 8½" sheets to fit the format of my sporadic correspondance assembling magazine, @RtH*Le. (Each @RtH*Le was unique, and in addition to a handmade cover, artworks from other artists around the world, and various other flotsam and jetsam, each contained a short letter from myself. "Correspondance" is a spelling adopted by many mail artists to emphasize the dance of images and ideas around the mail art network.)

On the wise advice of my editor, rather than following my own instinct to reproduce the text of the letters exactly as in the originals, some of the letters have been slightly modified to improve the literary experience of yourself, dear reader. Minor typos have been corrected, and my wild profusion of dashes and ellipses (ranging from 2 to 5 dots in the originals) have been standardized to some degree. Most places where significant portions of text have been omitted are indicated by ellipses in brackets ([...]), added text is in brackets, and a few paragraph breaks have been added. Other than that, the letters here are pretty much as I wrote them.

As someone who rarely reads books of collected letters, it seems a little odd to be publishing one. A rummage though the shelves and stacks of my personal library has uncovered only three: 1) *The Playwright and the Pirate,* a collection of letters between George Bernard Shaw and Frank Harris, which I acquired after embarking on this project; 2) *The Groucho Letters,* a collection of letters to and from Groucho Marx; and 3) *Marquis de Sade: Selected Letters,* most of which are to his wife, whom he refers to in one of them as "celestial pussycat" (which of course I had to use in a letter to my girlfriend at the time, although that letter isn't reprinted here). I am honored to join their esteemed company.

I hope that you find the letters reprinted here at least mildly amusing, and I hope they inspire you to begin cluttering the mailboxes of your friends and acquaintances with real, three-dimensional, tactile, delivered-by-uniformed-government-agents letters of your own.

1985–1988

demented remnants of light and ecstasy • The Life of the Theatre • giving birth to Disorientation • brilliant schemes for reorganizing everything • R. Crumb • balloon ride • Impeach Reagan rally • grocery clerk juxtaposition • revolution changing to family • angry and well-equipped • mystical taco experience • snail copulation • Wavy Gravy in the NCAA parade • "chocolate whiz-bang" • nuck

10 August 1985, Brenna Hoffmann, somewhere in England

Brenna my love:

[...] The juggernaut of time lumbers on here in the River City... life goes on. The sunflowers in the front yard are starting to bloom (as are the Chinese cabbage and the radishes. Long tall stalks of yellow & pink respectively) and so are the melons (cantaloupes? watermelon?) with big soft fuzzy orange flowers. The walnuts are coming on—there are 2 clusters of 3 walnuts each within reach of my southernmost window. The birds & squirrels are out in force, too—this morning I saw a cardinal and heard its strange and wonderful cry. Fleas we have a few of, though the kitties stay outside.

[...] the lack of your presence is a real & palpable thing—it walks the hallways at night, plays Joni Mitchell records sometimes, sits on the porch in the cool breeze of the evening and pets the cats. It's not something to make one feel bad, though—sort of calmly reassuring—especially since I know/hope/assume you're having a good time and learning a lot where you are. [...]

« I see we're all demented remnants of light and ecstasy
Derelicts in time trying to reconstruct with only faint recall
a lost message Peace Music Love Revolution Joy
This is the first day of the rest of your life
This is your Safe Conduct Pass There is Nothing to fear »
—Lawrence Ferlinghetti, from "Tyrannus Nix?"

see you soon,
all my love,
boog

12 August 1986, Frank Krug, Brookline, MA

Franko:

I'm alive. I'm at the Village Inn. It's in the wee hours of the morning. I just finished laying out the next Disorientation & I think it's turned out pretty good. I'll mail you a copy as soon as it gets back from the printer...

I'm going to have a place to live soon, Franko!—with a real address, and a room of my own. I'll have a telephone number again. I'll have a place for my friends to crash when they come visit, which Kurt says you might do soon...

It's sort of a rat trap—Anna & Mark & I looked at it a month ago & decided we didn't like it, but since then the landlord has dropped the rent and agreed to some quasi-major repairs, so J (& T & J) & I are moving in next week. It's on a quiet street & has a big back yard, even if it is kind of ugly... upstairs there's a room with a door about 4 feet high & the only light fixture is a pair of fluorescent lights mounted vertically on the east wall—the kids love it.

Right now I'm trying to decide whether to go back to J's house and try to get in (I've been staying there the last couple of days), go to the computer center and type letters until morning, or crash in my car. Being homeless in the middle of the night has definite disadvantages. Maybe I should go to Headquarters... or maybe I'll stay here until they run me out. [...]

I feel like I've just given birth, Franko—I feel like that after finishing every big publishing project. I feel like I should get to lay back awhile now & let other people wait on me & enjoy my new baby—In some cultures, though, there is a strange custom called the "couvade," wherein the mother gets up immediately after giving birth and starts working, while the father lies down in bed, receives the visitors, and is waited on by everyone else. This custom occurs in cultures on both sides of the Atlantic, in Africa & South America mostly, if I remember correctly, & is cited frequently by people trying to prove the existence of Atlantis. The rationale behind it, according to the anthropologists, is not sexism, but instead an effort to trick the evil spirits that might threaten mother & baby by putting dad in their place to take all the heat. Hmmm...

I must leave the Village Inn now and find someplace to sleep. My new address will be 431 Missouri. Our phone number has not yet been revealed. Come to Kansas, write soon...

love,
boog

17 August 1986, Steve Ballew, Derby, KS

O Steve,

Sorry I wasn't in town when you were here last weekend—I was down in Garnett (well, Westphalia, actually) for a Highberger family reunion. This weekend just past I was in Chicago. I went back with a friend who got busted there when we were in town for the International Anarchist Gathering, May 1–4. Yahoo...

The letter you sent had a cancellation advertising "Law Day USA Freedom Under the Law May 1"—yes May Day is Labor Day in every country that has one except the US & Canada—& here it's "Law Day." [...]

It's exciting to hear that you're getting so much time to work on your drawing—even before it was the best quality stuff I've seen anywhere in the area, & with time to make it more & better the possibilities seem endless... yahoo for all of us...

I just read an incredibly inspiring book by Julian Beck, late of the Living Theater. It was titled *The Life of the Theatre* and subtitled "The role of the artist in relation to the struggle of the people"—it used the theater as its dominant metaphor but most of what he talked about was applicable to artists working in any media—& we're all artists & the world is our medium... [...]

You said in your letter that you were typing because you were practicing in order to enhance future employment prospects... by some strange quirk of fate I got another letter the same day from another person doing exactly the same thing... I'm typing because it's more legible than my handwriting & I have access to a fancy typewriter now...

I want to come to Wichita sometime this summer to hand out anti-nuke leaflets at the KGE office—if we make it down I'll let you know when we're coming & try to stop in to see you. [...]

& I'd like to see the artwork that you're shelving on Mary's advice because I have absolutely no grasp on popular tastes & I'd probably like it. Working in color sounds good... even the disturbing imagery sounds good. Like Beck says, "We are a feelingless people. If we could really feel, the pain would be so great that we would end all the suffering... when the state heaps honors on art it is a way of saying this art is safe for the ruling class... beware of approval and official support."

Go ahead, disturb me.

boog

29 August 1986, Steve Ballew, Derby, KS

Steve-O:

Thanks for the kind words about Diso.—I may print them in the next issue—& there will be a next issue, maybe for spring—it helps me carry on & please don't forget I COULDN'T HAVE DONE IT WITHOUT YOU. Your contributions were essential to making the quality of the publication what it was.

About your doubts about employment options—give yourself a break. Everybody in America has compromised themselves somehow to survive. This comes up in anarchist circles a lot—some anarchos will criticize others for eating meat, but fail to notice that we all work at wage labor jobs & live in the money economy & accept the benefits of living in America... all I know is that there's nobody out here qualified to throw stones. Julian Beck said it like this:

All money is blood money.

Do what you need to do. You're a good person. That's all that's really important.

Another good point you made: we all worry so much about selling out that we never stop to be sure that anybody's buying... [...]

What you said about inertia & political action makes loads-o-sense. All the brilliant schemes for reorganizing everything are useless unless people are ready to do it, unless Joe Blow & Suzy Creamcheeze from down the street feel like it makes a difference in their lives, feel like it's something that they understand & have some control over. & that's where folks like you & me come in—before you reap you gotta sow & harvest's a long way off so we gotta sow, gotta sow... like Alexander Berkman says, revolution is the boiling point of evolution & here in 1986 America the water's not even very warm yet... so we tend the fire, & once the flames begin to catch, the wind will fan it higher... O Biko... [...]

peace,
boog

1 September 1986, S. Clay Wilson, San Francisco, CA

Dear S.:

Sorry about the fuckups in the article. I'll have to admit I'm not intimately familiar enough with your work to recognize the names of all yer characters but even so I should have been smart enough to avoid mislabeling Star-Eyed Stella as Ruby the Dyke. A brief glimmer of doubt crossed my mind as I was doing the layout: "This woman's s'posed to be a dyke? Oh well..." But I did it anyway...

The rumor that R. Crumb lived here for a few months way back when is a treasured piece of local mythology that was current even when I first moved here in 1977. It's too bad to learn it's not true. I guess this mention of it in the magazine will just reinforce the rumor, but somehow I don't feel like going to great lengths to correct the Error. I figure if enough people believe it, it must be true... whether it is or not...

The chicken on the envelope was Lance the Barking Watch Chicken. His adventures have been featured in such long-defunct local ragazines as "Snipes Monthly" and "Amok." Now he's mostly retired.

I met Pete V. a few days ago in the library. As I sort of expected he's somebody I've seen around for years but hadn't really talked to much. I imagine it's the same way with your other pals, too.

Thanks again for your help & the words of encouragement.

28 September 1986, X., somewhere in America

X. sweetie,

(After a short time out for a phone call from an old roommate who's now a lawyer in Maine & a few horsie rides for Jakie Neuhaus, young wrangler of the high prairie) Hello… every moment is an adventure, whether we like it or not...

Yesterday my folks went on their long-awaited balloon ride. It was wonderful just watching. They lifted off from the balloon people's place in Possum Holler (a little wooded valley just east of Pleasant Farm) & floated up, up, & away to the Southeast & ended up back in Kansas... in a field by a cemetery... then last night I went to the Houndogs show at the Rock Chalk. They're getting wilder & wilder... they opened the second set & played the first few songs dressed in big red bags & used dry ice for smoke effects. I brought a giant gourd with me to the show. It was about 2½ feet long and looked like a long, skinny, crooked watermelon or a mutant green bean... I left it as an offering for the band & it was incorporated into the show… at the end it was passed around to everyone in the room, then I gave it to Joe M. whose mission it was to take it home to the Rainbow House & leave it outside my sister's door…

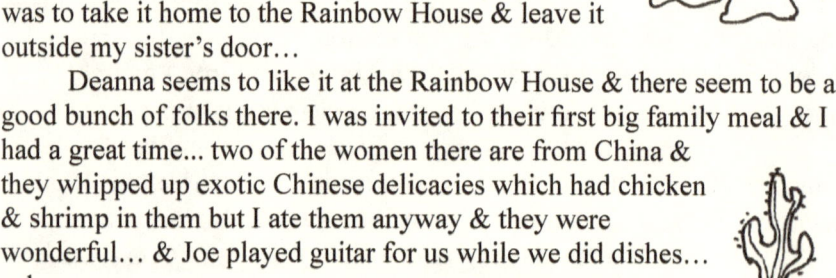

Deanna seems to like it at the Rainbow House & there seem to be a good bunch of folks there. I was invited to their first big family meal & I had a great time... two of the women there are from China & they whipped up exotic Chinese delicacies which had chicken & shrimp in them but I ate them anyway & they were wonderful… & Joe played guitar for us while we did dishes… yahoo…

This morning I went with Jean & Peter & the kids up to Dyche Hall for the Kansas Film Institute film festival where they were showing "The Song of the Sword" featuring Mark Parker, Keith Abrams, Clark Jamison, Ry Brown, Maria Anthony, & numerous other folks you would probably recognize. I was surprised at the quality… good acting, for the most part, excellent special effects, lots of neat images, good music... if you go for fantasy adventure stuff like that... & there were lots of good laughs in it too, it didn't take itself too seriously.

Shine on you crazy diamond...

I love you
boog

29 January 1987, X., somewhere in America

Kansas Day!

Hello X. dear friend absolute sweetie,,,,

Everything's OK, it was a sunny day very nice... [...] after work I went to look for somebody that wasn't home & so instead I sat on the porch of the Crossing & watched the cars go by & the clouds dance & the sun go down... & then to Rice & Beans, hung out with some folks, went home, made phone calls, nobody was home except Kurt who had worked all night last night & was ready to crash already so I said aha! a night free to write letters so I went & got some beer & hauled the typewriter out to the kitchen & put on some obscene Frank Zappa music & here I am... yow! ("This is exciting... I never plooked a tiny chrome plated machine that looks like a Magical Pig with marital aids stuck all over it such as yourself before...")

I have enclosed paraphernalia from the Impeach Reagan rally last week, a great success... more fun than any demo I've been to around here for awhile... a new @ in town, a young man named Tad that Ed met somehow, was Reagan, & played the part well. Somebody from Hashinger who I'd been talking to on & off for months about street theater was Col. North... & I delivered the rant ("Gee this is great... how about some bondage & humiliation?") enclosed ["Bedtime for Bonzo vs. The Joy of Cooking"], with a few minor variations... the megaphone was a little funky though & I was kind of out of breath so it wasn't perfect but it was something I'd been wanting to do for a long time... Dick was in top form, too, & it's been fun working with John Bode (he plays guitar for the Lonesome Houndogs—did you ever meet him?). Anyway it's good to have Tad around. It's brought a lot of new & needed energy into town & into the anarchist circle... he's keyed into the hard core scene but has a remarkable amount of tolerance for us hippies & unobtrusive types. [...]

Marko & I went to Des Moines in early Jan. to visit the Kindred Community & hang out... I was checking it out as possibly a place to move to & do new things... but I don't think so... firstly cause Des Moines is a <u>city</u> & I'm really becoming aware of how much I'd rather avoid that... & secondly I'm just not dedicated enough to spend all my time cooking & cleaning for other folks & live on $10 a month over food & shelter—I've got too many bad habits. So at this point I'm prepared to slog through another semester here, but I haven't enrolled yet... [...]

David Epstein burned a copy of the Student Senate rules & regulations at his last Student Senate meeting as president in November... I'm going to try to get a picture of it for the front cover of the upcoming <u>DISORIENTATION</u>.

love,
boog

6 October 1987, Rian Fike (a/k/a Alterior Facial Mandala, a/k/a AFM), Miami, FL

Hello AFM,

Yes, & what a pleasant surprise to get yer letter in my mailbox not so long ago. You ask for more juxtaposition, but it looks to me like you've got yer hands on a critical mass of it already. [...] I like what you say about the sixties: the metaphor I've been using is that it seems like the social/cultural upheaval of the late sixties/early seventies was like the first flowers of spring... they look beautiful & incredibly bright compared to the surroundings, but the first flowers always come too soon & get cut down by that last frost... but there will be more flowers and this time they will be here to stay... & now I would say that our job as juxtapositionists is to prepare the beds and sow the seeds for the coming spring's flowers & we can do that by scattering our ideas out far and wide even though some may fall on the stony ground and some fall by the wayside... & by building connections with other like-minded souls around the world... Juxtaposition...

I don't have any more juxtaposition to send, but I do think your contacting me was an important act of juxtaposition... oh, yes, & I'd be interested in finding out where you saw the manifesto. I'm always fascinated by how the networks work.

Sometime next year I may have time & funds to launch a magazine based around the juxtaposition idea. I'd like it to include things on all types & aspects of juxtaposition—anachronism, pentimento, non-sequitur, collage, zeugma, paradox... juxtapositions in space, time, language, ideas... articles by grocery store checkout clerks, mail carriers, librarians—I think working in any of those jobs would drive me insane because I'd try to assemble the items each person was getting & try to imagine what their reality looks like... fer instance, I'd be working in the express lane & some cat would come up with a bottle of ketchup, HoHos, a light bulb, & kitty litter & I'd try to imagine how they fit into some sort of coherent pattern & of course they probably don't. Most American lives seem like collages but collages that just don't quite hang together, random accretions of plastic, shiny metals, animal by-products, miscellaneous junk... fibers & oils, special jellies, resins & gums, unguents, tinctures & ointments, husks, shells, woody stems, agglomerations & concretions, concatenations, saps & nectars, various insects preserved in amber, sports equipment (ancient & modern), vials, jars, boxes, flasks, casks, chests, trunks, marital aids, magnetos, armatures, gears & levers, lubricating fluids, wheels within wheels, wafers, abstract concepts, noble ideas, ice cream...

well, uh... I like yer stuff, keep me on the mailing list... if you're on the road & near Kansas, I have a couch... peace...

in juxtaposition,
boog

11 November 1987, David Zack, Tepotzlán, Morelos, Mexico

¡Hola David y compañeros!

Many thanks for the translation of the juxtapositionist manifesto. I've made copies and sent them to the appropriate persons, like the Boogers.

Our plans have changed again. We're leaving Phoenix somewhere around the 15th of December. So we probably won't make it to Tepoztlån until January sometime. But we're all looking forward to coming to Tepoztlån, viewing the Image Wall in the kitchen, toma-ing some cervezas in the Club Azalea. This milpa & wind cave business we'll discuss upon our arrival. [...]

I've been proofreading scientific manuscripts for money these days. It's boring as hell but it pays the rent. & I'm learning lots of new words: heterodichogamy, protandrous, perinatal, interleukin, oviposition. Now I just have to figure out what they mean...

My friend Mark and I threw the I Ching a few nights ago & we asked about the future of our magazine, Project 1313. The answer was revolution changing to family... hmmm. Sounds about right, actually...

I'll let you know as soon as we figure out exactly about when we'll be where you are.

bingo,
boog

28 January 1988, Headquarters, Lawrence, KS
(from Pedro Escobedo, Querétaro, Mexico)

Howdy friends,

Headquarters training can be very useful when you're living in a Volkswagen bus with 2 or 3 other people for 2 months. Especially when your traveling companions have been through it, too. "When you roll over in your sleep at night you kick me in the head sometimes... it makes me want to drop this cracked engine block on your foot." "Oh... it sounds like you're feeling angry and well-equipped."

boog

28 January 1988, Ed Rothrock, Lawrence, KS (from Pedro Escobedo, Querétaro, Mexico)

Ed—

A few days ago we had a mystical taco experience. We ate tacos at a little place in Pedro Escobedo and afterwards we realized that there had been a prime number of taco eaters (Frank, Brenna, and myself), we each had a prime number of tacos (5, 7, 11), and furthermore, these consecutive prime taco numbers all added up to a prime total taco number (23).

These were good tacos, but not good enough. Tell Meredith we're still searching for the perfect taco. We already have a JAR. See ya in February.

boog

19 March 1988, Rian Fike (a/k/a Alterior Facial Mandala, a/k/a AFM), Miami, FL

Lost in the Sauce
(literally & metaphorically)

Howdy Rian,

Well, it's true I'm a little lost in the sauce literally tonight as well as just metaphorically as usual since I've been sucking on some beers, Hudepohl Bock, just the thing for this late winter night.

A good paradox is paradise. Yes, yes, & paradise is a paradox... so you've been in frequent contact with Michael Behavior at NLU... any relation to Simone de Behavior? well, at any rate, it sounds like a good contact, perhaps I'd write every day but I don't think I could keep up the pace, besides I don't have that much meaningful information to communicate, I have to save it up & trash-compact it into manageable & deodorized packages... I guess that's basically a western cultural trait, holding it all in until there's—pow!—an orgasmic release, & then starting it all over again. Gregory Bateson talks about that cultural complex & compares it to Balinese culture in Steps to an Ecology of Mind, but though the Balinese avoid the boom & bust of western culture they pay for it in other ways...

Yes, we did climb pyramids in Mexico, my friend, no mere metaphors this time, we went all the way to the top. My friend Franko juggled on every level of the Pyramid of the Sun and on the top a man from Hungary gave him a Hungarian coin that was basically worthless but he said it would make the phones work which is something that very few of the Mexican coins in general circulation at the time would do...

You feel like a puppet? Tell me more about this... yeah, I realize the predestinarian element of the humpty dumpty/hindu pieces/god reassembling itself sort of way of conceptualizing things, but do you really subjectively feel like a puppet, like somebody else is pulling your strings? To me it seems like you're pulling on the strings as much as any cosmical puppeteer might be pulling on yours... sometimes its hard to tell who's driving...

It makes me feel really good to hear about your family and about the things you're doing with the kids at school. So many people in this network seem to not to be grounded in the places they're living... it seems like the mail network is a substitute for real living for a lot of people. I'm really glad to hear you say that your family is your first priority... it makes me want to meet them. Teaching kids & raising kids seems like the absolutely most important work that must be done, Rian, so I'm really happy to hear that someone such as yourself is doing both on a full-time basis.

Right now what I'm doing for money is proofreading scientific journals for a local company, Allen Press. Earlier this week I got to proof an exciting but heartrending article about snail copulation. It seems that in certain types of helicid snails, only individuals whose shells twist in the same direction can successfully copulate, otherwise their shells get in the way and the genital pores on the sides of their heads can't come into contact. Mirror-image snails have been known to follow each other around for days, even weeks, all in vain. It seems to me that this process probably takes place in humans, too, although on a more abstract level. God knows, we all have our shells... but I can't tell if mine is dextral or sinistral... not that it matters all that much... Another drawback of this job is that I have to proofread the Journal of Animal Torture, otherwise known as Neuroscience. If I was really consistent with my principles I'd probably have to refuse to work on that journal any more because so much of the research they publish involves hurting animals... but right now the job pays the rent... but how much are my principles worth if I only stick by them when it's convenient? I dunno, Rian, it's a dilemma...

Angel Tech sounds like it must be the ticket, what with both the recommendation of yourself & the good professors quoted in the ad. I'll get my hands on a copy as soon as possible... although I'll have to take the Leary plug with a grain of salt. I got to see him when he was here in town for the "River City Reunion" last September... he shared the bill with Jello Biafra & in comparison came off as an old acid casualty, although I really hate to use the term... nah, Leary's problem wasn't acid it was just general lack of substance... he was funny, but Jello was funny as well as biting the meat that matters... I'll read the book as soon as I can.

Yeah, I suppose I'm "Into" "'real'" politics... it's like a disease... I have this goofy idea that if good-hearted people get together & work together we can change the world & make a space where can all go furthur... & that's going to take some nuts&bolts-type organizing.

I'll enclose some info on a prisoner in Arizona I've been working with. It's one of the few things I'm doing these days I can point to & say, look, here's something I'm doing that's having a real, positive impact on somebody's life... which isn't to say that the other work isn't important... is the underground really making a difference? It's making a difference for me... it can make a difference or not, it seems, by whether it exists for itself or whether it helps each of us working in our different communities bring the fire of creation & the lust for freedom & life to the people we see every day. If we can't do that then we're just pissing in the river & the river is dirty enough as it is...

My bathtub is probably full now, no there's not much water pressure in this my crummy downtown apartment, time to get clean... looking forward to another AFeManation...

boog

17 April 1988, Guy Clark, Chicago, IL

Howdy Guy my friend,

Yes I'm back now in the land of toilet seat covers and all-nite bowling alleys. The trip [to Mexico] served one of its primary functions which was to blast me out of some of the deadly ruts I was getting into before I left, but it's been challenging keeping it that way since my return—ruts never sleep. I'm still living in my crummy downtown apartment until summer arrives & I can find a place with a porch and a yard but in the meantime here I am. It's a rainy day and you can hear the sounds of cars driving on wet streets. The reggae show's on the radio and the air is thick with sage & frankincense & myrrh, meaning my roommate Costas is having a poker game tonight. Ah, what a groovy lifestyle...

But I have a good excuse to be elsewhere tonight since I'm going to the airport to pick up my sweetie who's been out to Boulder visiting a friend of hers who just got out of jail for being one of the first group of women to break into the Nevada Test Site & head for Ground Zero. [...] Yep, that's been a new thing in my life lately... I've been wildly in love with a wonderful woman named Mary... she's got bright eyes & a sweet, sweet smile that makes we want to evaporate into clouds of pure joy... I guess I've still got it pretty bad... well, anyway, that's been helping me stay out of the ruts and I've been learning & growing a lot & it's been giving me lots of energy for going out into the world & fighting for life... I deny death! Or like you say so well in letter #3, point 5: "why shouldn't we struggle w/ death? we grapple w/ life the whole way through, & death is a much less impressive foe." [...]

Yes & this college town has been awash in a fetid fervor of freedom these days, what with the basketball team doing its thang so big. Perhaps we were the only people in the city who didn't watch the Big Game, instead we got a bottle of wine & headed for the old Theta Chi house to watch the sunset. This place is a gutted concrete shell on top of a hill in the middle of a little woods right in the center of town and from on top you can see for miles. We could have kept track of the score of the game if we wanted to because every time something happened a roar swept over the whole city from thousands of windows. It was like we had our own cheering section as we made out on top of the world and every good move brought roars and screams of delighted approval. Later driving home the streets were deserted, no cars anywhere, like the town had just been hit with a neutron bomb or something. But as soon as the game ended, the whole downtown was flooded with hordes of hooters and honkers who were screaming happy and congratulating each other for happening to live here while the basketball team did well. Right on! Free to PARTY! I <u>love</u> this country... yes, & this week they had a big parade & 60,000 people flooded into town. We hung out the windows & sucked on beers and watched the action. The big surprise was seeing Wavy Gravy, of Woodstock and Hog Farm fame, come rolling by, a big fat bald hippie with long wavy brown hair, wearing a rubber nose & clown makeup & a "Beak 'Em, Hawks" T-shirt, lolling on the back of a convertible like a drunken maniac, wildly waving a "Nobody for

President" bumpersticker at the J-hawk fans. What a hoot!

Have you been in contact with AFM in Miami yet? [...] He's one of the charter saints of juxtaposition, I think. Tell him boog sent ya.

boog

23 November 1988, Jana Svoboda, Beaumont, TX

Hello jana,

Yes, I'm still alive. I think. I don't have a particularly good excuse for not writing for so long. I haven't been particularly busy & I think about getting in touch with you almost every day. Some days I've even come close to sitting down & writing, but I guess this isn't horseshoes. Few things are. Life is a gamma ray, old chum...

Most of all I suppose I don't want you to think I'm one of those people who gets caught up in a relationship & forgets about everyone else & ignores his friends. I most assuredly haven't been doing that, since I haven't been in a relationship for several months now. I've been traveling some, so that's partly an excuse, but mostly I've just been bad. To the bone. But I'm here now.

[...] And now I hear from Costas that he's got a job & is going to San Francisco. Lawrence won't be the same. I need to call Khalila & Aaron soon & see if they've got any going away party plans. This is something that needs to be done up right. It's the end of an era... remind me to get busy on that, OK?

So what are your plans like? Have you found a graduate program that you can hang with? Guerrilla epistemology? Psychic engineering? Cybernetic semiotics? Home ec? I don't know how this is connected, but I hear from someone that Norm Forer was one of the 5 finalists for the Hope Award. He didn't get it, but I'm sure the prospect of it would have had Archie Dykes rolling over in his grave, if he was dead.

And speaking of Norm Forer, I've been doing a lot of work on Disorientation recently (I thought I had turned the thing over to some other people but ("Chocolate whiz-bang," says Brenda in the kitchen) I got roped back into doing it again. One more time. Yeah, yeah, that's what I said last time...). & we're doing articles on some "KU Alumni They Don't Tell You About" again, & this year Ron Kuby's one of them. I interviewed him by phone last week. (That's how we got here from Norm, because Ron used to work for Norm.) Anyway he's a lot of fun to talk to & is doing lots of good work with William Kunstler in New York. I had this notion that there was a great herd of attorneys working for Kunstler but it's just Ron & Bill, representing an incredible array of famous victims & radical fringe elements: one of the people Bernard Goetz shot at, some Puerto Rican nationalists convicted for various acts of political persuasion involving guns and bombs, the Native Americans who took over a newspaper office somewhere in North Carolina recently, the people busted in the Tompkins Square Park riots in New York recently, the Yippies, Leonard Peltier, etc. He tried to talk me out of becoming a lawyer.

Oops, I haven't said anything about that yet. I'm scheduled to take the LSAT on Dec. 3. I've shelled out the money for it & everything. I haven't studied for it though. I guess I'm still pretty ambivalent about it. Ron says, "It bothers me to see creative people go to law school." I've gotten mixed reactions from other people. I asked my Dad if he'd still speak to me if I became a lawyer & he said, "I talk to lawyers every day." Hmmmm... The reasoning behind this is that it would be a way for me to go back to Garnett & still be able to make a living. Plus it would give me some appearance of legitimacy (so to speak) that I wouldn't have otherwise & that's essential for some of the organizing I'd like to do there. Still I'm not sure that's enough justification to sacrifice 3 years of my life. Plus it sounds really reminiscent of the reasoning that got me into engineering school, & we all know how that worked out. A lot of the motivation for this is probably me starting to feel old & feeling like I ought to be doing more with my life, to stop squandering my talent & time like it seems like I'm doing now. I'm not sure how much of that feeling is coming from outside & I'm internalizing it & how much is coming from within. This time I think a lot of it is coming from within. I'm feeling really directionless & when it comes down to it the stark truth is that even the wrong direction <u>is still a direction</u> & thus can have a certain sort of appeal... I dunno, Jana... I haven't committed myself to anything other than taking the test yet, though... we'll see...

& the kicker is that I've been feeling really restless lately too which combined with directionlessness is a real kick in the head. I've been taking advantage of my easy situation & traveling some. I got to go to California for a few weeks recently. And Oregon. Somebody I met at a couple of the anarchist gatherings was passing through town on the way to LA so me & my friend Mikey went along for the ride. LA was like hell. It was really beyond my imagination."Oh that motorway livin'... ain't it good to be so free?" ask the Kinks on the stereo now. I put them on after I started thinking about LA 'cause there's a song at the end of this side called "Celluloid Heroes" that says,"You can see all the stars as you walk down Hollywood Boulevard/ Some that you recognize, some that you hardly even heard of/ Some that suffered and struggled and died for fame/ Some who succeeded and some who struggled in vain." Or something like that. We saw all the stars on Hollywood Boulevard: Bud Abbott, Sammy Davis, Jr., Angela Lansbury, Bette Davis, Pinky Lee. We sat on a bus stop [bench] and watched Mexican street gang members chasing each other down the middle of the street trying to kill each other while the prostitutes behind us huddled around the moneymatic machine. And the cops drove around & around & eyed us suspiciously. Oh Hollywood, you elegant slum! At least it had character, more than the rest of LA rolled into a little ball together like a piece of Wonder Bread. Hollywood was the crust. Everywhere we went reminded me of a Frank Zappa song: Palmdale, Irwindale, El Segundo, Laurel Canyon, 3:30 in the afternoon...

We rode the Green Tortoise hippie bus up the coast, stopped at Santa Cruz long enough to buy a bagel & take a leak, then on to San Francisco where we spent a grand total of about 12 hours. We wanted to throw a bowling ball off the Golden Gate Bridge but we didn't have time. We did get a bowling ball when we were in Eugene with Brenna, it was bright blue & said "Darlene." We tossed it into the Willamette River in Corvallis & the goddamn thing floated. We followed it downstream for a ways & then lost it, presumably it's on its way out to sea & will wash up on the shore of some remote Pacific atoll where it will become the center of an elaborate cargo cult & Darlene will be their blue goddess... or maybe not.

"Everybody's a hero, & everybody's a star, & everybody's in show biz, no matter who you are." That's the Kinks singing now. I was on nationwide cable TV a few weeks ago, or so I hear. I was in a video that a local resident named Roger Holden filmed this summer. It's loosely based on William Burroughs's *Nova Express* & the music is by somebody called Schloss-Tiegel. Or something like that. My role is that I wave a sign around & thereby destroy the Clay-mation monster that's threatening the world with destruction. Pretty inspiring stuff, huh? I haven't seen it myself yet. I've had plenty of opportunities, I just felt unsociable the night they premiered it on campus & didn't feeling like seeking somebody with a TV and cablevision at 2 a.m. on a Friday night when it was on TV. Someday. Roger promises me a copy for my very own. Yee-haw...

I live in a real house now, with three cats in the yard, life used to be so hard, etc. It's been a little scattered with the onset of winter & midterms but mostly it's a really supportive place. Plus I'm eating well again. Tonight was an incredible sort of pesto soup & oat-rice patties. Lauren cooked them! Yum! Plus some apple-cinnamon rolls that my roomie Brenda baked at "Amazing Grains" which is the new name for the bakery behind the co-op which is now a co-op composed of Nan & Brenda & a woman named Irene. & 2 of my other roomies bake at Paradise... there's a whole lot of bakin' goin' on... & we finally turned the heat on yesterday so, although we're not baking, we're certainly beginning to thaw out. We already had a serious snow but it hasn't been very cold & today was almost perfect. Weatherwise.

Well, yow... a lot of words... have I redeemed myself yet? I hope. I think about you a lot, I know you can't tell that by looking in your mailbox, but it's true. I value your friendship a great deal & hope you'll do a better job of keeping in touch than I have... all my love to you and your family—

boog

3 December 1988, Brenna Hoffmann, Eugene, OR

"I falter before the task of finding the language which might adequately express the incalculable paradoxes of love."

– C. G. Jung

Moi aussi, mon cherie, moi aussi...

Hello sweet dear Brenna my friend,

& many greetings to you this fine cold Kansas night. I've been reading Jung, as you can see. I borrowed the copy you gave to Mikey. I just finished it, even including the Seven Sermons of the Dead. Jung says (as you might recall): "The older I have become, the less I have understood or had insight into or known about myself," but,"The more uncertain I have felt about myself, the more there has grown up in me a feeling of kinship with all things." I have kinship with all things and I took the LSAT this morning. I did it, Brenna. I massively fucked up one section, but I aced several others so figure I probably did well enough to get into KU. Now I just have to convince myself to apply. I tell people what I'm doing & I get a really wide spectrum of reactions, everything from enthusiastic handshaking approval to uncontrollable laughter to stares of disbelief. Laughter is the most common. That seems like the proper attitude. I just hope I can maintain it myself.

I had a very cosmopolitan dinner tonight. I was invited by my friend Sumaya from North Yemen who used to produce documentary films in Kuwait. The guest of honor was an Armenian political scientist from the Soviet Union. It was at the house of a Lebanese/Armenian/French woman who lives in an apartment where the Sanctuary used to be. Plus there were a few Americans there, how blasé... I brought wine, German and Bulgarian. It was juxtapositionist heaven... & to think that it happened on Michigan Street... in Kansas... so there was lots o' good food: orange lentil soup (orange lentils are just hulled lentils, I learned tonight. Is this true? That inside every brown lentil lurks a heart of orange?), an interesting broccoli/almond/ tomato/yogurt concoction that was probably some sort of ethnic but I didn't ask. And rice, & hummus & pitas. & PUNKIN PIE, made by Z., the Lebanese etc. woman, that was precisely yummy (the PIE, that is). And after it was everybody's bedtime I went to catch the last hour or so of BCR at the Bottleneck, where I got in for a dollar & drank a beer & found something to hold on to & shook myself in general syncopation to the wild jazzlike music until I forgot who & what & where I was even just for a brief moment because what's music for if it can't do that? And now I'm home, typing some gibberish, a letter to one of my best friends in the entire universe which might also be gibberish too (the letter, not the friend, you unnerstand...) but this is IMPORTANT gibberish because it's for you...

And speaking of gibberish, I ran across a very interesting word while I was proofreading a few days ago. It was in an article for an upcoming issue of the Journal of Phycology. About algae. Anyway this was a neo-Latin kind of word, a species name but I forget the genus, and after I read it into the tape recorder I had to stop for a minute because I was laughing. Here, you try it, the word was this: canaliculata. If you're not laughing yet, try it again only being sure to pronounce the second to last *a* as a long *a*: eh. There. And the answer, of course, is yes. Your place or mine?

All bad jokes aside, I still falter before the task of finding the language which might adequately express the incalculable paradoxes of love. I think it must be a sign language though. Like Ferlinghetti says, "Making love with bodies was a means of proving that life existed. Making love with bodies was a kind of speech to prove it, a language of being. Saints could prove it without bodies, I needed mine..." I am not now nor have I ever been a saint. & as a prospect for the future it seems neither likely or appealing. [...]

And I don't think I'd have it any other way, really, because it seems like that's what life is: unrealized desire. Yearning & seeking but not achieving. Like Alan Watts says, "The goal of love is always union with its object," and it seems like that union of love fully realized is ultimately stasis & death. I've seen lots of relationships work that way, in fact. But with love not fully realized, with desires unfilled, there is motion & life. I'm alive, I'm alive! Boundaries are important. I'm glad there are two of us. But yearning for the one keeps my wheels turning & I'm looking forward to summer when it will be warm & my wheels will once again turn me out towards you & the ocean (& speaking of which, I've got something to pass along to you. I don't know why it's still in my head but I probably won't be able to get it out until I write it down & send it far away. It's a marketing slogan for a certain masseuse you told us about when we were in Corvallis: It's not the meat, it's M'ocean. There, now I can forget. Feel free to pass it along to her. If law school doesn't work out, maybe I'll go into advertising...)

Anyway, in the meantime, you should write to me. The postcards you sent soon after we left really made me smile, & now they're up on the image wall in the dining room. Your prose really sparkles & creates warm, bright, clear images for me. I'd like to see it in more than postcard sized installments but I'll take what I can get.

I got to babysit for little Alex for about a half an hour recently, an intimidating prospect indeed at first, but it was all pretty easy in reality. He just sucked on his bottle for a long time & then went to sleep. Life is relatively uncomplicated when you're 10 weeks old, I guess. Oh, yes, here's another story: Did I ever tell you about "nuck"? Why of course I did. But just to refresh your memory just in case, it's a new preposition that Gregor Felke & I invented (if I remember correctly) that means "partially but not wholly submerged or contained in." Like, "the pestle was nuck the mortar" (or is it the other way around?), or "She stuck her tongue out at him so that it was nuck her mouth." Etc. Anyway little Alex had a pacifier to suck on, & guess what it said on it: NUK. They spelled it wrong, but the meaning was clear: nuck. Contentedly sucking on the pacifier nuck his mouth, little Alex smiled a great smile & thought great thoughts way too big for a ten week old baby but that's OK because soon he would grow up and go to school so they could carve his thoughts down to fit the little boxes they had prepared for him. Recess, peanut butter, cartoons on TV. Skateboard, rocknroll, styling mousse. Big house, fast car, credit card. Rest home, Ex-lax, cartoons on TV. Somewhere wheels are turning...

Enough gibberish. This sheet of paper is almost full. I will accept the natural limit imposed by this constraint & stop writing very soon. Boundaries are necessary. Without tension & distinctions there is only jello. Desire is the motor of history. Somewhere wheels are turning. WRITE ME LETTERS. If you want. I miss you, Brenna, though you're with me always. In heart & spirit if not in flesh. My heart sings now. I'll talk to you soon. All my love to you & your roomies & Oso & Montgomery & anyone else important in your life I might have forgotten. Shine on you crazy diamond.............

boog

1989–1990

Babes in Toyland • Free State Brewery opens • beat without GLEET • bean-holding moon • Fester wedding • dog buried in Sade • silence is the loudest noise • my heart thinks in a language I don't understand • Roxanne puts on the red light • Elvis was a timid boy • Locke's ontology of money

2 February 1989, Tad Kepley, Ulysses, KS

Alright now Tad,

Glad to hear you're alive and well and probably under police surveillance—everything's normal.

The raging debate on technology is usually too vague to be meaningful. Asking whether "technology" is good or bad seems about as useful as wondering if two legs are better than four. Humans use tools & if they didn't (or if they had four legs) they'd be something entirely different. I've already ranted about this in print so I'll just copy an article from gentle anarchist #11 & send that to you. I'd like to hear what you think. I'll just run through what I think are the main points again though:

1). Instead of talking about "technology" in vague generalities, we need to ask specific questions about specific tools & techniques in specific social contexts.

2). What we need to ask are questions like: is this technology compatible with nonhierarchical social relations? with a decentralized economy? Is this technology environmentally destructive? Does it fill a real need? Does this technology empower the people that use it or does it make them more dependent on things they can't control?

3). Every technology is a <u>social relationship</u>. With sufficient will & organization we can control technological development instead of vice versa.

The g.a. article is really just an outline of what maybe someday will be something more readable & more backed up with evidence & convincing arguments. In the meantime there it is. [...]

A couple of nights ago I saw the Wipers at the Bottleneck, also Babes in Toyland from Minneapolis & Cows from NY. Rocknroll. The Wipers were good, & I liked some of Babes in Toyland's noise, but more than that I enjoyed watching them play. There's something strangely androgynous about seeing women doing macho guitar posturing, something dangerously erotic like the little orange beard a woman I met at the Chicago gathering had. I fell in love with the bass player who was making love to her guitar right on stage, but that's all over now. Easy come, easy go.

[...] I'm still trying to save thirty bucks to pay the application fee for law school. I suppose I could if I really wanted to, but 30 dollars is a lot of beer. If you know what I mean. And beer will get you through times of no law school better than law school will get you through times of no beer.

Keep in touch. wahoo,
boog

1 March 1989, Costas Orountiotis, San Jose, CA

Howdy Costas,

[...] So you're in the fast lane now? I'm not sure I could keep up the pace... When BC was living in East Lawrence he called it "life in the left-hand-turn lane"... that's more my speed. [...]

SORT Saturday (a recycling fair) went over really big... hundreds of people came out to the fairgrounds & we collected tons & tons of trash... 7093 pounds of glass, to be exact, & the last I heard Till-Star was still weighing the rest of the stuff.

The Free State Brewery opened last Thursday, & the beer is great. They've got three kinds—a wheat beer, "Ad Astra Ale" (to the stars through ale, right?), and "Walruff's Bock" named after the last brewery in Lawrence that shut down a hundred years ago. Yum. I saw Rick Frydman working behind the bar last night. I took this to be further evidence of the enduring value of a KU law degree. [...]

I was down by the river this morning watching them tear down trees, the ones the eagles used to perch in. The restraining order keeping them from doing it got thrown out yesterday and this morning at 6:30 or so they started bulldozing. A few people tried to stop them, but it was too little too late. 4 people got busted. There was a picture in the Journal World tonight of two police officers looking up at Keith Abrams in a tree. It was hopeless but I'm still glad somebody did it. I suppose we need gestures like that to inspire us until the time when enough people come around that we can actually do something. Anyway watching the big yellow machines pushing and clawing at the trees made me really sad—and all for a fucking cut-rate shopping mall. How many places are there where you can see bald eagles in a city? One less now...

As I'm sitting here typing I'm waiting for the bathtub to fill—some things change, some things stay the same. I miss that old place—not much, but I miss it. & I miss you too, my friend. [...] Take care & I'll see you soon.

love,
boog

14 April 1989, Lauren Jaben, Minneapolis, MN

Hello Lauren,

When I sat down to type tonight I imagined you reading this letter and remembering how you used to walk by my door & always see me hunched over the typewriter wailing away with my one typing finger at speeds known but to few, and I imagined that making you smile. And I also just imagined you reading about my imagining (like you're doing right now) and that making you smile & laugh out loud—just a little, ha ha—like you used to always do. All this smiling & imagining... I miss you. [...]

I figured my taxes today & much to my surprise I realized that I owed 700 dollars in Social Security taxes. Oops! I decided that the best way to deal with this would be to file for an extension and leave town right away. I'm going to New York & DC in about a week. Vicky's going along for the trip to New York, but I'm coming back by myself. There'll be plenty of time to be hopelessly in debt after I return. And I'll still wangle a way to come up and see you in July. I talked to C. last week about our summer plans. We tentatively decided to go to the anarchist gathering together, so I would come and get her in Minneapolis & then we'd go to Washington & Oregon & California. Of course I'll allow plenty of time for visiting all my special friends in Minneapolis. I hope we can talk Brenda into going to Oregon with us too, but it depends on what her vacation schedule is at the bakery.

We finally got Disorientation to press on Monday, after Brian and Mike Mader and I spent 3 all nighters doing layout, in your old room. We hauled the kitchen table up there so we could keep Brian company while he typed on the computer as the rest of us played with scissors and glue. You'll get a contributors copy. Somebody else laid out the graffiti contest pages & they decided not to use the Stan & Jocelyn BOXCARS BOXCARS BOXCARS picture but we heisted one of your drawings from the last Diso so you ended up being a contributor anyway. It's really jam-packed this time, and the layout is slicker than ever, which isn't really saying that much but we typeset most of it this time with a real typesetter so that was quite a treat. Now that it's finished I have my life back again, but I still have to figure out something to do with it.

I played Scrabble with Julie on Wednesday. She beat me, even though I made the words ZEN, EYES, and FEZ all in one play, with Z on a double letter score, even. Counted twice, twice! 74 points! I want a rematch! Richard Brautigan wrote a story about playing Scrabble once. It's called "Ted" and I think it's in *The Tokyo-Montana Express*. It's about him being upset that his friends beat him at Scrabble even though he's a world-famous writer. Ted is a word that means "to spread for drying." He goes off at one point making up sentences showing how people might use the word "ted" in their daily lives: "Will someone please <u>ted</u> the cowshit?", etc. While we were looking up a word in the dictionary we came across the word GLEET, which means to emit a mucous discharge from the urethra. I encouraged her to use it but she picked it up right after she put it down because her conscience would have bothered her if she beat me with GLEET. As it turned out she beat me even without GLEET and has a clean conscience to boot.

I tell Charlotte [the cat] sometimes that I'm going to put her in a jar, but somehow it's just not the same. Give old Slim a scritch on the belly for me, OK? and Jagular, too. Peter you can do whatever you want with, but be sure to tell him boog says howdy. I'll see you soon...

boog

19 June 1989, Lauren Jaben, Minneapolis, MN

Lauren dear,

Well now it's the full of the moon again & I presume that it's the same full moon that's smiling down upon you even as I type. We gave Brenda a gift certificate for Natural Way and today she bought crescent moon earrings and Julie saw them and said that when the moon is in that phase you say that it's holding water, because it's sort of bowl shaped I suppose. Well tonight Brian made gazpacho and burritos and Julie wasn't entirely hungry so she made a burrito with a part of a tortilla and as it happens it tore out in a sort of crescent shaped piece that resembled a water-holding moon except it was holding beans instead. So that's the way it goes on an almost summer solstice Monday here at the Big House in Lawrence, Kansas. Same as it ever was... same as it ever was...

And this year is the fiftieth anniversary of the Wizard of Oz (The Movie) and so Liberty Hall showed it for a week just here recently. And of course we organized a grandiose extended family expedition to go bask in our cultural heritage. We all noticed things we hadn't seen before, like that the scarecrow is carrying a gun when they go off in search of the Wicked Witch of the West. I think Mary noticed that one. I had several guests at the time & of course we brought them along, too, so that now they can go home & tell everyone how everyone in Kansas watches the Wizard of Oz & that's all they talk about. My friend Madeleine from Toronto grew up TV-less and had never seen it before. Jake from Kentucky teaches history at a community college & told about an essay he'd read that argued that the whole thing was a Populist allegory about turn of the century politics. I read it today and for the most part it seemed pretty plausible. He identifies the scarecrow with farmers, the tin man as eastern workers (who are turned into robot slaves by the wicked eastern industrialists, i.e., the witch). The year the tin man stands rusting in the woods is the depression of 1893. William Jennings Bryan is the cowardly lion. The great Oz is the president, any president. In the book Oz isn't really green & shiny, it just looks that way because they make everybody wear green glasses, and when Dorothy takes hers off everything is grey and ugly, just like Kansas. (By the way, L. Frank Baum lived in South Dakota.) In the book Dorothy's shoes weren't ruby but silver, and this represents the populist crusade for free coinage of silver, and of course the yellow brick road represents the gold standard of the Republicans, and in the book it isn't bright & shiny like in the movie, but is full of holes which the scarecrow keeps tripping over & falling into cause he hasn't got any brains.

Hmmmm... this reminds me of a joke I read in Peanuts once... Linus, Lucy, & Charlie Brown are laying in the grass looking up at the clouds, and somebody asks "What do you see in the clouds?" Linus says, "I see the stoning of St. Stephen." And Lucy says, "I see George Washington crossing the Delaware." And Charlie Brown says, "I was going to say I saw a horsie and a duckie, but I changed my mind." Well anyway, I decided to read the Wizard of Oz again [...] and I like it. In it you hear the Scarecrow say, "I cannot understand why you should wish to leave this beautiful country and go back to the dry, gray place you call Kansas." And you hear Dorothy reply, "That is because you have no brains. No matter how dreary and gray our homes are, we people of flesh and blood would rather live there than in any other country, be it ever so beautiful. There is no place like home." To which the Scarecrow responds, "Of course I cannot understand it. If your heads were stuffed with straw, like mine, you would probably all live in beautiful places, and Kansas would have no people at all. It is fortunate for Kansas that you have brains." I want to say this to Eric before he moves to New York on Saturday. I'd say it to you, too, but it's too late. I also want to say to Eric, "In New York the acoustics are good for laughter, for life is all external, all action, no thought, no meditation, no dreaming, no reflection, only the exuberance of action. No memory of the past, no looking back, no doubts, no questions." I suppose he'll like it there. For a while.

I read [this] in the Diary of Anaïs Nin, Vol. 2. There are 7 or 8 volumes. It takes up a foot of space on the library shelf. That's how I got into it, wondering why there was so much of it. I've been really impressed with it. The writing is really amazing, and it's been full of revelations, among the first of which is that she wasn't a Russian man, as I had somehow come to believe, but instead a woman with a Cuban father and a Dutch mother who grew up in France and New York. Most of her friends are famous artists and writers (now, anyway, they weren't when she started writing about them) but unlike so much of the incestuous, self-aggrandizing beat literature, it doesn't matter that her struggling writer friend is Henry Miller or that her insane actor friend is Antonin Artaud, it's the way she writes about them that makes you want to keep reading and reading. Julie gave me her book "Spy in the House of Love" to read after we talked about her on the way to see the Benton exhibit in Kansas City, which was way cool. I used to not like Benton's painting at all but sometime after I came to college I fell in love with it, probably about the same time I learned to appreciate Gaudi. [...] I feel a little sad for Julie because so many of her best friends are leaving—You & Eric, & I guess Marvel is leaving soon too. Anyway Lawrence is still here. The dog and the city...

OK, and now I've just resurrected your last letter from its secret tubule along with the Law School Admission Test pen you sent which is kind of amusing because I paid those fuckers over a hundred dollars and I didn't get a pen... You talk a lot about boats. It makes me think of Anaïs Nin again, who lived in a houseboat on the Seine for a while until they made her move it up the river when World War II started. It was old and creaky and came with a drunken wooden-legged captain and a dark, sullen young lad to run the pumps. It also makes me think of Annie Dillard who I saw in New York with Donna's sister Carol (oh yeah—I went to New York. More later...) and read from her book American Childhood and told jokes, not necessarily in that order. Her father had a boat and ran away from their home once to float down the river to New Orleans and live on nothing but jazz music. To be a jazzetarian. Anyway he got about a hundred miles out of Cincinnati before he decided to sell the boat and come back. New York was a nice place to visit, but... you know the rest. Travel stories I'll save for when I come visit you, except to offer the opinion that I'm sure Atlantic City was modeled on one of the lower levels of hell. [...]

I'm sorry I'm so bad about staying in touch. I sunk into a deep funk after I got back from New York and only recently have I crawled out from under my rock. And then I was really busy, having let lots of responsibilities pile up for a long time. But I'm in tip top condition now. Even in tip top condition I'm still pretty erratic, though, so please don't judge how much I miss you by how often you see a letter in your mailbox. Give my regards to Peter, Theresa, Renaldo, Doug, Dave, Jagger and of course Slim. I'll see you soon, all my love,

boog

Brenda & Vicky's little cat <u>Lemon</u> crawled into a <u>jar all by herself</u>–

Be sure to write about me in your diary because someday I'll be famous for pioneering the "stream of unconsciousness" technique in writing and you too can have a prime number of volumes of your diary published and take up a foot of shelf space in libraries everywhere...

22 October 1989, Gareth Rowell, Niagara University, NY

hello Gareth,

Law school is more fun than being poked repeatedly with a sharp stick, but not much. Anyway, it keeps me off the streets.

In lieu of going to the National Lawyer's Guild regional convention in Kansas City Saturday, I went with Mark Parker to Kathel Miller's wedding in Oskaloosa. It was at the chapel at Old Jefferson Town [...] The crowd was mostly relatives and Festers (or Rennies, or Fairies, depending on who you talk to—Kathel has been following the Renaissance Festival/Fair circuit ever since she left 1614 [Kentucky], and that's where she met her new husband), and me & Mark Parker & Sky Lister. A strange brew, indeed... the reception was at the Eagles's Lodge in Oskaloosa... All around the walls they had a number of little boxes with lights that provided dramatic backlighting to Aubrey Beardsley-like paintings of inspirational allegorical themes: Truth, Justice, Equality,

Home, Country, Loyalty, etc. One of them was turned off when we got there and Mark Parker turned it on: God, it said. On the back wall was a picture with no name, dressed in a black flowing robe that covered his eyes, carrying a sickle, with tombstones behind him. Death, I presume, although they couldn't bring themselves to say that. I pulled the switch and turned that one off as we left, and as I turned around everyone was dancing in a circle and the ceiling fan above was spinning in a circle and the bingo board looked down benevolently on the whole scene and it was a happy wedding indeed. It made me think of a Gregory Corso poem, as weddings often do:

> O God, and the wedding! All her family and her friends
> and only a handful of mine all scroungy and bearded
> just wait[ing] to get at the drinks and food—

But for the first time in a long time everything seemed Right in the Universe... Me & Mark Parker, him in his blue blue suit with a pink shirt & me in my traffic court regalia, heading out into the sunset on the way home, comfortably buzzed by a couple of beers & a plastic glassful of champagne (which the Festers bumped together at the reception, yelling Clink! Clink! Clink!), rolling down unknown roads on the way home and discovering giant goats.

And in the meantime I'm in law school. I've been prosecuting in traffic court. Anybody who wants to appeal a parking ticket at KU can do so and can have free legal representation in the form of a first year law student. Prosecutors are first year law students, too, and the judges are 2-L's. The amusing part is that it's all sanctioned by the state—it's a <u>real</u> court, or at least as real as these things get. So far I'm 4 and 0—I've salvaged $110.00 worth of fines for the university—here I am pimping for the goddamned university and not even getting paid for it. I figured I'd end up selling out someday, but not for FREE. Seriously though it's probably better that I'm wrestling with these <u>moral ambiguities</u> now than waiting till I go back home & get stuck with being County Prosecutor. It's hard to keep things in perspective but Sean Santoro has been giving me lots of useful advice. As my 2-L mentor, Sean advises me to go listen to African music & not take it all too seriously. So I try. Tonight I went down to the Bottleneck to check out the "Disco Inferno" party for Mona Tipton & Jane Patrick & Frank Morris's birthdays. I stayed for about 15 minutes, as long as it took to get my fill of 70's nostalgia. The only good polyester is a dead polyester. Disco Duck. I love this country.

Time to crash, I suppose. I have Civil Procedure at 8:30 and will need to know the intimate details of rule 26(b)(3). Thanks for the letter—it was good to hear from you, eh? I wondered where you'd went, eh?

boog

16 December 1989, Glenn Elmer, Los Angeles, CA

OK now Glenn,

[...] I took a much needed & well deserved break from studying for finals last night & went to see BCR & the Lonesome Houndogs at the Bottleneck, it's a combination I've been wanting to see for a long time, the two weirdest bands in the area on the same stage for the same low price, a dynamic duo (a die-manic duo?) indeed. (It would be a great low-budget sci-fi movie: Teeny Boppers from Atlantis meet the Frat Boys on Acid.) [...]

Well, I have two stories tonight. Both are second hand, but both made me laugh. We'll see how they do on third use:

Tonight I had dinner with Anne Ogborn & her friend Fran—both are male-to-female transsexuals & are getting married soon with yours truly scheduled to perform the ceremony (they came to town tonight to check out Danforth Chapel). Anyway Anne talked to Jim Benson on the phone recently (Jim is still in Colby, if you don't know, still teaching math. And dallying with cowgirls...). Somehow Jim was roped into participating in a local "Dating Game", being an eligible bachelor and all. Jim, I hear, borrowed a costume from a friend who's a rodeo clown for the event. I can see it now: "Bachelor number 3, describe your idea of a perfect romantic evening." "I'm knee high to a grasshopper and covered all over with taco sauce!" Is Colby ready for this? Anne says it already happened, otherwise I'd be making plans to drive to Colby just to see it...

Story number two involves my roommate Pete while he was a projectionist at Liberty Hall. Pete went to work with Lauren & Peter's big black Lab dog Jagger who promptly fell asleep at the foot of the projector. Pete started the movie, "The Persecution and Assassination of Jean-Paul Marat as Performed by the Inmates of the Asylum of Charenton under the Direction of the Marquis de Sade," and went downstairs to watch, from which point of view everything appeared to be going smoothly. Meanwhile upstairs the film had broken after leaving the projector & instead of going onto the takeup reel spewed out onto the floor, on top of the sleeping dog, burying her entirely. 45 minutes later Pete goes upstairs to find a sleeping dog buried under 45 minutes of 32 millimeter film. Downstairs the action is reaching a crescendo as the actors are going wild getting ready to tear down the walls and break out of the asylum as upstairs Pete makes a bold grab to pull the sleeping dog out from under the film without waking her up and sending her howling off tangling & shredding the film. Pete was quick of hand & pulled it off & it only took two hours to put the film back together. The End.

I continue to be amazed & inspired by the events in Eastern Europe. Two days in a row this week the *New York Times* had pictures of beautiful Bulgarian women holding up candles in pro-democracy rallies. I think of Peter Gabriel's (or somebody's) song Biko: "You can blow out a candle/ but you can't blow out a fire/ for once the flame begins to catch/ the wind will fan it higher/ oh Biko". & now in Johannesburg Nelson Mandela is hobnobbing with Mr. de Klerk. The Nineties are going to be WILD, my friend, mark my words...

It's cold here now Glenn, that's COLD with a capital everything, the temperature has been in the double digits more often in the negative than the positive the last few days. I pity you poor Californians who don't get to experience real seasons... [...]

love,
boog

(my roommate Brenda has a friend who is a math grad student at Palo Alto, where they just found the biggest prime number so far. He sent her a copy. It covers 6 pages. 8½" x 11", small print, I-don't-know-how-many-hundred-thousand digits. For our law school finals, each of us was assigned a random 4-digit number to identify our exams with. I got 0277—PRIME. There is justice in the universe.)

17 December 1989, Josh Mars, Pacific Grove, CA

Hello Josh,

Silence is the loudest noise. Somebody else said that first but I believe it to be true. I heard it first as the dramatic end to a noisy performance art piece by mIEKAL aND & Liz Was at a place called ABC No Rio in New York. After the noise stopped I really heard the sounds of the city for the first time, even though I'd been there almost a week. And there's no silence as noisy as the one inside your head, like the one in my head after the beep on your answering machine. I work much better on paper, where you can't hear the silence between this sentence & the last.

I'm learning to walk on sharp knives. Someone else said this first too but I believe it to be true as well. I'm in law school now Josh. It's better than being poked with a sharp stick but not much. I'm in the middle of finals now & I'm finally realizing why law school finals traditionally make people so crazy. Once upon a time when I lived in a fine brick house with two cats in the yard, one of my roommates was a first year law student. One day right about this time he came downstairs with a glazed look in his eye, calmly walked into the kitchen, flipped the kitchen table over, then calmly walked back upstairs. He was one-quarter Penobscot Indian and there weren't any other Indians in the law school so he was invited to join the Black American Law Student Association even though he was as Caucasian as you or me. Tonight I studied for my property final until I couldn't stand it anymore. Why the fuck are they trying to teach me about property—it's like trying to teach someone without arms to juggle. It's possible, I suppose, but it's much easier with hands. And property would make more sense to me I'm sure, if I ever expected to have any. My way of talking myself into continuing to do it is by analogy—if you want to blow up a building the best place to start is by studying the blueprints so if I want to alter the nature of property relationships I should probably learn how the legal system deals with property. Sure.

I'm living in a fine wooden house again. It's the same old story—weird (but nice) roommates, vegetarian dinners, cats in the yard, big gas bills. From my bedroom window I can see where your old house used to be. There's a giant uglyplex full of college students there now. When I walk by it always makes me a little sad thinking of all the good times I had in the houses they tore down to build that thing. Like Spaghetti Wednesday. [...]

Steve Ballew was over for dinner tonight. We ate a spicy soup with GARBANZO beans and one of my roommates hung some of his drawings on our living room wall. He said you'd called & given him your new number & address. The last number I had was from when Steve & I got goofy on a big bottle of wine & called you up & left unintelligible messages on your answering machine & the next time I tried the number it was an all-nite plumber or a discount veterinarian or something. Anyway it's nice to know where you are again. I was in

California again this summer for the anarchist gathering in San Francisco but I didn't have my car again so I didn't have a way to get down to see you. I rode the bus out & caught a ride back with one of my roommates who was out there. I thought maybe we'd take the southern route home & be able to stop in on you but she wanted to go back to Seattle instead (or we tried to... the car blew up & we ended up selling it for scrap & flying home).

I hope things are going well for you in California [...] Let me know what you're up to. [...] Take care...

love,
boog

2 January 1990, Kate Steger, Minneapolis, MN

Hello dear sweet Katie my friend,

Your letter was just about my favorite christmas present so it's OK that it was late. You say that a proper, lengthy, descriptive epistle is what I deserve from you but I'm not sure I like the concept of "deserving"—who deserves anything? Did I deserve to break my neck when I was 15? Do I deserve to have a good friend like you? Did I deserve this sunny day? Anyway just seeing your name on the card was enough to make my heart sing, for I was afraid I had lost touch with you, and I know that the important details of just what the hell you've been doing with yourself the last year & a half or so will come in due time...

I liked the quote from the I Ching. Sure, my heart thinks, although it's usually in a language I can't speak & only vaguely understand. And like I just claimed moments ago, my heart does sing sometimes on special occasions but my experience tells me you don't have to think to sing & it probably even gets in the way so I suppose my heart's not thinking <u>all</u> the time. I know my head doesn't—that's how I got into law school.

Yup. Law school. I know it sounds crazy & it probably is. So far it's been one of the worst experiences of my life, although I'm not entirely sure why. It's not as bad as the Paper Chase (at least I don't think so—I haven't actually seen the Paper Chase but I seem to have heard about it a lot and it seems to be where most of the images I had of what law school would be like came from) but it's close enough. The whole thing is conceived as a giant brainwashing operation—they give you enough work to do so that if you want to do well you have to spend all your waking hours on it, they force you to be able to defend both sides of any proposition & totally wreck any ideas you came in with about good & bad, right & wrong, or up & down, then when you're totally disoriented & reaching out for something solid to grab onto, they have a ready made reality ready to hand you: The Law. A good job with a good firm. Swimming pools, movie stars... They even try to make you socialize & drink a lot of beer with other law students but luckily I have a houseful of weirdos to come home to. I'm glad I'm starting this at my ripe old age rather than doing it straight out of college. A lot of the kids are pretty intimidated about it all, but I feel too old & jaded to kiss much ass. One of my professors is a recent KU grad & I was his supervisor for a while when we worked together at the Info Center—so he doesn't intimidate me very much. & the Dean was on the University Senate Human Relations Subcommittee & sat through all the divestment hearings & I worked with him some then—he was convinced by the whole ordeal that divestment was legal & a legitimate response to the situation & wrote an article for the Oregon Law Review to that effect, which he just gave me a reprint of but I haven't had a chance to read it. Have we smashed apartheid yet?

So none of that answers the question of Why I would do such a thing. The rationale is this: I've been thinking about moving back to Garnett & this is one of the few ways I could make a living there. Plus a law degree will give me an aura of legitimacy that I wouldn't have if I went back now, and legitimacy & respectability are important for doing some of the organizing I want to do there. [...] I'm not sure there's anyone there who realizes they can get premium prices for organically grown food from city yuppies. I'm really tired of seeing little towns issue revenue bonds & give tax breaks to lure in factories that stay until the tax breaks run out then leave. If that same money was used to help local people create jobs processing local agricultural produce there might be some chance of building a sustainable local economy. Last year the mayor of Garnett was offering the place as a site for a toxic waste dump—that's not my idea of economic development. [...] So that's my naive and idealistic notion. We'll see what really happens. It's all subject to change on a moment's notice—I have signed no contracts.

So that's where my life's at, Katie dear. Pretty fucking crazy. I wish I could say I were handling it well (see how crazy I'm getting—I just slipped into the despised & archaic subjunctive tense) but I'm not. This law school thang has been like a chronic low grade infection of the emotions—my mood swings have gotten even deeper & wilder than they once were. I feel disconnected & isolated a lot of the time.

That's improved somewhat over break, but it's still there, lurking in the shadows. Perhaps by the time school rolls around again I'll be strong enough to wrestle these demons... I'm afraid though that if I can't exorcise them I'll just end up exercising them, because like they say, the things that don't kill us make us stronger & I presume this applies to Demons too...

Good Housekeeping took out a full page ad in the *New York Times* today to announce that this is the first day of the "Decade of Decency." This is just what I was afraid of. Already the decency police have staked out our house and will have enough to put us away soon. "Your honor, these people didn't flush after each use, failed to shave in numerous areas, listened to obscene musical recordings... I recommend a sentence of death followed by ten years of Leave It to Beaver reruns." The ad further went on to say these New Traditionalists it was warning about would "ignore the sizzle and demand the steak," no longer giving credence to mystical & subversive dietary ideas. I presume this to mean there will be an upswing in backyard butchering with Mom serving organ meats on special occasions. O Brave New World, to have the Good Housekeeping Seal of Approval in it... (on it?...)

I'd like to hear what you've been reading, Katie. Everything you've recommended in the past I've really enjoyed. I'm really enjoying having time to read again—for a while. The best & most dangerous book I've read in a while is *Erotism* by Georges Bataille—he argues that the sexual drive, the mystical religious experience, and the attraction of death are all essentially the same quest to overcome separateness. Also he talks a lot about taboo & transgression. *Shamanic Voices* was an interesting collection of interviews with native healers from around the world & contained this bit of wisdom from an Eskimo named Igjugarjuk: "True wisdom is only to be found far away from people, out in the great solitude, and it is not found in play but only through suffering. Solitude and suffering open the human mind, and therefore a shaman must seek his wisdom there." And I just finished a book called *the last farmer* which was mostly a good analysis of the forces ripping apart the family farm & the emotional side of leaving the country & trying to go back but it ended up being a rationalization by the author for why he wasn't going back to the farm & his happy ending had all of his brothers & sisters working for Dow Chemical or in Nuke plants. Supposedly this guy helped write the screenplay for "Who Killed Karen Silkwood?" but he also used to write for Rolling Stone. Enough said...

Jibber, jibber, jibber. All these words & still I haven't said the really important things: I missed you, I was happy to get your letter, come visit me anytime, I hope you're happy. Say hello to any of the thousands of our mutual acquaintances in Minneapolis that you might see, & shine on... [...]

love,
boog

14 February 1990, Rian Fike (a/k/a Alterior Facial Mandala, a/k/a AFM), Miami, FL

Happy Birthday Rian,

[…] Law school still sucks but my mental health has been much better this semester because I've been paying less attention to school. Once after I'd been up for a couple of days I let my roommates talk me into going to New York for the weekend to drop one of us off at the airport. This happened the last weekend in April or so & thus I got to see Mr. Guy. [...] New York took a heavy toll on Roxanne [the car], who now has a new name but has begun leaking out of every orifice. (The new name arose when the oil light began coming on for no apparent reason somewhere in Ohio & immediately after the Police came on the radio singing "Roxanne, you don't have to put on the red light...") Ah, how art teases life...

We rolled into Lawrence about midnight on Monday & I spent all the next day (May Day) running Bill Kunstler around town. It was all very inspiring for us few radical young lawyers-to-be. I set up a meeting between Kunstler & William Burroughs & getting to meet old Bill was one of the highlights of the day for me. He went out at one point to feed the stray cat in the back yard & for the most part could have been somebody's grandpa, but I did hear him talking guns with one of my friends at one point & really perked up when Kunstler was discussing a particularly gruesome & mysterious murder he was involved with.

OK, Rian, Back to Civil Procedure for me. Walk big, be one, remain in motion...

inertially yours,
all my love,
boog

29 May 1990, Guy Clark, New York, NY

"To be God, naked, solar, in the rainy night, on a field: red, divinely, manuring with the majesty of a tempest, the face grimacing, torn apart, being IMPOSSIBLE in tears: who knew, before me, what majesty is?"
—Georges Bataille, *The Story of the Eye*

And a Happy Birthday to You, my friend,

I know I should be writing this so it arrives on your birthday but it's too late now so fuck it. I tried to call but got no answer so I figured you were out traipsing around the dirty boulevards (I've been listening to Lou Reed lately...). & who should I get a letter from today, but Quarl (I thought it was Qarl...) Anderson... I heard it all from downstairs, the postwoman came to the door & asked, "Is there a Booger here?", that's how it was addressed & there was 20¢ postage due. Well it was more interesting than the axotomy of neonatal rat brain stuff I was proofreading furiously at the time. Anyway Q(u)arl says your new birthday is October 2, woops, I hope that wasn't supposed to be a surprise, if it was, act surprised, OK? & his day is Nov. 11—double primes, how auspicious, & Armistice Day to boot. Speaking of birthdays my friend Susie did my chart the other day & I asked her if I didn't like it can I be born again & get a new one? (I knew these Christians were up to something...) ("Give me your hungry, your tired, your poor, I'll piss on 'em, that's what the Statue of Libertry (sic) says." says Lou Reed)... anyway I'm just a Libra with an Aquarius rising, & the moon is in the 6th house, & I've got a Venus sextile Jupiter & all that. The upshot of it all is that I seek recognition in the public sphere & I should be a lawyer (that's what it says...)

Lawyer: Yow. I'm in the middle of the Defender Project now. We toured the prisons last week, Leavenworth & the state pen at Lansing. If you ever get busted, make sure it's for a federal offense, that's my advice as your attorney. My treat for the day was that I got to meet Leonard Peltier. He was hanging out by the law library at Leavenworth when we stopped by. So I slipped away from the group long enough to shake his hand & jabber a little bit. I mentioned that Kunstler had been down to speak at the school after they met & somehow that led to Christian Brando, who Kunstler is representing after he allegedly shot his sister's boyfriend (who had been beating on her, it seems). "He was a good kid," Leonard said of Christian. Oh yes, & the synapses are buzzing now, the MEETING FAMOUS PEOPLE synapse is firing wildly & reminds me that you asked about meeting Old Bill, so I'll dig out your letter right now. ::: OK, well it was a cozy scene at old Bill's place... Burroughs' two handlers, Bill Rich & James Grauerholz were there, plus Kunstler & me & Mike Tulis (current president of the National Lawyer's Guild chapter at KU & whose grandpa ran a gas station where Elvis Presley used to stop when he was a truck driver. Mike says his grandpa has sort of a Foghorn Leghorn voice and says "That Elvis, he was always kind of a timid boy."), and Michael Foubert, who did most of the organizing for the Kunstler visit. I didn't get to talk to old Bill much. I did mention that we were sitting in King Tut's Wa Wa Hut when someone announced that he'd just walked by & he seemed to be amused by that. He could have been somebody's grandpa, he asked my compadres polite questions about where they were from, etc., although the conversation with Michael drifted into weapons for quite awhile it sounded like. He got up at one point to put some cat food out for the stray that was living in the backyard. And Kunstler seemed to get a kick out of it. I was glad we could do something nice for him after all the hoops he jumped through for us. [...]

If you do the magazine & print my thing on borders, boundaries, and desire, please add this at the bottom:

"I know the idea is odious and alien to our culture that one would <u>deliberately</u> impose restrictions on movement and freedom of the body, but mankind throughout history has always done this. The lessons that can be learned and the life that can be led by doing this far transcend what can be learned by being <u>comfortable</u>. Being comfortable isn't necessarily living a 'good' life—that's the myth, but it's not true. Living an <u>uncomfortable</u> life is sometimes more satisfactory than a placid, bovine existence."

—Fakir Musafar

Yes, & finally—here's your B-day present. This 2 dollar bill I once sent to Eric. He took it to California and buried it in a jar on the beach with a note saying send it to me & get ten bucks back, somebody did—Eric can show you the documentation. So now the 2 dollar bill is back to you in New York and the spiral continues. If you want, tell me or show me what you do with the 2 dollar bill & I'll include it in the documentation for the project & send you a copy. Remember, an imagination is a terrible thing to waste.

Free your mind and your ass will follow,
all my love,
boog

7 August 1990, X., somewhere in America

Well hello now X., & happy between-the-bombs day,

What a long strange trip it still is...

And speaking of the Grateful Dead, now we know which one's dead, so which one is Grateful? Right now I'm listening to a tape made for me by one of my law school buddies, a young Republican Deadhead from Atwood, KS via California. His name is Rex & although I may razz him for the contradiction I perceive between his music & his politics, Rex is alright. [...] Rex taped this tape for me & I'm listening to it now, it's got (at my request) half a side of Wharf Rat, 3 different versions, "asked me for a dime, a dime for a cuppa cawfee... half of my life I spent doin' time for some other fucker's crime, the other half found me stumblin' around, drunk on Burgundy wine..."

And speaking of some other fucker's crime, I've spent the summer doing legal work for prisoners & liking it immensely. I've been hired on as a student director for the coming year, which means I get to do something useful at the law school for cash & credit & also I can quit Allen Press, which I'm coming to hate. Today I spent 7 hours proofing the *Journal of the Experimental Analysis of Behavior*, a magazine of evil Skinnerian bullshit. One article I proofed involved paying 5 people $525 apiece to live alone in a room for 30 days. Instead of being interested in all the things that would happen to people or go through their heads from living alone in a little room in a totally controlled environment for 30 days, the researchers in this article were concerned with some arcane bit of nonsense such as how well people's predictions of how much time they would spend doing particular activities corresponded with how much they actually spent. These Skinnerians are dangerous Nazis who must be resisted at all costs. They've found that under laboratory conditions they can control people's behavior if they manipulate the stimuli properly, but it doesn't work very well in the real world, so in order to control people they want to turn the whole world into a laboratory. It's the same thing that's happened to modern agriculture—they've found chemicals that work in laboratory conditions but not so well in nature so to make the chemicals work you have to recreate laboratory conditions in the field by killing everything in it. [...]

Tonight I went to El Matador with Donna & Steve Ballew for Taco Tuesday: 50¢ tacos. After that we went out to the county fair for the talent show, a scary demonstration of how much the local culture has been colonized and destroyed and replaced with plastic and cheap sanitized replicas of somebody's idea of what things probably used to be like—the emcee was dressed up like someone who might be a card dealer in a saloon in a bad western movie, the first act we saw was a pair of pubescent girls in skin tight pink leotard things (with a small but prominent midriff) writhing and dancing semi-erotically to canned disco music [...]

On the way into the fair, we passed a booth that said, "We're the picture-in-a-jar people!" We did not stop to investigate.

Patti Smith's on the jukebox now, she's pissing in a river & I certainly know the feeling.

I'm a new uncle now. My sister had her new baby a few days ago, Travis Jay Hattemer, 8 pounds 5 oz., black hair, way cute. They all came down to the family reunion the next day & of course were the hit of the day. Grandma was just about bursting at the seams with happiness, anyway I'm glad the pressure's off me. On the way back I almost killed grandma & the two older kids trying to avoid a dog in the road. The stupid dog stopped in the middle of the road when he saw us coming, then when I swerved to avoid him headed our way & we ended up in the ditch. Actually, it was a big wide ditch so we probably weren't in any real danger, but it still scared the peewater out of me (metaphorically speaking). This is the second time this year I've left the road at a high rate of speed—I got run off the road by a guy pulling a horse trailer on the way back from Minneapolis this spring. Cars are crazy. Next time I'll hit the dog. Actually, I have no way of telling what I'll do the next time I'm in a situation like that, but I do know that if I hurt or killed someone I loved as a result of trying to avoid hitting an animal—or for any reason—I'm not sure how I'd be able to live with myself. [...]

Things have slacked off a little lately—I've had a little time to read (most recently Peter Lamborn Wilson/Hakim Bey's book about mystical Islam and another Autonomedia book about Locke's theory of money—that sounds dreadfully boring, I suppose, but it's one of those idea books that jumps disciplinary boundaries & pulls in sources from all over, & besides money is still an idea that fascinates me—I can't pay the rent but now I know a lot about Locke's ontology of money—& like Allen Ginsberg says, why can't I go into a grocery store & buy what I want with my good looks?), & I took the WHOLE WEEKEND OFF last weekend, Mary & I went to Kansas, saw the Garden of Eden & Rock City, camped on a high bluff (oh yeah, I sent you a post card), anyway it was beautiful & was the most satisfying couple of days I've had in a while... and I'm sure we saw the Northern Lights...

OK, sweetie, that's enough for tonight, tomorrow I have to get up & go make phone calls & file motions & such. Call me, write me, take care of yourself. (Oh yes—you probably know this already, but our friend Stephen from England broke into a US military base and smashed up an F-111. If you didn't get a copy of the newzletter from his support group, let me know & I'll send you a copy).

I've been to Rock City,
boog

1991–1992

Jell-O history • Schrödinger's equation • Factsheet Five saves a life • you can't dechronolize yourself • Snake's Nest • long-distance telephone calls • into the garden of nuts • class war on the country radio • the lost city of Ubar • armadillopes • no rest for Huitzlihuitl • the heart needs constant attention • tiger in a tree • an Esperanto letter from Madagascar • too many hats or not enough heads • Kansas Populists in Topolobampo

3 April 1991, Lauren Jaben, Austin, TX

Howdy Lauren,

Tonight I was a good boy. I went up to school to work but all the machineries were occupied so I came home. And here I am playing with machineries again. Ruts never sleep...

The big news today was the Smithsonian Conference on Jell-O History. I'm not making this up. There was a "Jell-Off" contest for which the judging criteria were "level of disgust... political correctness, jiggle, odor and esthetics, which includes color, shape, and suspension of foreign objects." A tiered Jell-O rainbow cake won an award for being "the dessert your grandma would most like you to bring to her house." There [were seminars] on such topics as Jell-O wrestling, the history of vodka Jell-O cubes (which were traced back to a certain high school in California in the early 1980s), and "White Religious Cults: Jell-O and Little Marshmallows." Jell-O was invented by a carpenter named Pearl Bixby Wait in 1897. His wife, Mary Davis Wait, thought of the name Jell-O. The U.S. government has declared that Jell-O is not an animal product, even though it is made from animal skins and bones. "What," asks Steven Lubar, curator of the engineering and industry division, "could be more American?"

Drinking lots of cheap beer and climbing in trees to holler about basketball, that's what. And much honking of horns. KU was in the NCAA Final Four again this year, much to everyone's surprise. I have had some trouble distinguishing the NCAA tournament from the Persian Gulf War and I'm still not sure they're not all part of the same thing. I expected the Iraqis to make it to the Final Four this year, but even Army and Navy didn't survive into the semifinals. So much for the superiority of American technology—it's still no match for a good backcourt press. Everyone here is proud that the Jayhawks kicked ass, just like Our Troops. I love this country.

On a lighter note, Bob Isaacson has discovered Zoot Horn Rollo working in a used record store in Eugene, Oregon. Zoot Horn Rollo is a former member of Captain Beefheart's Magic Band and is featured on the weirdest record ever made, Trout Mask Replica. Bob is the goofy guy who used to work as events supervisor at the Kansas Union, the living room of the university, and is now out in Oregon working for a Lawrence company that seeks & destroys toxic wastes of various sorts. Bob says Zoot Horn is into more melodious stuff these days. "Pachuca Cadaver" and "Neon Meate Dream of a Octafish" are in his past now. (Fast and bulbous, got me?)

There are big changes underfoot at the house, but all the things you attached to the walls are still there. Brenda is going to have a baby, I suppose you have heard that. [...] Pete has opened a bike shop in the garage. Brian has put goldfish in the pond again, many people have planted garden, things are cleaner than they've been in a long time, talk of paint is in the air. Things are looking up at the Country Folks house. You'll have to visit soon.

Computers are weird, Lauren—I don't have the signal that the paper is almost gone so it's time to quit—I could be anywhere. It says "Page 1" down at the bottom of the screen, but it's in fuzzy shadow letters so I'm not sure I believe it. We'll see. Hello and hugs to Peter, communicate soon, vibrate at the proper frequency...

boog

PS OK, I checked—it's more than [1 page]. I had to PS so I could tell you about the smooth transition I was going to make, but forgot, between "Jell-O history" and "Brenda's pregnant." We were having a dinnertime discussion about baby names and the name "Pearl" came up. "What if it's a boy?" someone asked. I said I knew a man named Pearl, but Brenda wasn't convinced that it would be appropriate. Now that I know that Jell-O was invented by a man named Pearl, I believe her skepticism was justified.

12 August 1991, Costas Orountiotis, San Jose, CA

OK Costas,

I guess by now you've figured out that I'm not going to be able to take you up on your offer to help me get out to California to see you. Unfortunately the finiteness of time & space & other built-in limitations of the natural world & social reality have conspired to make it seem impossible. I guess if I took my quantum mechanics seriously I would have faith in Schrödinger & his magic equation and the nonzero possibility that it asserts for any given particle to be anywhere else in the universe in the following instant, and I would hold on to the hope that sometime next week every particle in my body would simultaneously leap to San Jose and find themselves in just the same relationship to each other as they are now, only in California. OK, it's possible—but I suppose it's not likely... [...]

I played at being a lawyer today, Costas, which was a vast improvement to proofreading articles about the viruses that algae get for Allen Press. Well, maybe. Today I was looking into an evidentiary matter—it seems someone was on trial for conspiracy to commit destruction of property and the judge allowed in evidence of the conspirators meeting in hotel rooms in Lawrence and signing oaths (concerning a matter not directly related) with thumbprints of blood & making pornographic movies with the defendant's wife. All of which was inflammatory and prejudicial to a vastly greater degree than it helped to prove the crime as charged. So I helped crusade for justice by doing research for part of the appellate brief. [...]

Mexico was wild & woolly & just like we left it last time except that everything was twice as expensive as it was last time, and it took me some time to adjust to this state of affairs. I'll spare you the story about watching the eclipse in the rain on top of a mountain, because I've told it too many times already & it's not getting any funnier—actually it was really funny, I was laughing so hard I could hardly stand up a lot of the time, & although others were disappointed I'm choosing to remember it as one of the best experiences of my whole life.

Here's another story that you as an environmental engineer might appreciate: Mexico is notorious for being buried in trash, almost everywhere you go you will find an even layer of shit, mostly the plastic bags that they sell everything from jam to beans to Pepsi in. Anyway, we were impressed that on the train from Irapuato to Guadalajara (24 hours, 800 miles or so, 1st class for 34,000 pesos, or about 11 bucks!) they set out cardboard boxes to put our trash in. A lot of the Mexicans kept throwing their trash out the window, like usual, but we were very conscientious about putting our stuff in the box. And then when we were rolling along somewhere in Durango the conductor [picked up the box, carried it down to the end of the car] and threw it out the window. I think you've picked the right career, my friend... cleaning this planet up is going to be the only growth industry for the next hundred years. [...]

boog

31 August 1991, Dave Buchen, Chicago, IL

OK now dave,

What a nice treat & pleasant surprise to hear from you out of the blue like a strange flower blooming in my mailbox, the seeds we sow always wait to be reaped, the chickens always come home to roost. Your letter arrived at a ripe & fertile time, a narrow window of opportunity—this week is the first time in months that I've written letters, they just started pouring forth out of nowhere for no apparent reason, but that will probably end soon when school starts up next week. So we'll STRIKE WHILE THE IRON IS HOT, as they say in the business...

[...] my friend Jim told me [a story] this summer when I saw him in New York, about how *Factsheet Five* saved his life: Right before he left he printed up a big stack of magazines called Rant/Rapture, filled with the works of a whole slew of local writers, poets, artists, cartoonists & musicians (there was a record insert). Anyway he tied up all his cash in this venture and they didn't exactly sell like hotcakes, so when he got to New York he was broke. Right about then, though, the *Factsheet Five* review of the magazine came out, so every day there would be a few letters in his mailbox, each with one American dollar inside, so he didn't have to starve. And then he sent the magazines out after he finally got a job.

Salvador Dali had a thing about eating as the highest form of awareness, & advocated "awareness of reality by means of the jaws." "There is nothing that cannot be eaten: at that time this was already one of my favorite expressions." "My edible, intestinal, and digestive productions were intensified... I wanted to eat everything and planned... to construct a large table of hard-boiled eggs that could be consumed." Dali goes to the bank and refuses to hand the teller his check because he is sure the teller will eat it... "and let our passions be devouring, but let's have a still greater appetite to live in order to devour them!" Yum yum!

I've been reading a good book, called *The Gift*, subtitled *Imagination and the erotic life of property*, written by a man named Lewis Hyde. He talks about societies based on gift exchange rather than commodity exchange, and describes gift exchange as "erotic" because it builds connections between people as opposed to commodity exchange which is more likely to do the opposite. He (dinner's ready... I'll be back...) (Time passes... marinated tempeh sammiches (the tempeh was marinated, not the sammiches, you unnerstand)) & fresh steamed green beans—yum, yum!) He says, "Gifts are best described, I think, as anarchist property." He looks at myths & the anthropology of primitive societies & argues that in all of them the fundamental theme is that gifts grow as they move, and if they don't move they perish. Now, though, he's off on an analysis of gift exchange as it shows up in the work of Walt Whitman & Ezra Pound, & my enthusiasm is beginning to wane...

I'm still not sure about this lawyer business, but I guess I'll follow through with it. I've got one more year to go but I still think about John Lennon a lot: "I don't wanna be a lawyer mama, I don't wanna lie." & that's what it's all about. Black is white, & white is black, and a good lawyer can prove it. Last year I worked with prisoners at the state pen & at the federal pen in Leavenworth. I liked the work, even though we always lost. Still I think I achieved more than I did with all the years of prison support work I did before school. It's important not just that they know somebody's watching, but that they know somebody with power is watching. & that's what I'm in this game for: power. I hate to say it that way, but it's true. It's not really anarchist talk, I realize (Is this the same person that used to insist that "The revolution is not to seize power but to destroy power."? Yes, I suppose I'm the same person—that's another long-winded metaphysical katzenjammer I won't get mucked up in tonight—but this isn't the revolution). The way I rationalize it is that the difference between political theory & practice is like the difference between being a scientist & being an engineer, & all those equations may look very elegant on the blackboard & the experiments always work in the laboratory but when you're out in the real world, out in the bloomin', buzzin' confusion, where everything is dirty and moist and sticky and there aren't any straight lines or round circles, then you have to fly by the seat of your pants, if it doesn't work the way the theory says you've got to get out & fiddle with the knobs & poke around with the pliers & screwdriver till you get it to go. So I still say I'm an anarchist in theory, but a populist in practice. And a lawyer.

Well, dave, I think it would be a fine thing if you would come to visit in January. I live in a fine old wooden house, a very very fine house, with four cats in the yard, life used to be so hard, etc., on a one-block long cobblestone street right by the park... and I live with four very good folks (well, three right now actually, another long story), but we'll have another by then because my housemate Brenda is due to have her baby in November (names are still being solicited: Alonzo? Berneice? Orion? Pristine? Oobleck?), so we'll feed you great steaming bowls of soup, borscht even, we'll give you a snug place to sleep, we'll ensconce you by the fireplace & give you hot rum & tell you stories, we'll give you things to bang on & we'll jam & howl & raise the dead (at the funeral home next door). Or something like that. Anyway it would be good to see you & I don't know when I'll be in Chicago again. I've already been scheming on how to get to SF, Oregon & Seattle over Christmas break, but even if I do I'll be back by the middle of January. Or even if I'm not here you're welcome to stay, but I can't promise you borscht. Or how are you planning to go west & how far are you going?

Enough, enough. Time to go have a beer. Or something. I hope all stays well in your life, there are worse things than being broke, as I'm sure you know. The clarinet is free... all my love to you & the Ooblecks.

remain in motion,
boog

8 October 1991, Tom Dougherty, Larned, KS

"You can't dechronolize yourself."
—from a radio show about (the late) Miles Davis

Yes, Tom, it's true, you can't dechronolize yourself—we're all stuck in time, prisoners of history and memory. And I suppose you can serve Memory or make it serve you—& you seem to do a fine job of the latter. Thanks for the birthday card. You're the one person who comes through no matter what (in addition to Mom, of course, and my sister). When it comes to birthdays, my memory no longer seems to serve me as well as it used to, but it can still conjure up pictures of the good times we used to have—I can hear you playing the piano, I can smell the bread baking in the oven, I can taste the Buckhorn...

Well, some things do change, I guess, & I have no fondness for the cheap-shit beer we used to drink. Tonight I'm sipping on some of my friend Clayton's "holy basil" beer—yup, it's got basil in it & is kind of honey-sweet & overall it's one of his better efforts. Clayton is a master of all that molds & ferments—he makes the best tempeh in town, I think, & gets pretty experimental with it, too: peanut tempeh, garbanzo tempeh, etc., etc. Sometimes I forget how spoiled I am living in Lawrence...

Scottish people must play lots of Scrabble, that's what I think. Almost every conceivable two-letter combination seems to be a Scottish word, according to my big nuclear-powered Webster's Third International dictionary: "ee" is Scottish for "eye", "ae" is Scottish for "one", and "oe" is a whirlwind off the Faroe Islands. "o-o-a-a" is a kind of Hawaiian bird according to Websters, but the Hawaiian dictionary I got at the public library booksale doesn't exactly agree. They like "ō'ō" as a kind of bird and "ā'ā" as "dwarf" (the " ' " is a glottal stop) but they don't run them together. Since it's hyphenated, though, it's useless for Scrabble, but Websters will accept "aa" (Hawaiian "a'ā"), a kind of lava. I'm sure this information will be of great use to you and impress your friends and confuse your enemies in the Greater Larned Scrabble League. Me, I get together with Dr. Bill every other Tuesday for a rousing Game—we play cooperatively & add our scores together & ponder the state of the universe. All in all it beats studying for law school.

Also at the booksale I picked up an English-Tagalog dictionary. Just now I looked up a phrase Mikey taught me, "mag bir muna tayo," which is supposed to mean "Let's drink beer first." Once again, the dictionary didn't quite agree. This time I trust Mikey. His high school was recently covered in volcanic ash, something so many aspire to but so few achieve.

I went home last weekend, & we all went up to eat at the Scipio bazaar, which was actually quite normal: same as it ever was. Good food, even though there was meat in everything but the mashed potatoes. Scipio definitely has the best sauerkraut in the area. A little brown sugar is the secret, I've been informed, but don't tell them you heard it here.

On the way down to Garnett I noticed that on the sign for the new Long John Silver's south of Ottawa they had flags that looked like this:

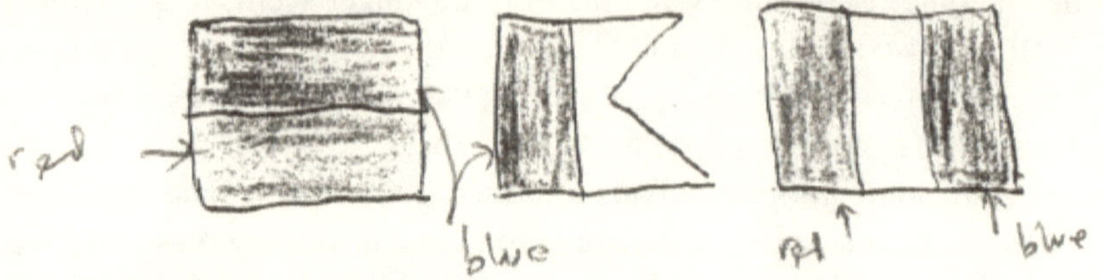

This looks very patriotic, of course, but I was sure it meant something so I looked it up in the folks's World Book Encyclopedia, and, sure enough, these are International nautical alphabet flags that spell out (you guessed it): "EAT."

I'd like to hear more about your trip Down Under sometime. I saw Kinky Friedman ("They Ain't Makin' Jews Like Jesus Anymore", etc.) at the Bottleneck last week. He talked about his recent tour of Australia & asked who in the place had been there—no one had—& it made me think of you. He sang "Waltzin' Matilda", which seemed to be in a different language: lots of stuff about jumbugs, tuckerbags, and billabongs, but I'm sure you can explain all of this now.

until soon,
boog

22 October 1991, Donna Eades, Seattle, WA

Hello Donna,

[...] Tonight was a potluck at Beki Dickherber & Chris Beneke's house. It was my night to cook so I made a huge lasagne in our institutional-size pan, my first attempt at the uncooked-noodle method. I missed the part about needing to cover it so the top layer of noodles was crunchy or pasty in some places but overall it was alright. Beki made crepes, Jenny brought banana bread, a woman named Carrie brought a pilaf with pine nuts & some bean dip, & Clayton brought more of his mystical & exotic beers—lemon balm & spearmint, I think. A good time was had by all. But there's nothing like a college town to make you feel old, especially when you are. Relatively, anyway. I had a long talk with Carrie, who's from a suburb of Chicago & in her fourth year of college & tomorrow had a paper due in a philosophy class, something about justice & Plato's Republic. And of course even before we told each other how old we were some back corner of my mind had cranked through the arithmetic & forced me to be aware of the vast gulf between us, or constructed it if it wasn't there already—but ten years is a long time, several lifetimes for me anyway, & I try not to pay too much attention to ages, but when I find myself in a place where I'm 50% older (or younger) than most of the other people around, it's hard not to notice.

Brenda is still pregnant, but not for Long. I'm really excited about being a new pseudo-uncle. She just walked by on the way to the bathroom—it's a comforting sort of surreal little vignette, to see out of the corner of my eye, a naked pregnant woman calmly walking past my doorway. Life goes on. Last I heard, Brenda is still intuiting a boy, & my sister says she trusts that sort of intuition, anyway it worked for her. They haven't chosen a name yet, as far as I know, but I can't wait to hear the final result. I hesitate to make any suggestions, because Brenda seems to take my jokes seriously, like "Aloysius" (that's Al-uh-WISH-us, in *New York Times* style), & I don't want to have live with the thought that I've caused some innocent young child to be burdened forever with a name that will make him/her an object of behind-the-back derision & mockery & subject of grade school beatings. So I don't suggest "Wanton," or "Pancake," or "Zydeco William Greatcheese Hammersmith of the Gods." (This reminds me of a story my high school Government teacher told, about a friend of his in the Navy named Oliver Wendell Turnipseed, who didn't like his name & decided to have it changed—to "Rebel Raider Turnipseed.")

I've been reading a lot, acting like I have spare time. I picked up a lot of nice things at the book sale: *The Name of the Rose*/Umberto Eco (actually I thought this was just an extended piece of pseudo-intellectual masturbation, but for some reason I read it all anyway), a book called *Snake's Nest, or A Tale Badly Told*, by a Brazilian writer named Lêdo Ivo, which is set in a backwater Brazilian port in the days of the Fascist "New State" of the early forties. Ivo is a high, wild, & pure poet & takes on life, love, death, fear, & hope: "She laughed when she made love," he says. "And it was to see her smile, and to accompany the trajectory of that smile until it changed into long sonorous joy, in that rising music of the sighs and syllables of an indecipherable language, that he began to make love with the lights on... As long as he was able to hear and contemplate, in the night more luminous than the very day, that laugh coming from the depths of ecstasy, he would be safe from danger and from death. Even when the laugh was transmuted into panting and silence, he felt redeemed and protected. He was a captive animal—but his cage was the eternity of a jubilation which had crossed the frontiers of sordidness and guilt, to liberate him and bring together around two tired or satisfied bodies all that was fragmented or dispersed. She would open her eyes, and in them, brown and without history, he could see only the brilliant substance of the hours, hard and unflagging as a diamond. ... Here I am above or beyond death, said the lawyer to himself... here I am fastened to life like one who clutches a handrail so as not to fall into the abyss of nothing. ... Between the long exultant laugh and the prolonged silence, life assumes the form of love and blazes like a sun... (etc.).

And I've read Milan Kundera's first book, *The Joke*, wherein he asserts that "Physical love only rarely merges with spiritual love."

And Ivo & Kundera have described with sharp & pointed accuracy the emotional terrain where I find myself these days. [...] I don't want to be a bachelor for the rest of my life, but I'd rather be alone than to get wrapped up with the wrong person. And then there's that pesky abyss of nothingness... Usually I'm not this befuddled & indecisive, I don't think, but I certainly feel lost right now... "Vanity, vanity, all is vanity," says the radio now, "We service ourselves like apes in a cage. We just end up with stains on our sheets and lines on our face. So baby, let's be Methodists tonight..." Or something like that.

The theory is that I'm going to enroll at 7:06 tomorrow (or today) morning, a scant 7 hours away, even if you round up, for my last semester at KU Law. No sadness here, not about my departure from that seamy hole, that hotbed of lust & debauchery & beer. The longstanding rumors of sexual impropriety at the school finally hit the papers Sunday—the top of the front page of the Topeka paper & copious column inches elsewhere, Uncle Gene & Dean Bob are squirming for sure. Four current & former KU law women have accused at least 2 of the law faculty of sexual harassment & nobody I've talked to doubts it's true. Names haven't been released yet but only a few people are implicated in the vicious gossip & I have no reason to doubt it—& no reason to pass it on, either. If you're interested I'll let you know all the gory details as soon as they're public. & in the meantime the director of affirmative action at KU has been accused of selling cocaine to a local man just before he beat someone to death with a golf club in a drug-maddened rage. And the KU student body pres is in the process of getting dumped for breaking some of his girlfriend's teeth. And when I get nominated for the Supreme Court I'll be sure to call you as a character witness...

I hope all is well in Wellsville, or Wuthering Heights, or

Württemburg or whatever that place is that you live. All my love to you & Bob, & hellos to Vicky & Steve & Enzo & Nick & Dana & Robert & all the ships at sea...

Until soon...
boog

14 November 1991, Sumaya Ali-Rajja, Paris, France

Sumaya, Mon cherie:

Long distance telephones still fill me with a child-like sense of amazement. The idea that you can say something in Paris and that can cause a little speaker to vibrate thousands of miles away in Kansas just blows me away. And the idea that I can talk to you at 5 o'clock while you're at midnight wreaks havoc with my basic notions of time. Usually I don't seek out this sort of wonder & amazement at 5 in the morning. I assume that if the phone rings in the middle of the night it's bad news and I don't want to hear it so if I ignore it maybe it will go away. So I tried that when you called and the ringing stopped—whew!—but then I heard the ominous footsteps coming down the hall and the quiet knock on my door and I wondered what horrible thing had happened to somebody I love, but fortunately it was you. And fortunately Wendy is willing to answer the phone in the wee hours of the morning, or I might not have gotten to hear your smiling voice after all these months & miles.

It sounds like you've had some adventures, Sumaya—and I'm glad you've survived them all. It sounds like you're embarking on another big adventure, too—marrying your Frenchman, that is—but I guess you've sailed these waters before so you know where most of the dangerous rocks are. You'll have to write & tell me more about him—Did you meet him in Yemen? What's his name? What does he do? Will he help do the laundry?

I had an adventure myself, last weekend, & I'm still kind of high from it. My roommate Brenda had her baby Sunday morning, here at the house in the room across the hall, and I got to be there with her. It was one of the most amazing & inspiring things I've ever seen, Sumaya. The whole process is so improbable, with all the pain & the blood & the kid trying to wiggle through a space that's smaller than his head—but then, all of a sudden, he slips all the way out, he cries, and he's sucking away at the breast like he's been doing it for thousands of years and just as sudden the pain is gone, replaced by indescribable joy, and everyone is laughing/crying, and it all seems perfect & natural & how could it be any different? He was a big baby, 9 pounds 10 ounces, with wise blue eyes and quite a bit of soft black hair. He looks like a little Buddha and is very quiet, and when he does cry it's not annoying (not yet, anyway) but just makes me smile. The midwife was really excellent—she's done hundreds of births and really knows her stuff. At one point, right before the final pushing, Brenda was getting tired & frustrated & Fran leaned over & kissed her on the belly. It made me wonder why people would want to have a baby in a hospital where they're so quick to pump you full of drugs or get out the scalpels and where you're with a doctor you've spent very little time with (Fran says that on the average an ob/gyn doctor will spend about 2 hours with a patient including the birth) & who wouldn't dream of kissing you on the belly and you wouldn't want him to anyway, and all your friends & family are banished to the waiting room where they pace up and down the halls and wait to hand out the cigars. We didn't have a good place to pace, so I kept myself busy by cooking almost constantly starting when Brenda went into labor, plus I kept some water boiling, because like they say in Gone With the Wind, "I don't know nuthin' about birthin' babies." But I'm learning...

The Mideast peace talks have been big news here and I'd like to hear what you think about it all. It seems like the more moderate Palestinians were the winners in the first stage, at least as far as public relations go. It amazes me that the Israelis are so arrogantly pushing ahead with settlements in the occupied territories, but I guess I shouldn't be—I just don't always have the energy to be sufficiently cynical sometimes.

I don't think I can come to your wedding in Cairo, Sumaya, much though I'd like to. I'm going to apply for a passport anyway, though, and wait for the travel fairy to come to my rescue. If you go to Oman, please send me a postcard. One of my life goals is to eat in a Chinese restaurant in every country on earth. Failing that, I want to receive mail [from every country, and once I have] achieved that my soul will leave my body and ascend directly to heaven. But you don't have to worry about accelerating my demise, though—we're getting new countries so fast these days I can't keep up. All my love to you, and I look forward to seeing you soon, one way or another...

boog

30 November 1991, E., somewhere in America

"I went down into the garden of nuts,
to see the fruits of the valley."
—God, Song of Solomon 7:11

Hello E.,

This is your Bible message for today. Please send your tax-deductible donation to the address below right away. Operators are standing by to intercept your prayer requests and take down your mastercard number. Wounds healed, diseases cured, & the dead brought back to life—call for a free written estimate.[...]

OK, I was just interrupted from this silly monologue by a pregnant woman breathing heavy into my ear. Jocelyn called to talk to my roommate Brenda... it sounds like Jocelyn may be finally starting labor, two weeks late. I hope so, for her sake. If it goes much longer she'll have to go to the hospital because Fran the midwife won't do homebirths that are that late because there's too high a chance of serious complications. Brenda had her baby almost exactly 3 weeks ago, in her room right across the hall. [...]

He was a heavy baby—9 pounds 10 oz.—and healthy & cute as a butt. I got to be at the birth & it was really inspiring & has gotten me all fired up again. The whole process still seems highly improbable, though—"How'd you get in there?"—and I wonder whose idea this all was. But I guess this isn't the only improbable process in the universe.

Reading springs to mind as another example—OK, there are these squiggly lines on pieces of paper, and they stand for sounds, more or less, and you look at the squiggly lines and translate them into strings of sounds, and those sounds are supposed to mean something, and furthermore they're supposed to mean the same thing to any of millions of people anywhere in the world. Crazy as it all seems, I've been taking advantage of my Thanksgiving vacation to read books that don't have anything to do with the law. *A Natural History of the Senses*, by Diane Ackerman, for instance. It's sort of like what would happen if Annie Dillard were writing a 17th-century encyclopedia—lots of facts heaped together without too much organization & all swimming in a soup of syrupy, lyrical prose. I'm not sure whether to love it or hate it, but I must be leaning toward the [former] (either that or I'm a serious masochist) because I'm almost finished. I did learn, however, that the word "porcelain" has its origin in the word for cowry shell, which in turn came from the word for the genitals of a female pig, "which is obviously what its silky texture reminded them of." Obviously. Ah, what one has to put up with in order to be a well-rounded individual...

OK E., it was good to talk to you the other night. [...] Ms. Ackerman says that "members of a tribe in New Guinea say good-bye by putting a hand in each other's armpit, withdrawing it and stroking it over themselves, thus becoming coated with the friend's scent"; since we can't do that I'll just say

hasta la vista, amiga
boog

6 February 1992, Brenna Hoffmann, Philomath, OR

They've discovered the lost city of Ubar, Brenna, that's the big story in the *New York Times* today. Well, yesterday actually.

"Ancient Sands of Oman May Be Fabled Source of Frankincense" is what they say. Eight ruined towers on the edge of the Empty Quarter, discovered at the center of ancient caravan tracks observed by infrared satellite photography. And some people say the space program is a waste of money...

The picture [above] is a street scene in a town in Yemen, sent to me by my friend Sumaya, who called from Paris today to gloat about the French being ahead of the Americans in the Davis Cup. The Davis What? Tant pis pour elles, as they said about Anne & Catherine in my high school French dialogue. "Tough shit! Who cares?" is a rough English translation. And so it goes...

We still have an empty room, Brenna. Think about it...

Last week I saw one of the weirdest movies I've ever seen. Dr. Seuss wrote the screenplay and it was filmed in 1958: "The 5,000

Fingers of Dr. T." Someone involved in the production was a flaming homosexual. Other than a couple of brief flashes, there was only one woman in the entire show, hundreds of singing and cavorting male extras, and 500 little boys... The protagonist is a little boy who is being forced to take piano lessons against his will, and dreams of the evil Dr. T, who constructs a giant piano made for 500 little boys in a Dr. Seuss–looking compound, complete with a dungeon for players of clarinets and violins who are dressed mostly in tight black pants and gambol wildly... "Dress me in limburger and Camembert cheese," sings the evil Dr. T. "Dress me in silk and spinach." All the little boys are made to wear little blue beanies with erect rubber hands on top. This is a truly evil film, Brenna, you must see it...

Iggy Pop is on the jukebox now, singing, "I am a passenger... I ride and I ride... I see the stars come out tonight... I see the city's ripped back sights... We see the dark and hollow sky... And all of it was made for you & me... so let's ride & ride & ride..." Indeed. We need to travel again, Brenna... to ride & ride & ride...

[...] I'm not home much, I'm instead off at school crusading for justice, working at the legal aid clinic & the Defender Project, pretending to be a lawyer. Dressing in uncomfortable clothes & being humiliated is almost a daily routine now. The latter part will get better with time, I presume, but until Zion comes I expect the former to be a problem. So far I've avoided buying a suit. Mikey says he'll loan me a suit, which will probably more or less fit. In the meantime I'm wearing some Salvation Army & garage sale jackets with some WalMart pants & calling it good enough. Thoreau said to beware of any enterprise that requires new clothes & this is advice I think about a lot these days. I need a fashion adviser... because I forgot to take the Dress for Success class...

but what is success? [...]

until soon,
boog

6 February 1992, X., somewhere in America

Hello X.,

I had a dream last night. Or was it the night before? I was in a high place, looking down over a city and a long road through the sand leading to a beach. Someone wanted me to go to the beach, but I was reluctant because I knew I would have to stay a long time and after a while I would get bored because it was just a beach. I wanted to go to the city instead. All of a sudden I was on the road to the city. I was lying on my chest on a cart that was about six inches high, and I was being pulled very rapidly by a small brown and black dog. We passed down a long straight road, with a low wall beside it that was also a bookshelf. Every now and then I would reach out as we hurtled by to grab one of the little laminated cards that appeared at random intervals on the shelves. The first one I remember said "SCOTLAND" on one side and had a picture of an official-looking building with lots of columns in front. The other side said "SEVENTEEN" but I don't remember what the picture was. The next card I picked up looked like this and then I woke up. I still haven't determined what it might mean... [...]

We have an empty room in the house. [...] Act soon, this offer may not last long. We have a washer, a dryer, and a baby. Good veggie meals 5 nights a week. Close to campus and downtown. Less rent than you're paying now. Hot and cold running roaches. Just sign on the dotted line.

I'm playing lawyer these days, X. I'm working at the legal aid clinic, dealing with landlord/tenant problems, juvenile cases, child support & divorce, that sort of thing. Plus I'm still working at the Defender Project, telling prisoners their cases are hopeless. Soon I'll be a real lawyer. I'm mildly panicked about it all, but I'd be even more panicked if I hadn't been working with Bob Eye and worked out this arrangement where he's probably going to send a lot of work my way. All I have to do is graduate and pass the bar. But I've never been very good about passing bars... especially if they have gold lame booths and women in white polyester dresses at a piano bar singing all your favorite boy- and girlhood tunes. I need to come visit soon... Maybe at spring break if I don't have to spend the whole time studying for my <u>Professional Responsibility</u> test...

Sumaya called from Paris today to tell me that the French were beating the Americans in the Davis Cup. «Tant pis pour elles», that's all I can say. And I saw sweet Julie Green tonight at the Free State, in her last night in America, for tomorrow she leaves for Japan to teach English. It's a small world, & getting smaller all the time. If I only spoke Uzbek, I'd drop it all and head east to make my fortune...

There's class war on the country radio stations these days X. I've been tuning in to Get Back to My Roots and to Keep My Finger on the Pulse of America. Sometimes it's hard to tell if they hate rich people or want to be like them, but they're definitely conscious of them. Conway Twitty has a song about a millionaire's wife who always wanted to be just a simple country girl and dresses up in skin tight jeans one night and goes down to the honky tonk and shakes her butt and has sex with Conway Twitty. There's another song wherein the narrator is driving along in his beat up pickup & a woman in a Cadillac makes eyes at him & he follows her to the country club & offers to buy her a beer but she says no because only members are allowed in here. To which he replies that he's a member of a country club (you can tell all your friends), country music is what he loves, at any honky tonk or roadside inn, etc. And yet another country singer says that uptown living ain't for him, because, as he says, "I need friends who don't pay their bills on home computers/ who buy their coffee beans already ground/ you think that it's disgraceful that they drink 3 dollar wine/ but a better class of loser suits me fine." Me too...

Mr. Thoreau said to beware of any enterprise that requires new clothes and this advice has been in my mind as I've started to assemble a lawyerly acceptable wardrobe lately. So far so good. I haven't bought a suit yet, but I did buy a pair of slightly-too-big made-in-China predominantly polyester WalMart kind of black pants recently. But also I have some shirts & a jacket that my sister got at the Oskaloosa Community-wide Garage Sale in a bag for a dollar that are really cool in a Levis "styled for young men" seventies kind of way. Way cool... Have I sold out yet?

Walstrom has been in town recently, except that when I went to find him at the oldest house in Lawrence recently, Mary Lisa Pike said she thought he was visiting his friend Ramsey in Kansas City. I arranged a meeting between him, Dr. Bill, and myself on the third floor balcony of the law school one day, thinking they needed that kind of action. We made this thing upon which I write. "Ruble flaccid" was a snippet of a headline out of the *New York Times* which I decided would be the name of my first-born child. Greg was working at a place called the Full Moon Cafe, which is in the restaurant space in the Casbah, which serves Middle Eastern food & where we absolutely have to eat the next time you come visit soon.

Call me. All my pre-Valentine's Day love,

boog

1 July 1992, Jana Svoboda, Beaumont, TX

Look, Jana–

there are ARMADILLOPE postcards —And armadillos (& armadillopes, I presume) are mammals—you can even see the hair all over this one. Armadillos always give birth to identical quadruplets of the same sex and are the only other animal known to be able to contract leprosy. They eat insects and "Diego de Landa, burner of many of the sacred books of the Maya, noted in 1566 that armadillo meat 'is very tender and good to eat.'" Another early pillager of Mexico, Bernal Díaz del Castillo, in his *Discovery and Conquest of Mexico*, remarks that "Oh! What a troublesome thing it is to go and discover new lands." Keep this in mind if you go to Mexico...

VIRGIL—I started reading *The Lives of a Cell*—[...] "A good case can be made for our nonexistence as entities," he says. Tell it to the judge, buddy, is what I say—

until soon, love,
boog

20 July 1992, Donna Eades, Seattle, WA

Hello Donna,

As you can see, I'm studying hardly for the bar. Actually, I have been studying during the day, but at night I revert to my true Self, like Dr. Jekyll (or Heckle & Jeckle, I'm not sure which). I've been reading Mexican history. I have read about Huitzlíhuitl, emperor of the Aztecs, who on his accession to the throne in 1391 was advised: "Do not think that you were chosen to rest, but to work." I have tried to tell this to myself, but Dr. Jekyll just laughs, ha ha. I have read of Empress Carlotta of Mexico, wife of Maximilian the unemployed Austrian prince who was installed as Emperor of Mexico by the Europeans while the US was distracted by the Civil War as part of a scheme to collect some bogus French loans. Maxi was soon chased out by troops loyal to Juárez and was shot; Carlotta succumbed to the family tendency to insanity and was locked up in a family chateau in Belgium. Once, she was discovered on the roof of the place after it had caught fire, yelling down at the flames: "It is forbidden! It is forbidden!" but the flames did not obey. All this is very interesting of course, but I suspect that none of it will be ON THE TEST. Farideh had a good visit, it sounds like; she told me that Donna is very nice but I knew that already. We sat down and did her taxes last week and I think the government owes her lots of money. We'll see. I miss you... Don't think I can make it in Aug., tho... Call or write soon... XXXOOO

boog

31 July 1992, Laura Fine, Springfield, OR

Hello Laura:

I took the bar exam this week; it was kind of like being forcibly sodomized. I think I'm going to sue them for intentional infliction of emotional distress while I still remember all the elements. I think it's a good idea to be required to review all the basics and to ensure some basic competence, but all in all it just seemed like a cruel and elaborate hazing ritual, and was no doubt designed primarily by people who grew up in fraternity houses. I'll let you know when they announce the results. I had occasion to dig back into the journals I kept when we were housemates at the Restaurant of Life. Those were the days, eh? I was either crazy then or crazy now, or both. The heart still needs constant attention, that's one lesson from those days that I'll always remember.

Until soon,
boog

12 August 1992, Marissa Hatttemer, Oskaloosa, KS

Dear Marissa,

I came up to visit a few days ago, but you weren't home. I was really disappointed that I missed you. Alex and Travis and I had a lot of fun, though. We played circus and I was a tiger. Then later Alex pretended he was a tiger and I was a tree, and for some reason the tiger was up in the tree (that means Alex was sitting on me). Then the wind started to blow (I started shaking and making wind sounds like I was a tree blowing in the wind) until the tiger fell out of the tree. We did this for a long time and I pretended that I wasn't tired (just kidding!). Your little brothers sure have a lot of energy, though. We also played catch for a while, then Alex and Travis played like they were dogs fetching the balls for me. They picked up the balls with their mouths and crawled over to me, and then they didn't drop them until I patted them on the head and said "Good boy!" They were really cute and I wish you could have seen them.

Deanna cooked spaghetti for supper. Yum yum! Also there was corn and salad, with cucumbers and tomatoes and peppers from the garden. I think garden vegetables are my favorite thing about summer—especially big, ripe, juicy tomatoes. Deanna sent a bunch of fresh tomatoes home with me, and also some pickles and tomatoes that she had canned. I can't wait to eat them all up!

I took my big test last week, but I don't know if I passed or not. I hope I passed so I can open up my office and start being a lawyer. I've had a little bit of a vacation and I've really enjoyed it, but I'm ready to start working again.

I hope that you've been having a good summer vacation. I was glad to see you at the family reunion and I hope I get to see you soon. Please write to me sometime to tell me what you have been doing this summer.

Love,
Uncle Dennis

13 August 1992, Rian Fike (a/k/a Alterior Facial Mandala, a/k/a AFM), Miami, FL

"We are what we pretend to be, so we must be careful about what we pretend to be."

—Kurt Vonnegut, Jr., *Mother Night*

Howdy Rian,

For the last three years I've been pretending to be a law student; lately I've been pretending to be a lawyer. I think this constitutes a clear *prima facie* case that I have not been careful. What have you been pretending to be?

Your phone message got to me solely by virtue of the fact that this is a small town. This is how I think it worked: the number you called belonged to my roommate Brenda before she moved in here; she had it at the house she'd bought with her lover Mike and used it after he left. When Brenda moved out of their house and into our house, Mike moved back into their house. We planned to have her number transferred to the new house, and told lots of people, including (apparently) yourself. Then we decided it would be collectively cheaper to leave the old number at the old house and get a new number for the new house, rather than moving the old number to the new house and getting a new number for the old house. So I don't think the number you called was ever installed at this place. Mike isn't living at the other place anymore, but he's renting it to a woman I know named Jane, who called up a couple of days ago and said a deep-voiced "Mr. Hamm" had left a message & a number. As soon as I realized it was a Miami area code, I knew it was you.

I've been enormously out of touch with our old mutual acquaintances & with the mail art scene in general. I saw Guy a few months ago—the folks at *Anarchy* magazine in Columbia told me about a lecture there by David Watson of the *Fifth Estate* that had been arranged by a group of anarcho-college students. It came at a convenient time so I went over to hobnob with all my old anarchist buddies & spent the night at Guy's place. It had been probably a year since I'd communicated with him, and other than a postcard I haven't been in touch with him since. Qarl sent me some interesting stuff in the mail, but I never responded, probably because I thought I was busy with some important legal project or other.

Every now and then I get in the mail a strange enormous mail-art paper called *Lo Straniero,* which always has hundreds of addresses of mail-arters from around the world; from time to time when I have something important to avoid I'll mail off odd letters to people I've never met in places I've never been: Iceland, Uzbekistan, United Arab Emirates, Peru, etc. So far I've had no responses from that particular activity, but it keeps me off the streets. I'll probably keep doing it anyway, because I still remember some vastly weird things I've gotten in the mail (like an Esperanto letter from Madagascar, for instance) that although I never responded made me very happy and gave me something to talk about for a long time.

THE NEXT DAY

It's too early to be awake, but here I am anyway. My girlfriend had a 7 a.m. dental appointment so I got up too, went down to my favorite downtown greasy spoon diner for no coffee, thanks, 2 eggs scrambled, hash browns, whole wheat toast & performed my daily ritual reading of the *New York Times*. Actually I don't read it, I just carry it around so people will think I'm some sort of groovy intellectual.

No big news today, but yesterday I read that John Cage died. "There is no noise, only sound," he says. "I think it is true that sounds are, of their nature, harmonious." Also he said, "I don't like meaningful sound. If sound is meaningless, I'm all for it." Cage was here a few years ago & I really enjoyed his performance—actually I enjoyed watching people watching his performance. If I remember right it consisted of snippets of a series of quotations he'd assembled and then reassembled through some sort of random operation, over and over again. There were some interesting juxtapositions and repetitions, but for the most part it was just nonsense, and I found it very amusing to watch a lot of the folks listening to it frowning with concentration & scratching their chinny-chin-chins and trying to impute lots of serious meaning to it. We picked up big stacks of copies of the program after it was over; I'll try to dig one up and send it along.

Did you vote for your favorite Elvis stamp? Young or old? I think that whole episode is a very good metaphor for the political process in general: No matter which way you vote, Elvis wins. Young Elvis or old Elvis, Elvis Bush or Elvis Clinton, Classic Elvis or New Improved Elvis or Caffeine-Free Elvis or Diet Elvis: the tip changes, but the iceberg remains the same.

I talked to your wife on the phone a couple of nights ago—in fact, I talked to her twice because I forgot to leave my actual phone number the first time—and I got the impression you were on vacation somewhere. Something about Michael Behavior and she was writing you a letter. If you end up in this neck of the woods be sure to call—we'll wine you (or beer you, anyway) and dine you and give you an actual bed to rest your weary bones upon. Likewise, I look forward to descending upon you some day in Miami, but I'm not holding my breath because it seems unlikely I'll have the wherewithal to go a-traveling anytime real soon, even though I'm a parasitic money-grubbing lawyer. Another great act of juxtaposition: poverty and a professional career, all at the same time. I'm sure the world will be a richer place for it, even if I'm not.

I hope things are well with you & your family & I look forward to hearing from you soon. I still wear the T-shirts you've sent and the burning flag/Statue of Liberty shirt never fails to instigate a conversation.

So we talk about Voltaire & Adlai Stevenson, & usually I turn around and show them the back of the shirt and explain that it came from my mail-art buddy

Absolute **F**reedom **M**andatory.
boog

12 October 1992, Brenna Hoffmann, Philomath, OR

"From where do you derive the definition of dignity?"
"I certainly would refer you to the federal regulations."
—from a KDHE hearing transcript

Invasion Day

Howdy Brenna,

Either I have too many hats or not enough heads. That's the way I feel these days, as my time is split between my job at the Kansas Department of Health and Environment, where I write final orders in administrative appeals, my commitment to the Indian Center, where it's hard to tell what I do other than refer people elsewhere, and my private practice where I do whatever walks in the door, whether I know how to do it or not. I'm finding the whole thing kind of stressful, especially after getting used to being lazy this summer, but I think it will get better as time goes by. After all, I've only been a real lawyer for a couple of weeks. I'll let you know how it goes.

I'm as old as Jesus now, Brenna, for good or ill. I hope I have a better 33 than he did. Glenn always placed great significance on living past 33—I think he already has—as it was a sign that one hasn't been chosen. Some other important historical figure died at 33, is my vague memory—Alexander the Great perhaps—but I can already look around and see a lot of people younger than me who have accomplished more than I have. This wouldn't be as important if I was at least having a good time, but I'm not sure I am. At least I don't have to wear a necktie to work.

I've still been managing to get some reading in, and this reminds me of an unusual literary-serendipitous experience I had recently. This summer for some reason, my mind wandered back to a footnote in (I think) O. Gene Clanton's *Kansas Populism* about a Kansas Populist who headed south after the Populist Party went bust and got involved in a scheme to develop the harbor at Topolobampo. I had the idea that I might do some research on this and try to get an article published somewhere, but of course I was lazy and did nothing about it. Then one morning I heard William Least Heat Moon on the Walt Bodine show, discovered his book *PrairyErth* was out in paperback, and soon after went down to the Raven to buy a copy. About halfway through, I came across a reference to the Kansas City, Mexico, & Orient Railway—a grand scheme to cash in on the China trade by building a railroad from Kansas City to a port on the Pacific 400 miles closer than San Francisco: Topolobampo. The tracks were supposed to go through Chase County, the place *PrairyErth* is about, but not much work was done there. The route in Mexico included what was to become the Copper Canyon train, but it wasn't finished until 1961 or so. The KCM & O went into receivership before the grand scheme could be accomplished, put under by American competition and the Mexican revolution. I found a mildly interesting book about the whole scheme, *Destination Topolobampo* by John Leeds Kerr, and it & *PrairyErth* both had vague but intriguing references to a utopian colony founded in the 1890s by Populist immigrants from Kansas. I work next door to the Kansas Historical Society now, so perhaps I'll get up the gumption to go digging around someday on my lunch break. We'll see.

It's madness here now, with all the kids going wild at all times. Dinnertime is pure chaos. To top it all off, we've instituted a new family tradition wherein the person who cooked the night before reads a poem at dinnertime. I started with "Marriage" by Gregory Corso, wherein he imagines getting married and living in the burbs and hanging a picture of Rimbaud on the lawnmower and pasting Tannu Tuva postage stamps on the white picket fence and when Mrs. Kindhead comes to collect for the community chest grabbing her and saying "There are unfavorable omens in the sky!" and when the milkman comes leaving him a note saying "Penguin dust, bring me penguin dust, I want penguin dust." Tonight Brian read from a book about iguanas that he found in the trash. It was one of the funniest things I'd heard in years, but I think you had to be there to really appreciate it.

OK, Brenna, it's after midnight and I have to tell someone about OUI in the morning (and we're not talking about the porno mag, this is Operating Under the Influence). So I'd better go figure it out beforehand.

As your attorney I advise you to write me soon.

I'm OK (& I hope you are too),

boog

The reverse [of this letter, not shown here] is a picture of a 75-foot tall concrete totem pole that can be seen outside Foyil, Oklahoma. Pete & I visited it on our little road trip to NE Oklahoma and SE Kansas. It's definitely worth a visit if you're anywhere in the area, for instance if you've stopped at the famous Woolaroc Museum or come to sample the healing waters of Lake Oolagah. Pete works in the new juice bar now—Herbivores it's called—on 8th St., just down from AJ's, which I think is called something else now, but is just as sleazy by any other name. At Herbivores I had an Elvis Parsley, which was very yummy. When you stop here at Xmas we will go for a drink. Hasta la vista…

4 December 1992, Eric Jeffreys, New York, NY

Howdy Slim,

I'm taking time from my busy Friday night of folding laundry and reading *The History and Social Influence of the Potato* by Redcliffe Salaman. It's one of those books that slices things a different way so you get a whole new perspective on things—a true juxtapositionist classic. Plus I'm learning lots about potatoes. For instance, potato starch is preferred in the paper and textile industries for coating and sizing. Popular potato varieties in the UK in the early nineteenth century included Manly, Ox Noble, Lumper, Cups, and White Kidney. To further accentuate this learning experience I got a bag of Art's & Mary's and ate most of it. Fortunately I wasn't doing something like reading Dostoevsky, otherwise I would have had to huddle in a corner of the basement, brooding, with a bottle of vodka, all by dim candlelight, of course.

There's trouble in paradise, Slim. My typewriter here sends out radio frequency waves over the electrical system that fucks up radio reception in any receiver plugged into the same circuit, so now my little boom box radio is giving me lots of weird hums & whistles & hisses in addition to the live Dead show they're playing on KKFI... oh, it's Jefferson Airplane now... Wooden Ships... I'd put on a tape but the tape player gave out a few months ago. But now that I'm a fancy lawyer I'm thinking about BUYING A NEW ONE. Even though I had to start paying my student loans back this month, and so far I've spent more on my legal practice than I've earned, and I'm only working 3 days a week for the government, I've still got more disposable income than I've ever had in my life. It's crazy. Now I can see how easily money corrupts & why people get sucked into these consumptive yuppie lifestyles. Just charge it please, on my GOLD CARD...

Well, while we're being corrupted here, Eric, I've got a proposition. Sometime this spring or summer I should come up to see you & we should hang out at the airport and get one of those stand-by flights where they drop you off randomly somewhere in Europe, then bop around for a week or so in a low budget fashion and come home. I might even be able to chip in for part of your ticket. Lao Tzu says that the journey of a thousand miles starts with the first step, but my experience tells me that a journey of a thousand miles starts with a CRACKPOT IDEA. Think about it...

And speaking of journeys of a thousand miles & crackpot ideas, I've been reading about a utopian colony largely populated by exiled Kansas Populists in the 1890's, in one of your favorite places in the world: Topolobampo. I've heard of a Kansas connection to the place for years, but only recently have I dug up anything substantial on it. You should give this place a second chance, Slim: if the Europe thing doesn't work out we should drive to Chihuahua, ride the Copper Canyon train over to Mochis, stay someplace other than the Apache 7, and go hang out in Topo for a while & see if we can find any remains of this utopian colony, then take the boat over to Baja and watch the sun dance on the big water. There are many, many places that need to be gone to...

They're branching out on the radio now—Adrian Belew followed by Poi Dog Pondering.

[...] more & more it seems to me like I had my shit together better five years ago. Is this just a normal part of the aging process or am I really regressing? (At dinner the other night we were discussing an old movie from the 60's—*Wild in the Streets*, I think it was called—where everybody over thirty is put into concentration camps and forced to take LSD. Jocelyn had the exquisite lack of tact to point out that I was the only person at the table who would qualify for this treatment. The more I thought about it, though, the more appealing it sounded...)

OK Eric, these are the months of my life... I'd be glad to pencil you in anytime... I'll have my machine call your machine. In the meantime, please let my strange travel suggestion burrow itself into your head like an evil worm that can only be killed by taking it back to the place it belongs...

Be well—

boog

1993–1994

les seins d'Hélène Lagonelle • Martian hillbilly music • the 50th anniversary of LSD • we're all 60th cousins • multidimensional Möbius strip • Garberville coincidence • Houphouët-Bouigny • RIP Frank Zappa • Biblical chicken pictures • four pounds of muscatel • Jeep the Pig • I type, therefore I am • intellectual promiscuity • the malling of Lawrence • a crow in the service of ghosts • Bell's Theorem • Columbus discovers the clitoris • a gallon of Desires • a mouse in the car

1 January 1993, Donna Eades, Seattle, WA

Dear Donna,

I talked to Mary Linn a couple of days ago. She says she handed the disk you sent over to computer experts who played with it and cajoled it and performed complex operations on it but couldn't find anything there. Please feel free to try again. I suppose its contents are all lost now in that twilight realm of letters imagined but never written, letters written but never sent, letters sent but never received, and missing socks that you only have one of. I think I was going somewhere with this, but Mulligan [toddler housemate] just came in & derailed my train of thought. She tells me she's cooking dinner all by her own self, and that we're having turkey for dessert. Also apple, pear, orange, and grape juice. Yes, and a tangerine and chocolate shake. Yum yum. Also she tells me that although they say that the little lord Jesus, no crying he makes (Jesus is one of her dolls), she has heard him say, "Mary! Mary!" (her full name is Mary Christ). Also he asks for coffee and beer. OK.

In the *New York Times* I read recently about a film that was shot last summer in Vietnam, based on Marguerite Duras's *The Lover*, coming soon to a theater near you. The book is supposedly autobiographical, & concerns her affair with a rich Chinese young business man while she was a relatively poor French teenager in Saigon. [time passes]

Now it is many days later and I have received your post card from Hong Kong. I have sent you a post card from Hong Kong as well. Anyway I looked in all the libraries and bookstores in town and some in Topeka and the only copy I could find was at the KU library but it was checked out. Eventually I put in a recall order, & it was well worth it. Her writing is really seductive, it reminds me of Ledo Ivo or Georges Bataille. For instance,

> I'm worn out by the beauty of Hélène Lagonelle's body lying against mine. Her body is sublime, naked

> under the dress, within arm's reach. Her breasts are such as I've never seen. I've never touched them. She's immodest, Hélène Lagonelle, she doesn't realize, she walks around the dormitories without any clothes on. The most beautiful of all the things given by God is this body of Hélène Lagonelle's, peerless, the balance between her figure and the way the body bears the breasts, outside itself, as if they were separate. Nothing could be more extraordinary than the outer roundness of these breasts proffered to the hands, this outwardness held out towards them. Even the body of my younger brother, like that of a little coolie, is nothing beside this splendor... Hélène Lagonelle's body is heavy, innocent still, her skin's as soft as that of certain fruits, you almost can't grasp her, she's almost illusory, it's too much.... those flour-white shapes, she bears them unknowingly, and offers them for hands to knead, for lips to eat, without holding them back, without any knowledge of them and without any knowledge of their fabulous power. I'd like to eat Hélène Lagonelle's breasts (I just realized this must sound much better in French: «Je voudrais manger les seins d'Hélène») as he eats mine in the room in the Chinese town where I go every night to increase my knowledge of God. I'd like to devour and be devoured by those flour-white breasts of hers. I am worn out with desire for Hélène Lagonelle. I am worn out with desire.

Me, I'm just worn out. I don't even remember what desire is any more. And who is this God she keeps talking about?

It may be that I'm just reacting badly to adulthood, but my mental health has not seemed very good lately. Nothing serious, like jumping-out-the-window serious, but it's been a sort of low-grade blah, a vague & general dissatisfaction. All I know is I need to change something in my life, but I'm not really sure what. A saner work arrangement would help, I think—I need to decide to either jump full time into private practice or give up and get a full-time government job. What's happening now is that there

YET ANOTHER INTERRUPTION. I'm back now with space music on the radio and a Belhaven Scottish ale by my side. Oedipuss is resting on the chair beside me, while Jezebel skulks and drools nearby...

we rejoin our letter already in progress…

is not enough time for me to do private work to pay for my basic expenses, so it's costing me money. I'm sure I'm learning a lot, though.

Oh yes, the Hong Kong postcard. As I presume you have guessed, I was not actually in Hong Kong. I got this postcard when I went to Philadelphia to do Doug & Theresa's wedding. We were wandering around Philadelphia's Chinatown and I saw these in a store there & I bought some, figuring they would come in handy someday. I sent one to my mother while I was in Philadelphia, and I told her on the card that I had gotten on the wrong plane and ended up in Hong Kong instead. I think she halfway believed it, though, and I had to promise never to do anything like that again. To her.

heart,
boog

31 March 1993, Dave Buchen, Chicago, IL

"'The horror, the horror!'"
—Mistah Kurtz

well now dave,

It's April Fool's Eve, and not a creature is stirring, not even the roaches.

Today I had to do some research at the law library at the Supreme Court building in Topeka. It was a cold rainy day. The grand promenade on the way up to the building was littered with the corpses of tiny worms. I wondered where they all came from and why they had died...

Many thanks for the beautiful Last Supper picture... a fine addition to the collection. It was very good timing, too... I expect to have it mounted in a prominent location by the time I cook our Last Supper on Thursday. This one was different than any I've seen before. The names along the edge of the tablecloth were a very nice touch. Also this one didn't have the rug with Chevy signs or the jug & stool for foot-washing. The ceiling detail was different than usual. Etc., etc. Anyway, when we open the Last Supper Museum as another roadside attraction, we'll be sure to have a little plaque reading "Donated by..." or "From the collection of dave buchen, Chicago, Ill."

By now you may have heard the rumor spread by Bob that I will be in town the weekend of the 10th & 11th to see your play. This is false, as I realized later that this day was Easter and I have family obligations. However, if you will still be playing the week after please call me & I'll be there... I need a road trip more than I have words to express it & your play got rave reviews. Plus I feel like it's time that I slept on somebody else's floor, just to maintain harmony and balance in the universe...

Bob says you're going to Czech (to Czech what? I still haven't figured out how to say this yet. "Going to the Czech Republic" sounds too awkward, "going to Czechoslovakia" sounds like I've been asleep for the last year, Czechia, Czechland, Czechistan all sound made up, which they are. Any advice you have on this matter would be greatly appreciated.). This sounds like a great adventure. If you send a postcard this will earn you another little plaque in the Postcards from Far Away Museum next door to the Last Supper building, or at least a spot on the Image Wall high up near the ceiling. Please tell A. howdy for me.

Spencer Subgum & I got to talk Tuva when he was here. It was nice to meet a fellow traveler. I'd appreciate it if you would forward the enclosed info on Frank Zappa & the Tuvans to him. If none of this makes sense ask Spencer to explain—he describes Tuvan throat singing as "Martian hillbilly music" & I'm sure you'd get a kick out of it. If none of this still makes sense and/or if you never see Spencer, never mind...

Anne Fausto-Sterling, writing in the *New York Times* recently, says there are at least five sexes. Kurt Vonnegut, writing many years ago in *Slaughterhouse 5* (or was it *Breakfast of Champions*?) says there are 7. My recent experience tells me there are zero, but that's another long story.

Some way or another, I'll see you soon...

boog

8 May 1993, Donna Eades, San Francisco, CA

Oh Donna,

This letter is long overdue. I've been composing it in my head for weeks. It used to start out with a somewhat hackneyed quote from T.S. Eliot: "April is the cruellest month," etc. Then it went into a discourse about the 50th anniversary of the first LSD trip and the 50th anniversary of the Warsaw ghetto uprising, both of which occurred in the same week. I was aware of the approximate dates of these two events before, but somehow it didn't occur to me that they had happened at the same time. The picture of Albert Hoffman wobbling goofily down the street of some Swiss town on his old bicycle and the Jews of Warsaw fighting Nazis hand to hand for their survival didn't go together for me, I guess. But the more I think about it, the more the two seem to make sense together, and seem to be among the important things that define the modern age: genocide and chemical consciousness alteration. (Mikey has come into my room now and the typing is helping put Cypress asleep. I hope the letter doesn't have the same effect on you…) Anyway, both of these happened before, well, murder and tripping did, but it took us until the 40s to apply mass production methods to them. That's it: genocide, mass hallucination, & just add the atomic bomb and you've got the last half of the twentieth century summed up perfectly.

It's been raining here. A lot. The weather has reminded me of an old Ray Bradbury story that I dug up & read tonight:

The rain continued. It was a hard rain, a perpetual rain, a sweating and steaming rain; it was a mizzle, a downpour, a fountain and a whipping at the eyes, an undertow at the ankles; it was a rain to drown all rain and the memory of rains. It came by the pound and the ton, it hacked at the jungle and cut the trees like scissors and shaved the grass and tunneled the soil and molted the bushes. It shrank men's hands into the hands of wrinkled apes; it rained a solid glassy rain, and it never stopped.

A few more days of this and it will be time to start building a large boat and collecting pairs of animals…

I was elected to the Community Mercantile Board of Directors as of last Wednesday. It looks like it's going to be one of those toughest-job-you'll-ever-love situations. We're scheduled to be in the new store at 9th & Mississippi by July 1, and Wild Oats can kiss our ass. We're betting the farm on this one, so it's got to work out. On paper it all looks good, but it depends on our sales more than doubling immediately upon our move. The analysts say no problem, but I've read half of their report and I still can't tell whether their estimates are based on objective information or whether they're just waving their hands a lot. We'll see... anyway, they had a keg of Free State beer over at the new place after the membership meeting last week, and even though it was still under construction that place had never looked so good. All I could think of was the time we went to the beauty contest there with bones in our hair and watched the young punks who were allegedly from some Swedish fashion magazine grading the local meat. Or the time, as student body vice-president, that I judged a toga contest there. I look forward to judging a *tofu* contest there instead. I only wish I could remember bowling there, like a few people slightly older than myself said they did.

OK Donna, time to go… I've got to go take a long soaky bath & think about important things & sleep & get up in the morning & go see my mother on Mother's Day. I hope your life is going well & I certainly think you should call or write soon & give me all the details. I hope to come see you sometime, because, like Zippy the Pinhead says: "I left my pants in San Francisco… There they wait for me… I hope."

all my love,
boog

11 September 1993, X., somewhere in America

X. dear:

"In conformity with the precepts *utile dulci, castigat ridento* (proceed from the useful to the agreeable), I will resort to a gastronomic farce to open a discussion of highly important matters." (to quote Charles Fourier.)

Yes, mock duck. I ate some of this stuff last night. My friend Elizabeth from law school fixed a weird but delicious curry featuring some funny little round mushrooms and this mock duck. It came in a can and was in the shape of a tiny, plucked duck. It was made out of seitan (Satan?), i.e., braised gluten. It was very tasty for such a perverse-looking thing. (It reminded me of *Eraserhead*.)

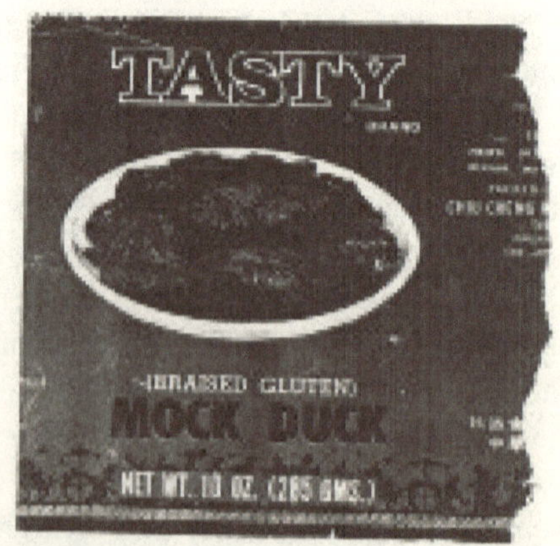

OK, now for the highly important matters… hmmmm … My trip up to see you & on to Dreamtime & Madison raised me from the dead, X. ... I hadn't realized how far away I'd gotten from where I wanted my life to be. I didn't use to be such a crazed workaholic... I used to like to have time to myself... I used to have fun... these things will come to pass again. I'm just a hippie in lawyer's clothing, & it's time to start taking some of those clothes off. I decided that I would pay more attention to feeding the creative side of my self & to relax & enjoy my life a little bit. Part of this involves having fewer jobs. I'm all but done at the Indian Center, just one case to wind up & then a hearing in a couple of weeks. I've pretty much decided to keep my flexible part-time job & give up on the full-time job they'd probably give me if I applied for it. I used to say to anyone who would listen that one of my life goals was to never have a full-time job. And so far I've achieved that—although there have been lots of weeks I've worked way over 40 hours—and this is no time to blow my record. Like we chanted in Chicago at the Haymarket gathering: 100 years of the 8 hour day is enough. On the other hand, I hope your new full-time job works out for you OK...

Dreamtime was way cool—I think you would like it there... I was a little put off at first, because I look pretty normal these days & a lot of the folks I dealt with there had a pretty serious hipper-than-thou attitude at first. But fortunately, I knew a number of people who were there & so I had reason enough to stay, & before a day was out all the groovesters seemed to have decided I was OK. It made me think a lot about the compatibility of a broad-based social revolutionary movement & an avant-garde art movement: the former has to include almost everybody & the latter is by nature exclusive.

Despite all that, I had a good time & I want to go back as soon as I can & I want you to come too. Liz & mIEKAL, the primary organizers of the place, are really great—no hipper-than-thou stuff from them & I'm really amazed at how they can live and work and raise a child (Zon, 4 years old, skinny & tanned with long braids & deep brown eyes) with almost no personal space. Things are so wide open there it makes 1614 look like a museum... but it works! I stayed at a place they called the Hotel, which was a big 2-story house with 7 or 8 bedrooms, 2 bathrooms, and a well-stocked kitchen—nobody was in charge but it stayed clean, food was prepared, & it was home away from home. And the school—it was like Drop City vs. a Doris Lessing novel I read once but the title of which I can't remember… anyway there was an embarrassment of space, endless rooms and objects—a clothes room, an electronic junk room, a music room, a paint room… a GYMNASIUM… some might say it was trashed & full of junk, but to my forgiving eye it just seemed to be bursting & reeking with potentialities & possibilities… It's not exactly what I want my hippie home in the country to be like, but I still want to visit. I got to hang out with Hakim Bey/Peter Lamborn Wilson most of one day, on a road trip off through the Driftless Zone, & he really helped jump-start my brain. & then all too soon it was over & I was off to Madison where I saw Chuck & Rick Sheridan and stayed with Jill

Innes, who was Glenn & my next-door neighbor at our sleazy downtown apartment 15 years ago.

[...] Time to quote Fourier again: "If one compares the immensity of our desires with our limited means of satisfying them, it seems that God has acted unwisely in endowing us with passions so eager for pleasure, passions that seem created to torment us by exciting a thousand desires, nine-tenths of which we cannot satisfy so long as the civilized order lasts." He therefore argues that the only truly functional society is one which allows the free functioning of the human passions rather than trying to thwart or deny them. On the basis of his observation of early nineteenth-century French society he concluded that monogamy was not natural behavior & the harmonious society would have to be structured so that free sexual expression could take place, part of which involved elaborate orchestrated public orgies. He also believed, however, that someday the northern lights would coagulate to form a ring around the north pole and that this would lead to the melting of the polar ice cap and the turning of the northern seas into "a kind of lemonade." So perhaps Fourier should be taken with a grain of salt. Cypress is here now & wants to type: cypress qqqqweeeeeeeeeeeeeeeeeeeeeeeeeeeeeeee eeeeeeeeeeeeeeeeeeeeeeeeeeeeeeeeeeeeeeeeeeeeeeeeeeeeeeee ee33333333333333333333333333334444444444444444 We'll it's not Shakespeare, but it's CLOSE...

OK… the Cypress interlude seems to have derailed my train of thought so I'm going to sign off & drink another one of these fine Israeli beers (Israeli Beers—isn't that a Cream album? (If you don't get this terrible pun, please try it on M.)) & read more Fourier or Chuang Tzu or about some obscure turn of the century utopian experiment in New Mexico. Normally I wouldn't support the Zionist occupiers but I'm celebrating the agreement with the PLO & hoping for the future. Besides, it's very good beer, Maccabee, it's called… and as you know one of the quickest ways to my heart is through the proper combination of barley malt, hops, yeast, & sweet pure water… which makes me wonder where the water for this beer came from…

Nonetheless, if you'll pardon my Hebrew: l'chaim...

Until soon…

boog

20 September 1993, Dave Buchen, Chicago, IL

Yo, Dave,

Welcome back to the land of the flea and the home of the Braves.

It was most pleasing to get yer postcard from Hungary. I don't know if you remember it, but it had a picture of wild masks with animal horns & bright colors, people wearing these masks & animal skins around a fire with an exotic domed building in the background. Nobody I showed it to could guess where it came from & I certainly wouldn't have without reading the back. It was very pagan, very Asian, very cool. But the blood of the Huns probably runs in all of us German types… Genghis Khan is our 60-times-great grandpa & we're all 60th cousins variously far removed. & the postcard from Kapolcs was cool too—why don't they have postcards this good in America?—I haven't checked the atlas yet but from the words on the back I can't quite tell where it's from. Hungary? Slovakia? Poland? The South Side? I'd like to sit down with you & some beers sometime soon & hear stories about your adventures. It's the next best thing to being there.

I was actually able to escape for six whole days to Minneapolis, Dreamtime Village, & Madison. Enclosed is the postcard I would have sent you if I'd known you'd been home. Bless us oh… Dreamtime was wild & inspiring. I got there just at the end of the Dreamtime Corroboree, but the energy was still high. Anyway, I really liked the energy at Dreamtime & I think you'd like it there too. Definitely a liberated zone, a temporary (or maybe a permanent) autonomous zone. I got to hang out some with Hakim Bey & that helped get the wheels in my head turning again. I've enclosed a copy of his *Radio Sermonettes*, which is the best political writing I've read in a while. The anarchist space you're putting together sounds like a project that's definitely consistent with the *immediatism* he talks about.

I think it would be just dandy if you & A. came to Kansas. I'm sure we'd try very hard to find you a place to live in a nice two story white house close to downtown & the university, with two cats in the yard, life used to be so hard, etc. There's a new hardcore bar just a couple of blocks across the park, and if you turn the wheels on the old red fire engine on the way there it makes eerie high-pitched whining noises that can no doubt be heard blocks & blocks away. Brenda & Mikey & I are in the process of buying our house here. We've got a pretty good crew here right now, at least it seems like it even though I'm not here very much what with meetings & work & hobnobbing.

It sounds like you've been doing some interesting reading. There's something fascinating about times of cultural transition, & the advent of refrigeration seems like one of those ignored but fundamental social changes. Personally, though, I'm convinced that future historians will divide historical time into two periods: pre-Spandex & post-Spandex. O brave new world, to have such fluorescent stretchy artificial fibers in it! One of my favorite movies of all times is about a historical transition like that—*Kid Blue*, with Dennis Hopper. It's about the rise of industrial capitalism and the end of the wild, wild West. Dennis Hopper is an out-of-work cowboy who gets a job in the new factory, where he sticks tiny parts on little geegaws. There's a great scene where Dennis Hopper is walking down the wild west street with the capitalist in his top hat, who has his arm around Dennis Hopper's shoulder & is explaining to him that he needs to get a job making silly & useless things in the factory so he can get money to buy other silly & useless things that other people are making in other factories. I saw it in the People's Theater in Garnett, Kansas, about 20 years ago with a total audience of about 4; I've only talked to one other person who'd ever seen it, at one of the workshops at the San Francisco @ gathering. I'm not sure I'd watch it again if I got the chance—it might turn out to be really crummy & I'd hate to spoil my memory of it as one of the best movies I've ever seen.

Well, the cows are starting to come home so I'd better crash so I can wake up soon & be at work. Welcome back, big hugs to A., & howdies to all the Subgummers.

yes,
boog

2 November 1993, Chris Beneke, Prague, Czech Republic

el día de los muertos

well now chris you don't have to believe this, but this is the second chain letter I've gotten from the Czech Republic this year. It seems only appropriate that I should send back to you the one I got from there (she used her U.S. address on it so you'll have to trust me on this one). I don't know what postage would be like on a paperback book from there to here, but I'm sure A. would get a kick out of it... perhaps if you sent it by very slow boat it would be affordable... I met A. last year when she came back and forth through town on both ends of an extended road trip with my anarchist buddy dave from Chicago. Dave I met at the Haymarket Massacre centennial anarchist gathering in 1986 & we've been anti-authoritarian buddies ever since. A lot of the names on the letter you sent sounded vaguely familiar, like I've seen them someplace in the *Factsheet Five*/anarcho/mailart subculture. I'm really fascinated by how these connections work, all these webs of acquaintances & correspondences... it seems like they should just expand & expand until they include everybody, but my guess is that it all sort of folds back in on itself like a giant multidimensional Möbius strip. Now that I think about it, the only book I've gotten back from this particular chain mail came from Beki (who got it via Donna Eades, I think, but I'm not absolutely sure) so you've probably already gotten a copy of it. Well, «tant pis pour elles» I say, «tant» fucking «pis pour elles.» (This is a line from a high school French dialogue that I still remember & for some reason it feels like an appropriate response in so many situations, even when it's not.)

The idea of imagining the connections made by a chain letter as it winds around the world reminds me of an idea that used to obsess me when I was a kid: I imagined what I would look like in four dimensions, and tried to visualize all the space I'd ever occupied as being occupied at once. This led me to do things like jump up and touch the ceiling in the corners of my room so I could be sure that I had completely filled it up—had occupied all the space in it. Whenever I travelled I imagined my 4-dimensional self as a giant worm oozing out into new spaces. I was reminded of this recently by an Italo Calvino book I picked up at the public library book sale, *If on a winter's night a traveler*. In this book was a computer program that counted words in books & spit out a printout list... by looking at the list you could tell what the book was about so you didn't need to read it. Anyway I imagined a list of all the words I'd ever written in letters to people & I imagined writing letters to people until I'd used every word there was & so the printout list would fill the entire lexicographical space. There: lexicographical—another brick in the wall. It's sort of like the idea in Arthur C. Clarke's "The Nine Billion Names of God," although I'm not sure what's supposed to happen after all these various spaces are filled.

Anyway, speaking of bricks in the wall, you missed the Lawrence cultural event of the season. Tiny Tim was here in town last week, and in addition to a trip down memory lane featuring all the great hits of the 20s & 30s the show included a Pink Floyd medley (featuring "Another Brick in the Wall" of course). Tiny also showed himself to be one of the world's premier Elvis impersonators—but the highlight of the show was probably his Sonny & Cher duet (even though his Sonny sounded more like Bob Dylan). Gregor Brune was the perpetrator of all this; I'll try to enclose a copy of his latest *Tiny Tim Times*. And I'll send Gregor a copy of the chain letter, so he can send Robert W. Howington, EXPERIMENT

IN WORDS, PO Box 470186, Fort Worth, TX 76147 a copy of TTT. Tiny Tim is an experiment in way more than words but I'm sure Mr. Howington can DEAL WITH IT. {The KJHK News at Nine O'Clock has a feature story about the "New Sense Museum," an open-air gallery somewhere in California that mostly features toilets painted in various fluorescent colors.}

Lil' Cypress is an experiment in words these days. He has a bigger vocabulary than I do: I came downstairs a few weeks ago & he was dancing and shaking a noisemaking thing. "Nice rattle," I said to him. He looked over at me with eyebrows raised & in a highly condescending tone said, "maraca." Of course he was right, the little rascal. And now Mikey has taught him to say "prestidigitator." I couldn't say sentences with that many syllables when I was his age. It'll just get him into trouble...

What a deal, my man! Putting on a play in Prague! Vaclav Havel watch out! We are young & life is sweet & it sounds like you're grabbing onto it [with] everything you've got. Part of me is jealous but the rest of me is excited as hell for you... I think I know what you mean about being overwhelmed by the transience of your community. Sometimes in Lawrence, too, I feel like an island in a swift, swift stream... but here I know if I stay in one place long enough everyone else will come by eventually, & there's no one who goes by that won't come back again. I think we're probably in the same community even though we're thousands of miles apart—everywhere I go I seem to run into people who know people I know—& the more I think about it it seems less like a swift stream than a briskly boiling soup. Yes, and we're all on the same side of the Möbius strip...

A lot of my knowledge about the world has come from the Hollywood Squares game we had in 5th & 6th grades (or was it 7th & 8th?) in Catholic school. The shortest will ever recorded, for instance, was left by some English guy: "All for mother." More kids were born in America from March 1959 to February 1960 (or something like that) than any other year in American history. The longest phrase without vowels comes from the Czech, "Grg prz strch prg," or something like that {It's 9:59 & we just heard a Tiny Tim station ID on KJHK}, which supposedly meant something like "Stick a finger in my throat." I thought this was something silly and contrived until I read *The Good Soldier Schweik*, in which every few pages someone would exclaim, "Well stick a finger in my throat!"

boog

6 November 1993, Brenna Hofmann, Philomath, OR

"Life is nothing but trading smells."
—Italo Calvino

hello Brenna,

The famous annual Lawrence Public Library book sale has come & gone again, & the line above is from one of my best scores, *If on a winter's night a traveler*, a shiny new hardback copy for 50 cents, cheap at twice the price. Among the other new things I brought home to my already overcluttered room included *Ringolevio* (the autobiography of Emmett Grogan, the San Francisco Digger who Richard Brautigan wrote "Death is a beautiful car parked only" about), *Innocent Ecstasy* (which fairly convincingly argues that Christianity created an ethic of sexual pleasure in America), and a Finnish-English dictionary. Yes, it was a very good year.

If on a winter's night a traveler was the best fiction I've gotten my hands on in years, and I think it's one of Calvino's best efforts. My reading of it was fraught with all sorts of little literary coincidences. For some reason I had been thinking about opening lines of books—I don't know about you, but the first line of a book will often make the difference between whether I buy it or leave it, or whether I read it or put it down. Anyway I was thinking about first lines of books one night while driving home from Topeka. The radio was on as usual, tuned to NPR. That night they interviewed Toni Morrison—this was just after she won the Pulitzer prize—& the interviewer asked her about her favorite first line from one of her books (I forget the answer) & her favorite first line from someone else's: "Call me Ishmael." That night at dinner we talked about this idea. Hardly anybody could remember a first line that grabbed them, other than the aforementioned from *Moby Dick*, or "It was the best of times, it was the worst of times," or Snoopy's "It was a dark and stormy night." My favorite, of course, is "We were just around Barstow, on the edge of the desert, when the drugs began to take hold." The next day I ran across a section of *If on a winter's night* that talked about—you guessed it—first lines. He mentions Snoopy & the narrator talks about wanting a book that "maintains for its whole duration the potentiality of the beginning"—& Calvino does it, too. [...]

Then that night I ran across a chapter in *If on a winter's night* where one of the characters has a computer that prints out a list of all the words in a book and how often they're used, very efficient you see, because instead of wasting all the time it would take to read the book you can just glance at the printout and see what it's about. Well, this idea fascinated me, & although I didn't have a handy computer program I decided to list the words in a copy of a letter I wrote to you recently. It's a small sample so the results are inconclusive, the only thing one can be sure that it was about is *I* (24) (30 counting *I've's* & *I'm's*), *my* (12), and *me* (4). For comparison purposes I performed the same operation on the most recent letter I could find that you had written to me. Anyway, we used the same 8 words most frequently, although in slightly different order. You spoke of love (2) and hope; I was concerned with time (8), work (2), and money. Your letter was about exaggerated excess exhilaration; mine about disabled disappearing discussion. You say *and* (28), I say *but* (8)—but nonetheless, let's not call the whole thing off. Trying to milk very much insight out of this exercise is probably dangerous, but if you notice anything interesting I'd like to hear it.

That's not all this computer program does—it also writes: you give it a list of words & it writes the book. I've started my novel already: endure (53), radiant (49), dreams (47), vast (38), soul (37), relentless (37), desire (37), mayonnaise (34), yearn (33), incomprehensible (32), flesh (31), heaven (31), burden (29), fuchsia (29), longing (28), wildly (27), blazing (27), incite (25), insight (24), joy (24), agog (23), prison (22), promise (20), sweat (19), sweet (19), fruition (19), bursting (19), uh-oh (18) … qat (5), mucilaginous (5), unguents (5), ornery (5), juggernaut (5), romeo (5), naugahyde (5), cellular (5), chartreuse (5), cursed (5), yahoo (5) … flaxen, iambic, pug, quincunx, pristine, aloof, molybdenum, ilk, … etc. The first line goes like this: "Radiant, blazing, his soul strained to bursting with a vast cellular longing, he cursed his very flesh—this prison this promise—and cried out to heaven for sweet release from the burden of a desire he could no longer endure." Etc. While we're at it, why not have the computer use the list of words to rewrite my letter to you: "Well howdy now Brenna, it's useless, I tell you. I've got a violently wild feeling from all the alcohol. I see the kids scrambling around on the mounds of old grain out back… more scenes from the hippie zone. This is a particularly goofy community..." etc. Oops, looks like we've got a glitch in the software…

In a similar vein, Richard Brautigan once counted what he called all the "rivets" in Ecclesiastes: "the first chapter in Ecclesiastes has 57 punctuation marks and they are broken down into 22 commas, 8 semicolons, 8 colons, 2 question marks and 17 periods." Etc.

Ah but enough of this silliness…

Lawrence has been the cultural mecca of the prairies lately. Diane di Prima was here on the anniversary of the day Jack Kerouac died, Tiny

Tim was here on C.'s birthday, Noam Chomsky is at the Union tonight. Diane di Prima was great—she told about reading her revolutionary letters off the back of a truck in 1960s San Francisco & read about her Italian anarchist grandfather from her yet to be published autobiography. My favorite line of the whole night, though, was from a poem written to her first child, waiting to be born. She apologizes to the kid for having to be born to a sloppy anarchist beat poet parent, but points out that this place has its advantages:

I can show you
baby
enough to love
to break your heart
forever

love,
boog

29 November 1993, Jana Svoboda, Corvallis, OR

"There is no excellent beauty that hath not
some strangeness in the proportion."
—Francis Bacon
(that's what I keep telling myself, anyway)

howdy Jana,

Your letter made me homesick for Corvallis even though it's not home. I think you've picked a fine place to live, bike paths, curbside recycling, micro-brewery and all... gonzo cuisine, whale watching, belly dancers and all. I've got lots of good reasons for staying in Kansas, though, even if I can't think of any of right now.

I called Brenna on her birthday last week & she said she'd seen Virgil & Zoe & William at the library. It makes me happy just thinking about the possibility of two of my favoritest people in the universe being able to bump into each other on a regular basis someplace far away. Bumping into people in places far away is one of my life's big pleasures, even if I have to experience it vicariously. I got to experience a little bit of it directly last weekend, when I went up to see my buddy Dave in Chicago. We went to a potluck/benefit at the Autonomous Zone, a new anarchist community space, where I ran into an old acquaintance from

Lawrence, who now lives in Chicago & had come to read her poetry there, & another person that I'd met at Dreamtime Village in Wisconsin in September. I guess it's not that much more of a coincidence than you or Virgil running into Brenna in Corvallis—I imagine that if you took all the people in North America that are plugged into the *Factsheet Five* sort of anarchist/mailart/marginal community and put them in one place, you probably wouldn't have a town much bigger than Corvallis. As I was writing this I stopped to try to think about the weirdest coincidence like this that I could remember, & none of them really seemed particularly unpredictable: for instance I shouldn't really be surprised to find somebody I met at a couple of the anarchist gatherings sitting outside of a squatted building on Avenue C in the Lower East Side, or to meet somebody on top of a semi-abandoned hotel (listed in the quasi-hip travel guides) in San Blas who knew anarcho-hipsters I knew in San Francisco.

The one coincidence that still rattles me happened while Brenda & I were stranded for 8 days in Garberville, California, a few years ago. This town was about five blocks long & 2 blocks wide, & at the edge of town the "US Out of North America" and "Trespassers Will Be Eaten for Breakfast" signs began—we were in the middle of pot country & they weren't interested in having strangers wandering by. So we got familiar with the town pretty quick. One day when I went to use the pay phone by the grocery store someone else was there first—a hippieish looking woman with a naked baby in a grocery cart. We both had a lot of calls to make, so for some reason we took turns, & while she was on the phone I entertained little Vartan. Her name was Nadia & she invited us out to visit her and her husband Dennis, who had parked their trailer on some "unowned" land outside of town. We didn't make it, somehow, & left town soon after. When I got back I had to dig through the mail that had accumulated in my post office box while I was gone—at the time I was spending a lot of time publishing *the gentle anarchist* & working with prisoners. One of the letters was a request to forward some correspondence to one of the prisoners I was working with. I read it, as I always do before forwarding letters to prisoners under my return address. The people who wrote the letter said that they were travelling, but expected to end up in Northern California—& it was signed "Nadia, Vartan, and Dennis." (Twilight Zone theme music here...)

So I bet you've encountered lots of people you knew in unexpected places (you encountered them in unexpected places, that is)—so tell me about some of the strangest. Ask Virgil, too. I'll try to ask other people & if I get enough responses I'll send them out to all participants.

I love your new address [on Bittersweet Place], Jana. What you've lost in space you've gained in postal coolness. It makes me want to write you letters, even more than I already wanted to. I thought about this on the way to Chicago—there was a song on the radio that went something like "Please forgive me/ I can't stop loving you/ don't deny me/ this pain I'm going through," which comports nicely with my theory of desire. It seems to me like what most people really want is to want—that the sensation most people crave is the aching, the longing, the yearning—& when they get what they want, the high that comes from desiring is gone. That's one connotation that "bittersweet" has for me—that feeling of almost being there that is so much better than just bitter or sweet.

I got to see Jill when I was in Wisconsin a few months ago—I don't know how many years it had been since I'd seen her—at least three, & longer than that since we spent very much time together. Her kids were so big, & so beautiful... & so was she, even without strange proportions. Seeing her really woke up dead parts of me... Has it really been 15 years since we lived in those sleazy downtown apartments? I guess there ain't none of us as young as we used to be...

We had a dinner for my folks for their 35th wedding anniversary this weekend (I guess [my] theory of desire doesn't apply here). We rented a hall in Garnett, invited all the relatives, had a big catered feast (with two kinds of meat), white sugar cake with blue sugar roses, champagne, the works. It wasn't exactly the kind of party I'd plan for myself, but they seemed to enjoy it. They spend all of their time doing things for other people, so I'm glad we got to do something for them for once. Can I interest you in some leftover jello salad?

The theory is that I'm going to be at work in Topeka at 8 o'clock this morning, so I'd better be a good boy and get some sleep. My schedule is actually utterly flexible—I can show up anytime I want as long as I keep up with the work—but I need the hours. Like Bob Dylan so profoundly says, "Time is an ocean, but it ends at the shore/ You may not see me tomorrow." Like I say, Time is a notion that ends with a snore—and you just might see me tomorrow...

bittersweetly yours,
boog

10 December 1993, Ray "Byrd" Brecheisen, Pittsburg, KS

"Who cares if you're so poor you can't afford to buy a pair
of mod a-go-go stretch elastic pants?
There will come a time when you can even
take your clothes off when you dance."

—Frank Zappa,
We're Only in It for the Money, 1967

Howdy Ray,

Yes, I too freaked out in Kansas when I heard that Frank Zappa died. I was on my way to my part-time job as a petty bureaucrat in Topeka when I heard it on NPR. I was pleased at least that they played the "Who could imagine that they would **freak out** somewhere in *Kansas*?.. **Kansas?**.. *Kansas?*.. Kansas?" line on national radio. If my memory serves me right (and it does, sometimes), that was the same day they announced that Houphouët-Bouigny had died—Houphouët-Bouigny, the former president of the Ivory Coast, Houphouët-Bouigny, the man whose name is never pronounced the same way twice, Houphouët-Bouigny, the man whose name looks like it should be the name of a rare but incurable and unbearably gruesome disease: "Oh God! The doctors say I've got... *Houphouët-Bouigny!*" (dramatic organ music here).

It was a pleasant surprise & curious coincidence to get your letter, because I'd been thinking about you recently. At my petty bureaucrat job in Topeka I review appeals of administrative decisions for KDHE and write final orders for the Secretary to sign (I'm not sure if I have a real job title, but when some people call me the "Special Counsel to the Secretary" I don't argue). Anyway, I have to read a lot of transcripts, and one day I was comparing the testimony of two witnesses for consistency. I made columns on my little yellow legal pad with the name of each witness on top. The first name was "RAY" and the second was "BYRD" and when I looked back I realized that I had written "RAY BYRD." So I thought of you. And in the alley behind the Landon building, which I walk through sometimes on the way back from lunch to take a shortcut by way of the freight elevator, is a sign for the "Byrd's Nest Café." The last time I walked through, there was a 24-foot cabin cruiser parked on a trailer behind the Byrd's Nest, a strange sight indeed to see looming above you in a narrow alley in the middle of a city in the middle of

Kansas. But I'm sure it's there for a very good reason...

I had heard that you were married, but this baby thing is news to me. Hullaballoo! Helluvadeal! I'm sure you're a very good dad, even at 2:30 in the morning. Your life is probably different than it used to be... [...]

OK, Ray, I'd better get back to work—I've got some frogs that are depending on me to have a motion for summary judgment filed by the 15th & I'm nowhere near finished yet. [...]

I'm sure the rails you ride are <u>still</u> rusted...

hobo chang ba,
boog

11 February 1994, Rex Erickson, San Diego, CA

Well Howdy now Rex,

According to the 1994 Smithsonian engagement calendar that a friend gave me for Christmas, Henrik Ibsen says that

> [y]ou should never wear your best trousers when you go out to fight for freedom and truth[,]

which is probably why lawyers always wear nice pants. Not me. Actually, it depends on who's judging what's nice and what's not. The trousers I have on now are perhaps my best, old jeans mended by my roommate Brenda with psychedelic print patches & one with a giant image of a strawberry. I don't wear these to court. To court I wear tan "Bugle Boys" that an old girlfriend gave me, a pair of black made-in-China pants that I got at Wal-Mart a few hours before my first full-dress trial advocacy class, and a pair of black wool dress pants that I paid 50 bucks for then kind of fucked them up by drying them too long because the timer on our dryer doesn't work any more. Since I wear these to court, I can crusade for freedom and truth while I'm there & still keep Henrik Ibsen happy. Fat chance.

Is it normal to be a lawyer for a year and a half and still be impoverished? I don't know, Rex, but why be normal? All I can say is that, in my humble opinion, you're in good company. I'm no poorer than I was last year, though, and I'm working a lot less. This is more what I had in mind...

Velvet Underground's on the jukebox now—"shiny, shiny, shiny boots of leather, whiplash girlchild in the dark... ermine furs adorn, imperious"—they don't write songs like this any more—"strike dear mistress, and cure his heart." The book this song is based on, *Venus in Furs*, is worth reading if you can get your hands on it. As pornography it's amusingly tame, but it's interesting inasmuch as he takes the Christian idea of suffering as a means of proving love and takes it out to its logical illogical conclusion.

Yes the passing of Frank Zappa was a great tragedy indeed—the modern-day composer[1] is off to that great utility muffin research kitchen[2] in the sky, all too soon. Who else will write for us such lines as

> Evelyn, a dog, having undergone further modification, pondered the significance of short-person behavior in pedal-depressed pan-chromatic resonance and other highly ambient domains. "Arf!" she said.[3]

or

> Ladies and gentlemen, the monster which the peasants in this area call Frunobulax (apparently a very large poodle dog), has been seen approaching the Power Plant... We can't let him reproduce! Somebody get the pants![4]

[...] I briefly considered the idea of trying to organize another Zap-Out, wherein we would play all of Zappa's records in chronological order without stopping, but I gave this up pretty quickly. The last time we did it was in 1982 or so & it took just shy of 24 hours. If we did it now it would take twice as long and I'm 50% older—it just wouldn't work. So I'll just close my eyes and dream of guitar notes that go reent-toont teent-toont teenooneenoonee[5] & which might irritate an executive kind of guy.[6] RIP, Frank Zappa...

So, Rex, what kind of music are you listening to these days? Still hanging out with those Mexican beet farmers? Do you go to many shows? Have you figured out how to be a human and a lawyer at the same time? Do you represent any bands? Questions, questions, questions, flooding into the mind of the concerned young person today...[7] Where can I get my poodle clipped in Burbank? Where can I get my stomach pumped? Etc., etc.

[...] Keep in touch, Rex, and tell me what your life is like...

string beans to Utah,[8]
boog

13 March 1994, Gregor Brune, Lawrence, KS

Howdy Gregor,

Thanks for keeping the *Tiny Tim Times* coming. Enclosed is my entry in the Tiny Tim drawing contest. I know it won't reproduce very well, but I'm submitting it anyway for your viewing enjoyment.

As you may have noted on the back, it's titled "Tiny Tim as a Chicken." Tiny might be pleased to know that this is sort of a continuation of a series of Biblical chicken pictures: "Veronica Wipes the Face of Jesus as a Chicken," "Moses as a Chicken and the Burning Bush," "Absalom as a Chicken," "Lot's Wife Turned into a Pillar of Chickens," "Salome with the Head of John the Baptist as a Chicken," etc.

I wouldn't worry too much about the FF5 review. Hell, if *Factsheet Five* had ever said that one of my publications heralded the downfall of civilization as we know it, I would have been *flattered*. I hope they're right.

Keep up the good work.

tiptoeing through the tulips,
boog

14 March 1994, Trout Fishing in America, Carpinteria, CA

Dear Trout Fishing in America,

I heard on the radio tonight that you got a new name for your high school graduation. Congratulations!

In one of Kurt Vonnegut's books one of his characters is elected president and randomly assigns everyone a new middle name constructed from the name of an animal, plant, or mineral plus a number from one to twenty: Zircon-12, Pig-4, Rutabaga-17, and so on. So now everybody had relatives all over the country—everywhere somebody went there would be other Zircons or Rutabagas or 17s. Just like real families, though, they didn't necessarily have anything in common or even like each other very much even though they had the same name. In your case, although you probably won't run into any other Trout Fishing in Americas, I imagine that you will find lots of friendly relatives you didn't know you had.

If you're ever in Kansas, I know where we can get four pounds of muscatel for a dollar and fifteen cents.

mayonnaise,
Boog Trout-13 Highberger

23 March 1994, Honna Veerkamp, San Francisco, CA

"It would certainly take a lot of celery roots to make a battleship."
—Richard Brautigan, in
A Confederate General from Big Sur

Howdy Honna,

Boy, are you gong to have a big plaque in a prominent place in the Last Supper Museum! The plate you sent arrived at the perfect time, too, because just that night we had three dinner guests who hadn't eaten at the house before, and thanks to you we had a Last Supper plate for each of them. Two of the guests were Amazing Grains bakers and one was a woman named Sarah who has been living in Matfield Green working with the Land Institute. Part of the time she works on a project analyzing the economics of the place—what goes in and what goes out—which I'm sure will find that the place is a colony, like a Third World country, and that the value of what is exported is much greater than the value of what is imported from outside. I was really excited to hear about this because it was something I had thought about for a long time, and I'm looking forward to seeing their results. The rest of the time, Sarah says, she runs a little coffee shop in Matfield Green and serves coffee to old people and listens to their stories.

Is it springtime in San Francisco? It certainly is spring here in Kansas, and it's making it hard to concentrate. The sun has been shining, the crocuses are blooming, the redbuds are budding, the college students are at Padre Island. I quit working early this afternoon and went wandering around. First I delivered (by Boog Post, of course) a copy of the announcement of the *Tiny Tim Times* Tiny Tim drawing contest [...] to a friend who lives by the park. At the park I saw the Co-op softball team practicing, so I went over to watch. Brenda is on the team and is very excited—she says she has never played softball before. She hit pretty well for a beginner, but she needs to work on staying in front of the ball when she is fielding. Brenda says they're sure they're going to win at least one game this year. After seeing them practice I'm almost sure she's right.

Cypress has been way cute, as usual. He finally got a little haircut and looks a lot different. I thought Brenda would put up more resistance, but when he said he wanted a haircut, she and Mikey gave him one right away. He's in that stage where he's experimenting with other identities: "I'm Papa," "I'm little Boog," "I'm a lepidopterist," "I'm Jeep the Pig," etc. Hmmm... some of those probably require a little explanation.

Jeep the Pig is one of those Vietnamese potbellied pigs that is the pet of someone down the street or a friend of someone down the street. I haven't actually met Jeep the Pig, but he made quite an impression on Cypress. The lepidopterist thing is probably my fault. He was in my room one day, pretending to be a butterfly, when I said something like "Uh oh! A lepidopterist! He's going to put us in a jar! Let's hide!" And of course he loves to hide so he started saying "A lepidopterist! We must hide" every time he was in my room, and we would have to crawl under the covers of my bed, or under my big coat, or under something until the lepidopterist went away. And now he's the lepidopterist sometimes, and I have to hide or run away. I've got to be more careful what I say to this kid—he's too smart for my own good.

Epicenter sounds like a cool place—it's on the list of Places I Must Go When I Come to San Francisco Next Time. I just got a stack of these Dreamtime Talkingmail magazines, so you & Epicenter should have one if you don't already. I got to visit Dreamtime Village when [I was in Wisconsin] last summer and it was really inspiring—it shook me out of my lawyer doldrums and made me remember that inside I'm still an artist like everybody else. I would love to create an energy center like Dreamtime here in Kansas and some days I think that buying our house is the first step in that direction. Is there any communication between the Epicenter folks and the people at Bound Together? Any animosity? A generation gap? I'm curious to know how the marginal scene works in a place that's big enough to have separate groups of radicals/marginals that don't all know each other. Do you know the people in Contraband? That's the name of the naked people on back of here who do performance art and such in the SF area. The guy in the middle on the bottom row is my buddy Keith, who I met at various anarchist gatherings & who out of the blue sent me the postcard that this picture was on a few months ago. I've been getting an amazing amount of San Francisco energy lately—the whole universe is conspiring to send me the message that I must come to San Francisco, but I still haven't figured out how.

I hope relationships aren't making you too crazy. When you said in your last letter that "Significant evidence suggests: possibly more trouble than it's worth," I had to laugh and cry because it was so true. Sometimes I wonder whether I'm cut out to be in a traditional full-time relationship at all, no matter how wonderful my partner is. I used to think things would make more sense as I got older but so far this has not been the case. But I guess my life isn't the only one that doesn't make sense. Soon I have to go talk to a client about child support, and then see if Fran is still awake. I will see you in San Francisco soon, if only in my head.

love,
boog

11 April 1994, Theresa Martin, Minneapolis, MN

Hello Theresa,

To answer your question: *my whole life* is an essay exam for which I am completely, absolutely, and thoroughly unprepared. [...]

And you're not the only one with rodent troubles. As you no doubt noticed, mice are eating my stationery. I wish they'd hurry and finish it off so I could get new envelopes with the right address.

It sounds like you've been crazy busy. If I had an ounce of empathy and compassion I'd probably feel guilty for having free time lately, but I don't. It's been an interesting experiment so far & I kind of like it. Lazy & no apologies.

Yes, & I've been restless, too... I've felt driven to go out wandering in the night... One evening at the brewery I got into a long discussion with somebody who offered to do my hair up in a beehive before I cut it off next (I'll send pictures); another night I ended up at our neighborhood hardcore bar across the park, listening to grungey metal music [...]; tonight I'm just listening to bootleg Zappa, drinking Mexican beer with limes, sitting in front of the one-eyed monster, working on creating the myth of my own existence... I type, therefore I am...

I've been reading about the myths of other people's existences: I recently finished a book about Louis Riel, a Canadian Métis revolutionary and religious nut. Up until 1870, apparently, most of Canada was still owned by Hudson's Bay Company. Then the Canadian government bought the company out and tried to incorporate the new territory, but met with resistance from the descendants of Indians and French fur trappers who had been living there for years without having to deal with a central government. Riel led a rebellion against the Canadian government in Manitoba in 1870 and again in Saskatchewan in the 1880s, but in the meantime was locked in an asylum for claiming that he was a "prophet, infallible pontiff, and priest-king." He also decided that the New World had been colonized by a boatload of Egyptians with their Hebrew slaves who ran aground in the Yucatán; the Egyptians went south and the Hebrews went north, and all the Indians are descended from them:

> Quand je vous parle, c'est la voix de Dieu qui sonne
> Et tout ce que je dis vous est essentiel.
> Je suis le joyeux téléphone
> Qui vous transmet les chants et les discours du ciel.

(When I speak to you, it's the voice of God that sounds
And everything I say to you is essential.
I am the joyous telephone
Which transmits to you the songs and speech of heaven.)

Later he renamed the days of the week and denied the doctrine of transubstantiation: "'You can't eat a man six feet tall,' Riel scoffed." Despite all that, Riel is apparently somewhat of a folk hero in some Canadian circles, and various leftists have tried to recreate him for their own purposes. But, like bp Nichol says,

its always these damn white boys
writing my story these same stupid fuckers
that put me down to try to make a myth out of me
they all sit at counters scribbling their plays on napkins
their poems on their sleeves and never see me...
They're crazy these white boys said louis riel

I first read about Louis Riel in (& the poem above is from) a way cool Autonomedia book called *Gone to Croatan* (& subtitled "Origins of American Dropout Culture"). In addition to Louis Riel it had essays on the Ishmaelites (a wandering tribe of Indians, escaped slaves, and white dropouts that lived in Indiana until the middle of the nineteenth century and appear to have inspired, among other things, James Fenimore Cooper's *The Prairie*, Little Orphan Annie, and the Nation of Islam) and on the "Lost Colony" of Roanoke, the residents of which apparently didn't disappear at all, but just decided to stop working for their upper class masters and went to join the natives in the nearby Great Dismal Swamp, where they still have the family names of Roanoke colonists and "still know exactly who they are."

Fran's sister Rita was back in town recently and told about somebody that a friend of a friend had encountered who had named one of their children "O Pale and Beautiful Smiling Jesus Smith," who I'm sure also knows exactly who he is...

The brand name on the pop machine at the Landon SOB (that's Landon State Office Building) is "Dixie-Narco."

This is all the news I have, except that I could probably keep gibbering for hours if the beer and the Zappa held out. Instead I'll just tell you that I've talked C. into coming to Lawrence on or about May 12 (she says she's riding with Laura) and it looks like I'll be giving her a ride back sometime in the following week. So I'll see you soon.

That's when I'll be able to tell you more about my friend dave's plan to bombard the *Reader's Digest* with stories that all contain the line, "And then before anything else could happen the ultimatum to France," selected at Random from *The Autobiography of Alice B. Toklas*.

I am the joyous telephone,
boog

23 April 1994, Donna Eades, San Francisco, CA

Hello Donna,

Mary says you're in China now, so I guess this will wait till you get back. Mary also says that Carol is in Morocco. 50 years from now there will be a PBS documentary about your exploits: The Travelling Eades Sisters, 7 pm on Thursday on channel 19, please call in your pledge of support for public television right away to help make our 2044 fall fund drive a big success, we wouldn't be here without lots of cash from you the viewer, etc., etc., and now back to our regularly scheduled programming...

The enclosed article is from an old issue of *Art in America* & was written by the person I told you about when you were here whose unpublished novel I'm theoretically trying to find a publisher for. I haven't copied the manuscript yet for various reasons... Crackerjack [Kid] gave me Zack's address. I had assumed he was still in prison in Mexico, but now he seems to be in a nursing home in Texas. I should probably contact him before I do anything else... I'll keep you posted.

I went to a lecture on child language acquisition with Mary yesterday, then we went out for beers & dinner at the Full Moon. [...] Mary says you want to have a baby—I think you'd be a great mom. All the Country Folks alumni are doing it: Lauren & Peter, Pete & Elizabeth, who knows, maybe more... I think I'm out of this game... I used to think I wanted to be a daddy someday, but [...] I'm no longer convinced that it will be a great tragedy if my genes aren't passed down to posterity. There are plenty of kids in the world already and I'm not sure I'm cut out for being in a stable, long-term monogamous relationship. I used to worry, in Gregory Corso's immortal words, about ending up "all alone in a furnished room with pee stains on my underwear," but no matter what happens I don't think I'll have to be any more alone than I want to be & I've already got pee stains on my underwear so I don't see that being married or having babies is of decisive importance any more. And anyway, some people argue that the most important mode of human reproduction now is intellectual rather than biological, and I've been so intellectually promiscuous that surely I've impregnated somebody by now... and even as we speak the bad ideas are growing inside their heads, multiplying, getting ready to burst out like viruses to find other ripe & unsuspecting hosts... burn this letter now before it's too late... [scary organ music here: cut to the secret underground laboratory] "ha ha ha ha..." [he wrings his hands with glee and flashes an evil, leering grin] "Tomorrow the world!... ha ha ha ha..." [strange chemical apparatuses glow and bubble] "Quick, Igor, to the laser printer!"

your mad scientist friend,
boog

3 June 1994, Jake Gibbs, Lexington, KY

What a long strange trip it's been, Jake,

& getting longer & stranger all the time. No wonder I'd been thinking about you lately. I hope this letter finds Delia as well as when you wrote last. Why does it take losing the things we love most to remind us how much they really mean to us? And why don't we remember to tell people how much we care about them until after they're dead? It sounds like you've been lucky to be reminded and then to still have her around. [...]

We finally did get a mall—an outlet mall down by the river. Fortunately, even though they cut down a lot of the trees that the eagles used to roost in, they seem to have come back. Last year the flood almost washed the thing away: close but no cigar. Somebody has printed a postcard showing the water lapping at its edges & I'll try to send you a copy sometime because I think you'll find it inspiring. And since then, another outlet mall sprang up like a mushroom on the north [side] of the river—I went up to Wisconsin for a week last summer and when I got off the turnpike when I got home I thought I was in the wrong place because this thing was almost finished and as far as I could remember it wasn't there when I left. And now somebody has proposed tearing down a block on the edge of downtown for a commercial/residential complex, and a couple of big discount chains are planning stores in a hub south of town where the bypass is supposed to go—which I understand is the new trend rather than the traditional enclosed mall with a couple of anchor department stores and a lot of little specialty shops. Feh! I haven't given up yet, but I've also been keeping my eyes open for someplace to flee if it gets too nasty here. As far as I can tell, though, this is happening everywhere. Lexington sounds like no exception.

You sound like anything but a slug, Jake. Teaching, Alfalfa, the dance school, the co-op, local politics—and most importantly, being a dad. Like I've said to a number of my friends, and as I still thoroughly believe, raising kids right is the ultimate revolutionary act. I live with a two-year-old—he was born here at the house—and watching him grow & learn & respond to the love & patience he gets has made me even more acutely aware of how much our survival depends on good parents, which I'm sure includes you & Nimi. [...]

I almost hate to admit it, but I've been reading Camille Paglia. She's very entertaining—she writes in epigrams, almost every sentence is quotable—but she's also full of shit up to her ears. She thinks people are inherently evil, that Hobbes was right, that feminism is bad for women, that western civilization is a good idea. I haven't read anything so infuriating since Milton Friedman's *Capitalism and Freedom*. I figure it's good to do something like this every now and then, though, so I don't get intellectually flabby. It seems important to see what the other side is thinking, plus it's nice to get a little ammunition to throw back at them, little gems like "The Devil is a woman," and "Freedom is the most overrated modern idea," and "If civilization had been left in female hands, we would still be living in grass huts." I can see the latter painted in big capital letters on the side of a bulldozer as it chugs purposefully down Deer Run Court, building a bright and shiny future for us all, amortized however over twenty years so if it falls down after that we really don't care. [...]

OK, enough whining & cynicism. My typing finger is about to fall off so I'm going to stop. I hope things are well & I hope I get to see you & Nimi & your beautiful children sometime soon.

love,
boog

20 June 1994, Jude Pate, Sitka, AK

almost solstice
Carta Blanca con limon
slow, sad, bittersweet song on KJHK

Greetings, Counselor:

This time I presume it's no false alarm because I heard it straight from Rupert himself: Congratulations. I had no doubts.

Your postcard was beautiful—many people have admired it, it hangs now on the image wall in the dining room among the Last Suppers and other postcards from far away (including one my friend Shelby sent from Anchorage that says

"Alaska is BIG, BIG, BIG!")

I'm not sure if I'm a crow in the service of ghosts or a ghost in the service of crows... or a ghost being serviced by crows. I suppose, like they used to say on TV, that only my hairdresser knows for sure. Well, I don't really have a hairdresser, but I'm going to try to get Anne to do that beehive this week. It's been hotter than Hays here for many days now and I'm ready to chop all my hair off so if we don't get it arranged soon it'll be too late. I saw her at the Brewery a few nights ago & she said that your dog had died—it made me sad to hear it, it's so far from home to lose such a good friend. My intuition or my imagination tells me that you found a special place to lay his bones to rest, someplace where his ghost can bark at the crows...

I've been legally busy again. The county has started construction on the western leg of the bypass even though they have agreed to issue a supplemental EIS for the eastern leg which supposedly will include consideration of alternative routes. So this week or early next I and/or the attorney for another party will be filing a motion for a temporary injunction. We've got some cases right on point and it looks like we shouldn't have too much trouble getting the injunction without an outrageous bond. Before that, though, I've got to file a motion to join the Kansas Department of Transportation as a defendant. I'm learning everything I always wanted to know about civil procedure but was afraid to raise my hand in class, but they don't teach you this stuff anyway so it wouldn't have made any difference.

In another interesting travesty of justice I'm representing somebody against the biggest developers in town who want to build a subdivision where his house is. First they tried to unilaterally cancel his lease, but we pointed out that they couldn't. Then they claimed his lease didn't include the acreage behind the house which he had been using with their knowledge for the last eight years, and they started bulldozing it. So we got an ex parte restraining order (after two days of running up and down the stairs at the courthouse on crutches—I had sprained my foot & could hardly walk) & the first judge recused himself because he was a member of the country club but we lost the hearing for a temporary injunction. I got beat up pretty bad—it was my first adversarial hearing of any complexity and I was up against Wint Winter, the probable next Attorney General. He's an excellent courtroom lawyer, quick on his feet—& I sucked eggs. It was certainly a learning experience, though. I think the best case scenario at this point is that we cut a deal for them to pay to have the beautiful old 1880s house moved off the property (and delivered to my client) in exchange for dropping the suit & terminating the lease. Justice, eh? There was a passage from a book I just read that I wanted to get into the record but I decided against incorporating it into my closing because it was a judge trial & it probably would have done more harm than good:

> When we Indians kill meat, we eat it all up. When we dig roots, we make little holes. When we burn grass for grasshoppers, we don't ruin things. We shake down acorns and pine nuts. We don't chop down trees. We use only dead wood. But the White people plow up the ground, pull up the trees, kill everything. The tree says, "Don't. I am sore. Don't hurt me." But they chop it down and cut it up. The spirit of the land hates them. They blast out trees.... They saw up the trees. That hurts them. The Indians never hurt anything but the White people destroy all... how can the spirit of the earth like the White man?... Everywhere the White man has touched, it is sore.

Kate Luckie, Wintu Nation shaman, quoted in Jack D. Forbes, Columbus and Other Cannibals 25 (Autonomedia, 1992), citing Cora DuBois, "Wintu Ethnography," University of California Publications in American Archaeology and Ethnology v. 36 (1935–1938) (emphasis added). Unfortunately, no amount of blue-book razzmatazz is going to give this any precedential value in the Douglas County District Court. But trees don't have standing anyway, and neither does the spirit of the earth. Plus there are lots of trees left, and if you've seen one tree you've seen them all, right?

Well, enough of this misanthropic raving. Life is good here—I've been managing to maintain a fairly good balance between work & play, responsibility & frivolousness, security & joy, lightness and weight, fulfillment and desire—well, maybe I could stand to go a little heavier on the fulfillment, but I have no intention of cutting back on the desire—that's not the kind of balance I'm looking for...

DAYS PASS...

The do is done. I'm tall enough to be on the basketball team now. I'll send pictures. [...]

See you later, litigator...
boog

1 October 1994, Becki Newburn, Ruacana, Namibia

Bula, Becki:

No wonder I couldn't find you in my atlas—it's amazing how much difference a few little letters can make. This atlas shows a "Ruacaná" in Angola, so I'm guessing that you're just on the other side of the river. Your descriptions of the people & the river were beautiful—they made my heart sing, made me want to come visit—& this of course reminds me to remind you that the definitive travel book on Namibia hasn't been written yet... earlier this year I read a book written by somebody who'd done a Peace Corps stint in Togo & who as far as I know was previously unpublished. If he can do it, so can you—if you need an agent let me know.

It sounds like you're doing good work & I admire your dedication—it makes me feel lazy & privileged—I waste so much time on such trivial bullshit & I have such petty desires: I want to sleep for another hour, I want a beer, I want some french fries, I want the new Bad Religion tape. Rather than engaging in any more whining, though, I'll just try to use your example as an inspiration to get my shit together.

Congratulations on being madly in love. *Who cares if he's the one?*, is the way I look at it—the high is the same either way & you might as well enjoy it. I've been going through the same sort of thing—I didn't think it was possible any more, at my ripe old age, but I haven't felt this goofy in years. The best thing about it is that she's somebody I've known for 15 years ("That's great—you don't have to worry about farting around her" says Anne at the brewery) but the worst thing is that she lives in Wisconsin. Otherwise it would be too easy, I suppose—& this way I get to do a lot of traveling.

Yes, & I suppose love is possible—Pete & Elizabeth seem to be making it work. They've done the big 3: house, marriage, baby on the way. I got to officiate at their wedding & I liked it because it had a lot more meaning to them than most ceremonies I've done have had for the people involved—they put a lot of work into it. As part of the ceremony, they recognized the 4 elements—earth, air, fire, & water—& for air they released two white doves—oohs & ahs all around. Grandpa Laufer belted out the Our Father in an impressive a cappella baritone, Peter Williams read a Pablo Neruda poem in Spanish & then Elizabeth's sister read it in English—it ended with "I want to do for you what spring does for the cherry trees" (yes!)—& when it was all over they rode away to Liberty Hall on a bicycle built for two festooned with tin cans & streamers, & we all lived happily ever after.

OK, yesterday was payday & I did buy the new Bad Religion tape & it's on the jukebox now. I don't buy prerecorded music very often, but every now & then some song or band will seize my head & I feel compelled to do so. These guys are cool—they're fast & their lyrics have words like "febrile," "palpitate," "supine," "vortex," "sagacious," & "recompense." Do you have access to a tape player? If so, I'd be glad to mail you any musics of your desire, straight from the infinite culture factory of America... just let me know...

I've been taking advantage of my relative leisure to play around with mail art—it's an easy & entertaining way to connect with people around the world. If you'll examine the envelope this is in you'll note a stamp that says "arte ala carte" which was part of a beautiful sheet I received from a woman in Connecticut, and a little brown stamp with a picture of a M. Gérard Barbot, who I've just started corresponding with. I have this theory that the universe is unfolding toward the point where everything is connected with everything else, to pure connection & consciousness, & the function of humans is to facilitate this unfolding in whatever way possible. This isn't just some sort of post-psychedelic delusion on my part, this is more or less what the physicists are saying these days. Do you know Jude Bray? She's our new roommate & her husband Daniel is a quantum mechanic & is living in Chicago where he's wrestling with the implications of the Aspect Experiment which has proved Bell's Theorem, which, as I understand it, says that either: 1) every particle in the universe is interconnected through a faster-than-light field; or 2) physical reality doesn't exist. & this is science... either option is OK with me but I have this idea that if it's the latter that's true I don't have to worry as much about sweeping my room or paying off my student loans.

OK, enough gibberish for one night. In the morning I will get up & go see my parents, & we will go to the Catholic church bazaar in Scipio, Kansas, where we will eat sauerkraut, green beans, roast beef with mashed potatoes & gravy, & ho'made pie & where Mom will no doubt want to play bingo. Well, it's the only indigenous culture we've got, so we might as well enjoy it, is the way I see it—it's better than McDonald's & WalMart, animal flesh notwithstanding.

I'm glad things are going well for you—what a blessing to be able to realize how sweet this life can be—please write & tell me more stories...

love,
boog

10 October 1994, Jill Innes, Madison, WI

Invasion Day (observed)

jill dear,

What a guy, that Columbus. Not only did he single-handedly initiate one of the most horrible genocides in human history, he also comes back from the dead once a year to stop the US mail. Between him and our vicious mailperson-eating Shih-Tzu dog, I may never get a letter from you again.

Speaking of Columbus: did I tell you about the other Columbus I read about recently? Renaldo Columbus was his name, and he claimed to have discovered the clitoris in 1551. *I'm not making this up*! Apparently several other good doctors of the time (all men, of course) disputed his claim & said they found it first, but just like the other Columbus none of them seem to have consulted the people who were already there. [...]

All my paragraphs are ending with ellipses tonight... I suppose it's the only honest & realistic way to end a paragraph... I feel like my life ends with an ellipsis right now... or more correctly, I should say it *continues* with one...

It makes me smile to think of you rolling around Madison on your bicycle—I imagine streets wet with drizzly rain & covered with fallen leaves, & you with a heavy sweater & a contented smile & your hair flowing out behind you. I wish it was something I could do with you, but I've learned to reconcile myself with not getting everything I want. Every now & then I think about getting a three-wheeler, but somehow I never get around to doing anything about it. I'm going to try to make it to the police auction this weekend, though, in search of a bicycle for my nephew Alex for Christmas, so maybe I'll keep my eyes open. I used to really love to ride bikes. When I went to see my folks last weekend we went to the church bazaar at Scipio (seven miles north & one mile east of Garnett) & it reminded me of the time when I was in eighth grade or so when I set off on my old beat-up one-speed to ride to Scipio &

Greeley—a round trip of 25 miles, the last 5 of which I did on a flat tire. In my later years I would amuse myself by passing cars on the highway, which I did by starting out at the top of the hill around Eighth Street and pedalling as hard as I could in tenth gear so that I was going well over thirty by the time that I got to the flat spot around the Dairy Queen. No helmet, of course—I think this was before they were invented. Ah, youth...

Youth... this reminds me of a cartoon I saw recently that I meant to alter & send to you, but it got recycled before I got the chance. It had a picture of a man up in the clouds with outstretched arms, flying, & he was thinking something like, "I'm too old to be doing this." The caption was: MID-LIFE CRISIS. I had intended to alter it so that it said, "I'm too old not to be doing this!" & to add: "Sensory overload is wasted on the young!"

Ah, jill, my love... I look forward to overloading my senses with you soon. [...]

boog

22 October 1994, Jill Innes, Madison, WI

jill dear,

I bought a gallon of Desires today. $14.98 at the hardware store on Sixth Street. I had resolved to paint the porch floor a deep purple, & this afternoon I went in search of paint. I was browsing through the purples when I came upon color number F334—"Desires"—and even though it wasn't exactly the color I had in mind I no longer had any choice. So we painted the kitchen table with desires tonight, and by the time you come visit the porch should be painted, too. I look forward to greeting you [...] on the porch of desires [...]

The weather was incredible again today, and Maggie suggested a picnic for supper... this got transmuted somehow into just moving the table out into the side yard. It was great—eight of us dining by candlelight under the cornflower blue sky: bright orange shepherd's pie & a spinach salad with Jude's ginger dressing, washed down with a bottle of tasty Chardonnay I'd received as part of a wedding fee. Maggie's sister & Cypress entertained us with the cello, the dogs chased each other, the sky slowly grew darker, the tensions of the last week drained away. I can hear Monsieur Brillat-Savarin saying, "They are so good-natured! They have such sparkling eyes!" Despite its madnesses, this life is surely sweet...

And how much sweeter it would be with you here as well, my love, and how I long to see the sparkling of your gourmand eyes... and the rest of you, too: "The tongue of man," and woman, too, old B.-S. surely means, "by its delicate texture and the membranes with which it is closely surrounded, clearly reveals the sublime nature of the functions for which it was intended." I couldn't have said it better myself.

The next day:

I read your last letter over & over again because it made me smile so much, & it made me think, too.

The client you told me about sounded like more of a blatant racist than I've had to deal with in a while. The racism around here these days is generally much more subtle. Sometimes I wonder if we'll be able to get rid of it as long as the idea of racism is in our heads. I try to treat everybody I meet with the same decency & respect, but there are still times when a voice in my head says, "Look! I'm not being a racist!" like it is some sort of unusual accomplishment. It makes me feel good to see your kids interact with their friends and I wonder if the idea of racism is in their heads, if they are conscious of not treating people differently because of their skin color or whether it just comes naturally.

I just read a pretty good book called *Tent of Miracles* by a Brazilian author, Jorge Amado. It talks a lot about racial problems in Brazil, and it seems to advocate miscegenation—a really nasty-sounding word for people of different races having babies together—as the best solution. The protagonist causes a big stir at one point by printing a book exposing the black and native blood in all the supposedly lily-white ruling class families in the area. And that fits with what I've read elsewhere—that almost everyone in Brazil is a mulatto or mestizo of some shade or another & it makes me want to go there & see all the beautiful people & see if it is possible for people to live together peacefully even though they don't all look exactly alike. [...] From looking at my dad & my uncles with their reddish skin & aquiline noses I used to suspect that there was some secret Native American on that side of the family, but now I think it's just my imagination. The most exotic thing in my family tree is a couple of Luxembourgers, but I like this so much that now when people ask about my ancestry I tell them I'm Luxembourgeois (actually, I think the proper adjective is "Luxembourgian," but it's my ancestry so I'll say it how I want). [...]

boog

9 December 1994, Shelby Shanks, Houston, TX

Hello Shelby,

I have a mouse in my car. It's a long story: We've got mice in the Country Folks house, and being good wild-eyed hippies we don't have traditional mousetraps that snap! shut and crush their little spines, no, instead we have a very p.c. live trap that works like this:

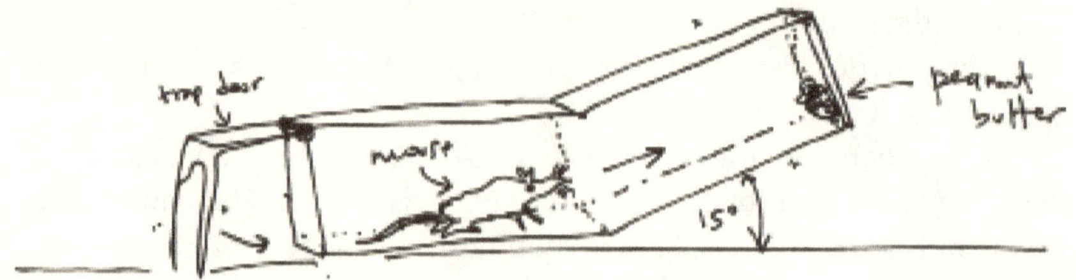

The right end is tilted up off the floor, and as the mouse approaches the peanut butter (Good to Eat!) the trap tilts forward and the trap door snaps shut. Then we take them out and release them in somebody else's neighborhood.

So I'd caught another mouse a couple of weeks ago and I went up to campus by the stadium to let him go, & (oops!) before I got him out of the car the trap snapped open & the little fucker scurried under the seat. So I left the door open after I got home, figuring he would find the outside, but a couple of days ago I started to notice things that had been gnawed to bits on my dashboard, on the floor, etc. so I figure he's still in there somewhere... (so I have set the trap) [...]

Well, Shiner's on sale now here in Kansas, & I'm in the middle of one even as we speak. Like the old song says:

> I can think of nothing finer,
> Than to drink a couple Shiners
> in the morning—

Or something like that...

Jeff at the liquor store has given me a copy of an interesting new magazine that's sitting in front of me on the desk now. It's got a fairly straightforward title: BEER. Everything you wanted to know about the new American microbrew revolution but were afraid to ask. There are over 350 small breweries in America now, it says—are there any in Houston? I was in California & Oregon in August & it was beer heaven, one place called the "Bombs Away Cafe" (my friend Brenna said it opened during the Gulf War) had 21 different microbeers on tap, plus 5 or 6 more seasonal specialty beers. I thought I saw the world through beer-colored glasses, but these guys at BEER magazine really take the cake. There's an article, for instance, about a visitor to Northern Iraq, who plots & struggles to have a couple of six packs of rare Iraqi Scheherazade beer smuggled across the border. "Beer or death?" he muses, "Beer or death?" Hell, why not both?

I haven't see Sally in a long time, but I would have paid money to see her in black & white striped Lycra pants. It's good to know that there are other attorneys who still aren't a lawyer inside. I still don't feel like a lawyer inside, & I trust it's the same with you & Chris.

Hasta la vista, babies—
boog

1995–1997

King Tut's Wa-Wa Hut • worthiness of dreams • postcard from Budapest • 13 has always been pretty good to me • a short art biography • luxurious squandering • Mister Boogie • memo(random) • 6 pairs of pants • Free State Firebirds • quop • PJ Harvey on Yugoslav radio • Vermin stamp • this beast called love • a Nazi submarine covered with snails • fromage à toi • cheese money • Tiny Tim's funeral • showdown in Chocolate • printing with body parts

16 January 1995, Paul Hilmarsson, Eskifjörður, Iceland

Howdy Paul,

[...] Yes, Lawrence is the home of William Burroughs, not to mention Custer's horse (Custer was an American general who was famous for being wiped out by Native American warriors at the battle of Little Bighorn in Wyoming in 1876. The horse was named "Comanche," and they used to describe it as "the only survivor of the Battle of Little Bighorn" until somebody finally pointed out to them that a lot of Indians survived, too. After the horse died they stuffed it & now it's on display at the Natural History Museum at the university here) and Einstein's brain in a jar.

[...] The only time I've been in Burroughs' house is when I helped arrange for William Kunstler to speak at the university in 1990 and I set up a meeting between the two of them. [...] I had been in New York a couple of weeks before and was hanging out at "King Tut's Wa-Wa Hut" across the street from Tompkins Park in the Lower East Side when an old guy in a white suit shuffled by. Somebody shouted "There's William Burroughs!" and most of the bar cleared out to go see him. I told Burroughs this story, & he seemed to be amused, because he, of course, had been in Kansas at the time. [...]

Well, Paul, I know even less about Eskifjördur than you know about Lawrence. I read a cool book last year called *Last Places* by a guy named Lawrence Millman; he arrives in Reykjavik and travels to Sprengisandur, Mödrudalur, the Odádahraun, Akureyri, Grimsey, Isafjördur, and other places, but I don't think he ever makes it to Eskifjördur. I'd love to visit Iceland someday—I've heard that Air Iceland stopovers in Reykjavik are free—but I don't think I'll be able to manage it any time soon. If you're travelling through next year we'd be glad to put you up. [...]

Cheers,
boog

29 May 1995, X., somewhere in America

"The landscape of the plains, if such there is, assumes the form of our own dreams, the shape of a chimera; it becomes sterile when the dream is unworthy."

—Ezequiel Martinez Estrada,
X-Ray of the Pampa

Howdy X.,

Sometimes I wonder if my dreams are still worthy—often it seems like they've been ground down by the years & made small & smooth & unobtrusive. It's good to hear that your dreams are still big... [...]

Okay, okay, I'm being too cynical—I haven't turned into a complete slug, even though some of my plans are kind of conventional these days. Yes, I'm planning on living as part of a more or less nuclear family & helping raise 3 kids who like to watch TV & eat hamburgers, but I still also dream of going to Uzbekistan (or maybe Vietnam or the Yucatan or...) and I still want to work on building an exuberant, sustainable, free society... even if it means being firm & patient with 3 kids who like to watch TV & eat hamburgers. Babylon hasn't sucked me in yet... [...]

R. called a few days ago—it was good to hear his voice. I guess he and V. are splitting up again, but he still seemed OK. I've probably babbled to you about this before, but talking to R. of course made me think about all of our interconnections & about the set of all my lovers' lovers & what an incomprehensibly odd group of men & women they are, & of course it made me wonder how many levels you have to take it out before we're all connected in a sordid circle of contagion & desire. [...]

And all that is probably why I'm so intrigued by mail art—I'm fascinated by how the networks work—who corresponds with who corresponds with who, who introduced who to who, etc. And did I tell you that I went to see a band called Smut at the Replay Lounge a couple of months ago? They're three women from Minneapolis & of course the one I talked to after the show used to be in RABL [the "Revolutionary Anarchist Bowling League"] & knew you & K. & K. More little circles... [...]

home, home, & deranged,
boog

10 August 1995, Lisa Mandelstein, San Francisco, CA

Hello Lisa,

Thanks for the cool postcard from Budapest by way of Prague. It sounds like you are having too much fun, but I'm sure it's just what you need. I'd love to hear stories sometime... Where else did you go? How did you travel? Where did you stay? How cheap was the beer? This juxtaposition of Budapest and fun makes me think of an old Zippy cartoon in which a detective Zippy wearing a Dick Tracy hat is interrogating a bearded lady, trying to poke holes in her story, & he says to her, "Quick! Sing me the Budapest national anthem!" Or something like that... I could probably find this old comic book somewhere in the piles of debris in my room & check out the details, but I prefer the security of my own twisted memories.

My travel plans have been shifting... for various reasons, Jill & I are going to Mexico instead of California or Oregon. I'm disappointed that I won't get to see you, but I suppose I'll be able to drown my sorrows in cervezas y frijoles y playas. (I just realized how beautifully alliterative this would be in English: beer & beans & beaches.) I'll send you a postcard. And Jill still hasn't been to San Francisco, so we'll have to come visit eventually. I haven't gotten to go to Wisconsin for a while, but her 9-year-old son Max was here for 5 days last month. We had a great time. He liked to go hear music, so we spent several nights at the Full Moon, jabbering with people and playing cards, and the last night we were there he put a dollar of his own money in the tip jar for the band. What a guy. [...] Our relationship is still working great, but it's starting to look like we won't be living in the same town anytime soon. So I'm sort of in limbo, but as limbos go it's not so bad—I've been in worse. So I'll keep going forward & taking one breath at a time...

I'm not going forward very fast, though—I sprained my ankle on Monday & haven't been able to get around since. I did go to the doctor this time, though, & I should be mobile by Monday. In the meantime my roommates are taking amazingly good care of me—feeding me pesto & hummus, fetching me beers, emptying my pee jar. The joys of communal living...

So here I am, reading, writing letters, trying to find better things to do than play solitaire on the computer. I've just been reading the latest issue of a magazine that I would subscribe to if I wasn't so broke, called *Experimental Musical Instruments*. I'm musically illiterate but it still fascinates me. The last couple of issues have included articles on tubulongs (aka "conduit marimbas"), the Banjo King (a man who played up to 6 banjos simultaneously while juggling them), growing bamboo for instruments, Stroh violins (violins with trumpet-shaped sound radiators) and related instruments, and a musical piece composed entirely from the sounds generated by prying apart, crushing, melting, and cutting up a transistor radio. I'd be glad to send you their address; I think they're located up in Marin County somewhere. Nicasio... again, I could check my map, but prefer to persist in my illusions. Hopefully they will inspire me to construct some of these weird devices someday.

About my only creative activity recently has been playing with mail art, making pseudo postage stamps (some more pseudo than others) and sending them to other strange people around the world. A character called the Crackerjack Kid has invited me to exhibit at the Electronic Museum of Modern Art (EMMA). I don't know if I've been uploaded yet, but if you're out surfing, EMMA is at http://www.dartmouth.edu/pages/user/cjkid/EMMA. One of the stamps on the outside of this letter was made by a guy up in Mill Valley & you will recognize the clown; who knows what else I will stick on there. Anyway it keeps me off the streets, not that that's a big problem this week.

OK, enough rambling. I suppose you can tell I've been locked up in my room for a long time. Anyway, it made me smile to hear from you & I look forward to seeing you. Please give my best to Alan, and shine on you crazy diamond.

love,
boog

Oh yeah, another thing I meant to tell you... I was doing a volunteer shift at the co-op last month & I was assigned to count vitamins with a woman who I thought looked remarkably like you. It turns out that her name is Lisa & she lives on our block. Strange but true...

13 August 1995, C. Avery, Kansas City, MO

Hello Avery:

After I got your card, I counted the number of times I'd moved: 13, not counting all the places I crashed when I was basically living in my car once upon a time. Thirteen has always been pretty good to me, & I hear that 13 is a lucky number in India. I hope this move wasn't too much of a pain in the but, like Céline asks, "Can there be joy without disorder?"

love,

boog

21 October 1995, Aleksandr Z., Samarkand, Uzbekistan

Dear Aleksandr,

I don't speak Russian so I hope you understand my English without too much difficulty.

Thank you for the invitation to participate in your mail art projects. [...]

I was interested to see all the American cartoonists on your Exchange list—are you a cartoonist as well? S. Clay Wilson lived here in Lawrence many years ago, & I interviewed him once for a magazine I used to publish. He's quite a character. Once in an art class here he posed naked as Jesus on the cross. Those were the days...

I have also enclosed a copy of *A Juxtapositionist Manifesto* to explain the art movement I belong to, even though I'm probably the only one in it. All mail artists are juxtapositionists, though, whether they know it or not. Our job is to keep making more & more connections until everyone is connected. That is why it pleases me so much to have made this connection with you, my friend...

до свидания,
boog

A SHORT ART BIOGRAPHY OF BOOG HIGHBERGER
(FOR ALEKSANDR Z.)

March ? 1965 Kindergarten art class. Chastised by teacher for following instructions. We were gluing handles to paper bags for some reason or another. I brought a bag that already had a handle, but put glue on the bag anyway. Teacher was not amused.

October 1969? Won a school-district-wide contest for Halloween pictures made from natural objects, but was disqualified for using prohibited materials (stick-on gold stars).

November ? 1973 High school art class. Chastised by high school art teacher for drawing a shoe with two shadows, even though there were two light sources and we could both see two shadows. "An object only has one shadow," she says. OK, teacher, sure...

May 1978 Dropped out of architecture school. Went into engineering.

June 1983? Participated in mail art project sponsored by Joe Schwind of Kansas College of Collage. Received a decorated folder with 50 photocopied posters which I immediately stapled to the front of a local tavern with the assistance of a friend on a weekend pass from the state mental hospital.

Jan. 1988 Visited mail artist David Zack at the Immortality Centre, Tepoztlán, México.

Feb. 1990 Brain Cell 170.

Oct. 1994? Mailed bowling ball to Eric Jeffreys, Brooklyn, NY.

Oct. 1995 Sent artistamp sheet to Aleksandr Z.'s "Exchange" mail art project.

22 October 1995, Gerardo Yépiz, Ensenada, Mexico

Howdy Gerardo,

Thanks, as usual, for the packet of cool stuff you sent. I love your stamps. Is that your tongue & nipple? I also really like the arte postal Mexico triangle and the Ray Johnson diamond. I've been pasting them on letters to friends around the US & around the world... I'll send you a list someday, so you'll know where your stamps have gone.

I visited your home page a few weeks ago, at the free terminal they have at our public library. Way cool. Two friends of mine from San Francisco are driving down to Baja this week & I told them about your home page, about Café Café & about Señor Salud. Maybe you'll see them wandering goofily around Ensenada...

I just got access to an old perforator so I've started to crank up my artistamp activity. Enclosed is one of the first group of sheets I perforated on the new perforator. I'm also starting a new series titled «yuxtaposiciones norte/ latinamericanos»; I downloaded your picture from your homepage & I would like to use this for a stamp if it's OK with you. Yes, & if you need any perforating done, just let me know...

I've been reading George Bataille lately, *The Accursed Share*. This guy is definitely the political economist for the mail art movement: He says that the real problem of <u>general</u> economy is not how to allocate scarce resources but how to use the excess energy that a society can't use for reproduction & growth. "If a part of wealth," he says, "is doomed to destruction, or at least to unproductive use without any possible profit, it is logical, even <u>inescapable</u>, to surrender commodities without return... if the excess cannot be absorbed in growth, it... must be spent, willingly or not, gloriously or catastrophically... I insist that there is generally no growth but only a luxurious squandering of energy in every form!"

I eagerly await your next glorious, luxurious squandering...

Cheers,
boog

28 November 1995, Lauren Jaben, Austin, TX

Howdy Lauren,

[...] Thanks for the collage portrait of Lucy bug—it's good to know that you still have time to make things even though you're a Mom. "Bug" seems like a fine name to me, & it reminds me of one day a few summers ago when I was driving by the old crack house down at the end of the block & for some reason I stopped to talk to a man who was standing on the corner. He asked me for a ride somewhere & I said sure. On the way there I asked him his name & he said "Bug." I laughed & said that's funny, my name is "Boog." "Boog?" he said, & looked at me like I was weird... This has just reminded me of Helmut & Yo-Yo in *Night on Earth*... have you seen it?

Yes, & as time goes on I discover more & more boogs. "Boog" means "bow" or "arch" in Dutch, "Bóg" means "God" in Polish (my little dictionary that I got for a quarter at the public library booksale this year says that the vowel is " 'oo', but very short"). Bob Fuller (of Brendy & Bob, who I married (to each other) last summer) has shown me a book that described and had a picture of the burning of the Böögg (I'm not making this up), a harvest-time (I think) tradition in Switzerland. Brian says that while searching unsuccessfully for my entry in the cyberstamp exhibit I think I told you about he discovered a couple of Boogs in Sweden. In Mexico City Jill & I found a book of comics featuring a guy named "Mister Boogie"—he's a kind of sleazy detective type, & his nickname is "El Aceitoso." And the list goes on...

Yes, Mexico... we had a great time & I'm already ready to go back. Yes, we made it to the Museo Frida Kahlo in Coyoacán, & it was wonderful. I had heard that there weren't any of her paintings there any more, but there are actually several, including "Viva la Vida," the still life with watermelons which (I think) was her last painting. One of the coolest things at Frida's house was her & Diego's collection of retablos, which completely covered all the walls of one of the rooms. After wandering through the house we sat in the garden & petted the cats. The momma cat had only three legs & she was meticulously grooming one of her kittens... I hope you get a chance to go to Mexico City and farther south sometime soon... every couple of hundred miles farther south you go, it seems like it's a whole nother country... [...] The girl on the left [in one of the enclosed photos] was named Elódia (although I'm not sure I'm spelling that right) & she was incredibly sweet—Jill wanted to take her home. The kid on the right was kind of a brat, though—he ripped off one of the bracelets that Elódia sold us, & the other kids called him a chingar until he gave it back. […]

boog

Oh yes... Lucy bug has been posted on the image wall downstairs for everyone to admire...

December 1995, Robin Crozier, Sunderland, England, UK

MEMO(RY)

FROM: Robin Crozier
TO: Boog
DATE: 16 : 12 : 95
SUBJECT: What do you remember about 10 : 12 : 95?

I don't remember anything at all about December 10, 1995. My calendar is empty for that day except for 2 notes: One reminds me that it was my friend Joe's 37th birthday, but I'm sure I did not call him or write him on that day. The other note says that I made a directory assistance call to Kansas City, but I have no idea whose phone number I was looking for. The rest is just blank: Blank like snow.

So I guess I could make something up, but I'll tell you about November l0, 1995 instead. My friend Jill and I were in Mexico City. The day before we had visited Rene Montes & his wife Françoise——————>>>> but that's another day and another memory. We got up late that morning and had breakfast in a little cafe near the zócalo, after an aimless walk from the Hotel Isabel, on Avenida Isabel la Católica. Through a series of miscommunications Jill ended up getting peaches & cream & a big piece of chocolate cake for breakfast. I'm not quite sure what I had: eggs with chorizo, maybe, but whatever it was it wasn't as memorable as the chocolate cake.

After breakfast we walked to the subway station at the zócalo and took the blue line train to the General Alaya station. A man walked up and down our car selling a big thick slick fashion magazine of some sort for what—10 pesos?—very cheap compared to what it looked like it ought to cost, & very expensive for the Mexican subway. We caught a bus from the subway to the center of Coyoacán & walked to the Frida Kahlo museum. It was beautiful—we wandered through the part of the house with her & Diego Rivera's paintings, and I was amazed at their collection of retablos—images of scenes of sickness & tragedy with thanks to this or that saint for the miraculous cure or rescue they helped achieve. All the walls of one room were covered with them. After that we sat in the garden & relaxed & petted the cats, one of whom had 3 legs & some scraggly-looking kittens. Later in the market we had "eskimos"—sort of like milkshakes—I had rompope (sort of a rum-flavored butterscotch affair) and Jill picked zarzamora because she liked the sound of it. It turned out to be blackberry (or something very much like it).

That evening some guys were playing South American music in the plaza, there was a warm breeze, the church by the plaza was lit up in the dusk, my friend Jill was beside me and for just a moment I had one of those rare, high flashes of pure joy & a feeling that everything was OK in the universe...

I could go on & on with pages of detail about everything we saw & did that day, but I won't. I'm more interested in why my memory is so much more vivid about this day than about a day a month later... or yesterday, for that matter... one was blank, the other could fill pages... Is my daily life that boring & mundane when I'm not traveling? Or is there something about traveling that shakes you into awareness, that jazzes your circuits with electricity & burns in the smells and the sounds & images, sort of the way they program read-only memory chips? And if that's the case, what am I doing sitting here in front of this typewriter? Well?

5 January 1996, Angela Weiss, Tacoma, WA

Hello Angela,

Thanks for the recycled lawyer pants—they're perfect for a recycled lawyer like me. I just tried them on and I'm wearing them now & they fit just fine, & look pretty snazzy, too. By some weird twist of fate & Christmas, I now have six pairs of pants with no holes. This I believe is an adult lifetime record for me, & I'm sure I will have wrecked them all by the end of the year. [...]

What a hoot it is that you found another Boog in Tacoma! Is he a long oo Boog or a short oo Boog? I think I'll send one of my cards: us

Boogs have to stick together. Recently I learned that "boog" (pronounced with a long oo) means "bow" or "arch" in Dutch and that "Bóg" (pronounced with 'a very short oo') means God in Polish. Today I got a postcard from Tom Dougherty with a picture of him standing with an odd-looking bicycle in front of a big triumphal arch with what looks like the Eiffel Tower way in the background: Tom & boog. [...]

The card you sent was beautiful—I've always been fond of pointillists, like Seurat & Steve Ballew & that other French impressionist whose name I can't remember who painted that picture, the name of which I can't remember either, of well-dressed 19th-century people in the park. At least one of the women is holding an umbrella. You know... Anyway I'm glad to see you have an outlet for your creativity, & I feel flattered to receive something that you think is one of the best you've ever done. Me, I've been making these silly artistamps (that's what the people who make them call them) like the sheet I've enclosed, & trade them with people in places like New York and Mexico and Connecticut and Argentina and Switzerland, anyway it keeps me off the streets. I just got ahold of a really cool perforating machine from a friend who bought it a long time ago at a print shop auction, & I've been having lots of fun with it. Jill & I went out to meet one of my artistamp buddies in Mexico City when we there in November, & I've agreed to perforate some things for him, so in addition to punching lots of little holes in things, this funky old machine is helping build international understanding & solidarity, too.

I've probably babbled enough—I miss you, I hope I get to see you soon, keep writing,

love,
boog

11 March 1996, Pitch Weekly, Kansas City, MO

Dear Pitchfolks,

Thanks to Frank Doden for the news that the future students of Lawrence's new Free State High School have chosen the "Firebird" as their mascot. OK, Frank, so the kids have chosen a kind of Pontiac for their school symbol—what can you expect, when their parents named the place after a brewery?

Sincerely,
Boog Highberger

8 May 1996, Jill Innes, Madison, WI

"In the coffee shop a waitress said, 'Of course I will bring beer if you insist, but I think you should try the mangoes.' [...] the waitress returned and set a tall glass before me. 'There we are, the classic fruit of the monsoon,' she said, then stood back with folded arms, watching. The contents of the glass were a warm, glowing orange; faint hints of fire indicated that perhaps crystals from the sun had been dropped like sugar lumps into the blender too. It smelled of flowers and, mixed in with the wonderful mango tastes, the fruit gave off hints of cinnamon and rare spices. I finished every last drop."

–Alexander Frater,
Chasing the Monsoon

jill dear,

No matter what I read, it seems, something in it turns my thoughts to you. Later on in the book, the author sits in with a bunch of Indian men who are discussing their favorite varieties of mangos like wine connoisseurs. In some parts of India, before the fruits of a mango tree could be eaten, it had to be married to another tree, usually a tamarind or a jasmine. I hope the mangos are ripe in the Yucatán in February & March...

And the mango is the appropriate fruit here all of a sudden because the monsoons have arrived. [...]

Tonight was Scrabble night with Dr. Bill. We learned at least one new word: QUOP. It is some sort of British slang for "throb": "My head really quops." Sure. Anyway, as long as it's in the dictionary, we'll use it. [...]

my heart quops for you... all my mango love,
boog

19 May 1996, Predrag P., Kragujevac, Serbia, Yugoslavia

Howdy Predrag,

Thanks for your last letter. I'm sorry that it has taken so long to write back. Лучще поздно чем никогда! I have been busy, and I needed some time to think about the things you said about the fighting in Bosnia. In the news reports in this country, Milosevic is generally considered to be responsible for starting the war by inciting Serbian nationalism in the late 1980s. From what I read here (I don't read just the mainstream press and I don't get any of my news from TV), every side in the war has been guilty of atrocities, but the Bosnian Serbs seem to be the worst. I am aware that Croatia had a Nazi government during World War II and the current Croatian government is supported by the US government even though it has committed evil acts against both Serbs and Muslims in Bosnia. It's hard to know where the truth lies, but after I thought about it for a while I realized that we don't have to agree about what the truth is in order to be friends or to exchange mail art. As long as we keep exchanging and talking to each other, we will understand each other better and our truths will be broader and deeper and more alike.

Musically, we are already very close together. If you play all the bands you listed on your radio station, I would listen to it all the time. I am especially glad to see that PJ Harvey has made it to Yugoslavia. I saw Cows once at a club here in Lawrence called the Bottleneck, along with Babes in Toyland. I have met Michelle Shocked a few times. The first time was in 1984. I was vice-president of the students at the University of Kansas, and we were trying to start a "white bikes" program (like they used to have in Amsterdam, where a lot of bikes are painted white and left around town for people to use for free). Michelle Shocked passed through town on the way to a protest at the Republican party convention and came to one of our "white bikes" meetings. Later she sent a poem and a report on the protest to *the gentle anarchist*, a magazine I used to help publish. She also showed up at a couple of the North American anarchist gatherings held in the US and Canada in the late 1980s. If you like Michelle Shocked, I think you will like Ani DiFranco. She is not as well known as Michelle Shocked because she has refused to deal with big record companies and does her own production and distribution. I will send a tape or CD soon, if I can (I'm short of money right now). If I do send a tape, I would appreciate in exchange (if possible—don't worry about it if you can't afford it) a tape of some Yugoslavian music that you like. In the US, bands from non-English-speaking countries rarely get any airplay, but I am interested in hearing music made in other countries.

In the meantime I am enclosing some bus, train & airplane tickets from my trip to Mexico last November, a sheet of artistamps, and maybe a beer label or two. I look forward to hearing from you soon.

your friend,
boog

12 August 1996, Vermin Supreme, Gloucester, MA

Howdy Vermin,

I'm glad you liked the stamps. [...] As for the perforations I have access to an old one-line-at-a-time pedal perforator. A real pain in the butt for large quantities, but it works OK for small batches. A local print shop might be able to perf them for you at a reasonable price. I have a thing against selling stamp sheets, but I sell my labor to lots of folks so if you can't find a willing print shop I'll perforate them for you for cash. It takes a lot of time, though, & it's kind of boring so I'd need to make around 10 bucks an hour to not be grumpy about it, which works out to something like 75¢ a sheet for the small ones and 50¢ a sheet for the big ones. Plus printing. But I'd be happy to send you small quantities in the mail from time to time in exchange for other odd flotsam & jetsam or just for the hell of it. Let me know. [...]

It sounds like the St. Louis scrub-in was a big success. & the last time I saw the Sears Tower it looked like it needed a good flossing, so I think you've got your work cut out for you. Thank god someone is concerned with the moral hygiene & dental rectitude of America.

I have brushed. Amen.

Your pal,
boog

22 August 1996, Guy Clark, Columbia, MO

Genny Cream Ale
"Spit" by NY Loose on the rocknroll radio
rain

Howdy Guy,

I just reread your letter from mid-June—yes, I've been in that crisis. Still there, maybe. One of my responses to it was to go to law school, but as your attorney I advise you to be smarter than me and not dig this kind of hole for yourself. I know that this society tends to equate annual income & moral worth, but I tend to think if you're getting paid more than 5 figures chances are that somebody's getting screwed over to make the payments on your Beamer & your hot tub. Even though I'm doing worse than I used to, I still think the goal is to live as well as you can on as little as possible. (Although Georges Bataille may have changed my mind about the occasional necessity of wild consumption & squandering of resources—have you read *The Accursed Share*?) Anyway, I think you're doing good work.

A friend of mine who lives here now used to be the community garden co-ordinator in Columbia—Kelly Kindscher—he's written a couple of books on edible plants & he works at the Kansas Biological Survey these days. Lawrence has a community garden now, with one plot right by the co-op & another at the Indian Center, but we're a long way from having a paid coordinator. I'm still on the board at the co-op, & it has been really hairy for the last couple of years. Our managers have lasted an average of 6 months each & we're periodically teetering on the edge of bankruptcy. Last month we had to lay off a staff member who had been with the store for 20 years—and I got to tell her about it. But I think we're finally on the upswing, we've got a new manager who is a local & who has managed the store before, I think we've finally got our expenses under control, we're getting a beautiful mural on the side of the store that should dramatically increase our visibility, and Wild Oats seems to have given up on taking big losses to undercut our prices. So we'll see. It hasn't been fun, but I like to think it's going to be worth it in the long run.

And what is this beast called love that eats our hearts and spits them out and makes us act like teenagers and drive hundreds of miles and we dance when it says dance? I'm reminded of an old live Patti Smith tape that somebody here used to have: "love is so sweet, love is so pure/ love is something that you must endure." It's all a mystery to me, and

I'll leave on my next love commute to Madison in a week and a day... This time I have a co-commuter—through the mail art network I just met a man who has moved to my old hometown, Garnett, Kansas, & his ex-wife is teaching at Taliesin, the Frank Lloyd Wright school/studio in south-central Wisconsin. We'll probably stop at Dreamtime Village, & I may finally meet Malok—did you ever correspond with him? He was on one of AFM's lists years ago. This new connection with Eric has been fruitful in lots of ways—he has loaned me a strange 3-wheeled bicycle that he built—it's got a sort of bucket seat, the pedals are stuck out in front, and the two front wheels steer by way of a handle bar that pivots under the frame. AND I CAN RIDE IT! Today, I took my first real bike ride in over 20 years—what a sweet, sweet feeling to be able to move without hurting or driving, to cruise, to glide... freedom. This could change my whole life...

Well. I have to pretend to be an adult tomorrow, so I'm going to sign off & hope to see you soon. Please keep in touch.

namasté,
boog

30 November 1996, Edgardo-Antonio Vigo, La Plata, Buenos Aires, Argentina

Querido amigo Edgardo,

Muchas gracias por tu carta ultima muy cálida. Es verdad, el año tiende a terminarse. Para mí, he sido muy bueno en muchos aspectos. Nuestro amistad y nuestra correspondencia especialmentes han enriquecido ma vida. Me has dí mucho inspiración y felicidad, y estimo mucho tu paciencia.

Recientemente, recibí cartas de dos otros de tus amigos—Mario Gemin y Bernard Cathelin. Mario me mandó algunas hojas de sus artistamps—estan muy bonitas. Mario me mandó tambien una fotocopia de una foto de él y tú y dos otros a un galería (¿conosces este foto?—trataré te mandar una copia—¿es la mujer tu esposa Elena?), Bernard me mandó un sobre muy lindo con un dibujo de Mercurio, mensajero de los dios. Se mandé algunas hojas de mis artistamps y se dijo que un amigo de Vigo es un amigo mió.

Los narrativos mordaces de Fontanarrosa me interesan mucho, pero no estoy cierto que podría apreciar completamente su estilo literario. Si me mandarías un de sus narraciones, trataré lo leer, pero si me dirías algunos títulos de los narraciones, buscaré las traducciones ingleses.

Hoy, al biblioteca universitaria, ví "Boogie" en un revista méxicana, "Proceso." Fontanarrosa es dondequiera...

Ayer, el "New York Times" incluyó un articulo sobre la busca de un submarino nazi en la Patagonia. Vidal Pereyra (¿el inodoro Pereyra, tal vez?) dice que vió el submarino en el marzo 1980, y estaba cubierto con los caracoles...

Este noche, ellos dicen que nevará, 8 a 15, o tal vez 20 centimetros. Envidio tu tiempo de verano... espero que to tienes un solsticio bueno...

All my love and respect to you, my friend (and to you, Elena, if you are translating this),

y abrazos fraternales,
boog

[Dear friend Edgardo,

Many thanks for your last very warm letter. It's true, the year is tending to finish up. For me I've been very good in many aspects. Our friendship and our correspondence especiallys have enriched ma life. You have I gave me much inspiration and happiness, and I really appreciate your patience.

Recently, I received letters from two other of your friends—Mario Gemin and Bernard Cathelin. Mario sent some sheets of his artistamps—they are very nice. Mario also sent me a photocopy of a photo of him and you and two others of a gallery (Do you know this photo?—I will try to send you a copy—Is the woman your wife Elena?), Bernard sent me a very beautiful envelope with a drawing of Mercury, messenger of the god. I sent himself some sheets of my artistamps and he told himself that a friend of Vigo is a friend of mine.

Fontanarrosa's mordant narratives interest me a lot, but I'm not sure I would be able to completely appreciate his literary style. If you would send me a of his narrations I will try it to read, but if you would tell me some of his narrations, I will look for the English translations. Today, to the University library, I saw "Boogie" in a Mexican magazine, "Proceso." Fontanarrosa is wherever…

Yesterday, the "New York Times" included an article about the search for a Nazi submarine in Patagonia. Vidal Pereyra (the Inodoro Pereyra, maybe?) says that he saw the submarine in March 1980, and it was covered with snails...

Tonight, they say that it will snow, 8 to 15, or maybe 20 centimeters. I envy your summer weather... I hope that your have a good solstice...

All my love and respect to you, my friend (and to you, Elena, if you are translating this),

and brotherly hugs,]

7 January 1997, Eric Farnsworth, Garnett, KS

Howdy Eric,

Please accept the enclosed *fromage à toi* as a small token of my extreme. I got this here Krafty cheese for the mail art project the blue invitation for which is enclosed: I made them some edible money in the form of a rubberstamped piece of cheese. Do you know this Sagebrush Moderne? He wrote back & said he liked the cheese, he had thought of TURNIP MONEY himself, & regretted that they hadn't gotten many intriguing submissions yet. I'm sure that, if you want, you can tickle his fancy...

I got the GO CARD documentation from K. Frank Jensen yesterday. It was very nice to be on the same page with you and very nice to see two Kansans on the short list of contributors. All we need to do is to get Tim & another person or two to be regularly active to create the illusion that Kansas is some sort of wild mail art mecca. No problem.

Thanks very much for the Sto Zvirat tape. I played it on the way to work today & it made me happy. I'm probably more partial to them because they're speaking a language I don't understand & because the Hungarian/ska juxtaposition is so improbable & perfect.

I'm getting excited about Mexico already—I'm glad that it has worked out that we get to travel together again. And to Mexico, to boot. Yahoo! Mazatlán sounds like a good destination, but I'd like to go to at least one place I haven't been before. Mexcaltitlán or Zacatecas would be nice, or Barra de Navidad or Manzanilla. We can play it by ear. The Lonely Planet guidebook says that there is a hotel or two in Mexcaltitlán now. On the other hand, Zacatecas is alleged to have the most baroque cathedral in Mexico, and an aerial tram up to the silver mines on the edge of town. Then again, I wouldn't mind another stay at the mostly abandoned Hotel Misterioso outside of San Blas, where lizards run among the fallen coconuts & horses graze in the beachfront courtyard. I'll try to bring my big Mexico map when I come down on Sunday so we can plot & scheme & dream.

Dinner on Sunday is still up in the air—Dad's birthday is a couple of days after & there may be extra relatives around—I don't want to overwhelm Mom—but it still may work out. [...]

My car was in the shop for a few days over the weekend, & your bike made my life dramatically easier. So I made it to the co-op board meeting & got to go out & eat Vietnamese food & pick up my mail, all thanks to you. So thanks again...

hasta pronto,
boog

25 January 1997, Sagebrush Moderne, Glenbrook, NV

Howdy Sagebrush,

Glad you liked the cheese money. I'm curious to see how it evolves:: My guess is that it won't rot, but will just sort of shrink up into a dark orange crusty thing: legal but not so tender. I like the Wonder Bread idea, & I will try it as soon as I can get a hold of some without actually buying it (I admit that I did buy the cheese, but Wonder Bread would be going too far, even for Art...). If anything interesting results I'll send it along. I like your turnip currency suggestion, and just in case you're money hungry I'll send along a turnip recipe I recently received from a painter friend in Dodge City. She cooked us some and they were yummy. [...]

Hmmm... If I remember correctly, I put pyramids on the back of the cheese dollar, & it just struck me how appropriate that is, because every currency system really is a pyramid scheme at heart. I'm meeting with somebody in a couple of hours who's interested in a local currency system—something I've been interested in for quite a while—& it looks like there might be enough local interest now to get something off the ground. Most of these things just use computer-based accounts but I hear that in Ithaca they're printing actual currency. If you're not already plugged into this action I can send you more info if you're interested.

Until,
boog

16 February 1997, X., somewhere in America

"If I was a moon I'd expect the wolves to howl at me, wouldn't you?"
—David Zack

OK, X.—

The above quote is from one of Zack's old "correspondence novels," a copy of part of which I received in the mail from a guy named buZ blurr who lives in Arkansas—this part of the novel was about buZ (aka Russell Butler), & Zack rambles about his visits to buZ's house in Arkansas. buZ is the person who connected up me & Eric, the guy who just moved to Garnett & who built the three-wheeled recumbent bike I've been riding around. Eric & I & Jill & her 14-year-old son Oliver are going to Mexico next week. & on the way back, after we drop Jill &

Oliver off at the airport in Dallas, we're going to stop in & visit buZ. The connections just keep getting twisteder & twisteder. [...]

Thanks for the photo of Tiny Tim. I told Gregor at the co-op that you went to Tiny's funeral & just the thought of it made him very happy. I wish I could have gone with you—I could use a recharge of that unconditional-love-for-all-the-nuts energy. I certainly don't have it like I used to—I guess it has come in spurts at various times of my life, but these days I feel like Jesus yelling "Heal yourselves!" And realizing, of course, that I need to heal myself, too... [...]

Have you read *Venus in Furs*? I found it very amusing. [...] I also recommend *Psychopathia Sexualis* by Krafft-Ebing. It's full of stuff like:

Case 66. X., age thirty-eight, engineer, married, father of three children, married life unmarred. Visited periodically a prostitute who had to enact, previous to coitus, the following comedy. As soon as he entered her compartment she took him by the ears, and pulled him all over the room, shouting: "What do you want here? Do you know that you ought to be at school? Why don't you go to school?" she would then slap his face and flog him soundly, until he knelt before her begging pardon. She then handed him a little basket containing bread and fruit such as children carry with them to school. He remained penitent until the girl's harshness produced orgasm in him, when he would call out: "I am going! I am going!" and then perform coitus.

It's sad what some people will do for a laugh, but Krafft-Ebing almost always works for me.

OK, X. ... I need to pretend to be an adult tomorrow... I have a lot of little things to wrap up before I leave town... I'll try to send you a postcard from Mexico.

I am going, I am going,
boog

5 April 1997, Elizabeth Wilmot, Buena Park, CA

Lion that eats my mind now for a decade knowing only your hunger
Not the bliss of your satisfaction O roar of the Universe how am I chosen
In this life I have heard your promise I am ready to die I have served
Your starved and ancient Presence O Lord I wait in my room at your
    Mercy

—Allen Ginsberg
from "Lion," in *Kaddish*

Well now Elizabeth,

The Lion has finally won. Allen Ginsberg died this morning, at least that's what they say on our new micro-radio station (KAW-FM, 88.9 FM, 5 watts or so), broadcasting out of the basement of (aptly-named) Liberty Hall tonight. So I pulled out *Kaddish*, which includes a poem of the same name that Ginsberg wrote about his mother's madness & suffering & death. "There, rest," he says. "No more suffering for you. I know where you've gone, it's good." At least we can hope...

Yes, I know where you've gone, & I'm sure it was good. I can imagine you raging around London, & I'm sure your next letter will be juicier than the last. I just hope you were careful in those snicklewaiths...

You may or may not have gotten a postcard from my latest journey by now:: I spent a week and a ½ or so in Mexico:: Chihuahua, Mazatlán, Durango:: with Jill & her 14-year-old son & my pal Eric from Garnett. [...]

The narcopolicias were out in force this time, & instead of ignoring gringos like us like they used to they singled us out for special attention (this was easy because with the exception of the Barranca del Cobre train we were always the only gringos on the train or bus):: I had my bags searched twice & I got frisked once. (This was understandable, of course, because the US government was hammering the Mexican government over narco-cop corruption at the time, & it was on the front pages of the papers every day.) While we were on the train from Durango to Torreón one of the narcos asked me <<Parlez-vous français?>> even though he spoke English & it was fairly obvious that we were Americans. I tried to answer him in French, but it all came out in Spanish so I gave up fairly quickly. This guy was young, very Spanish looking, & obviously well-educated:: we speculated on what he must have done to get himself stationed in Chocolate (the little town where we got stopped) to search the 2nd class train every day. He kept asking us why we were taking the train, he thought it was very suspicious... I told him it was porque no me gusta la television... because our previous trip was a spectacular mountain bus ride from Mazatlán to Durango during which we were continuously assaulted first by a big-budget kung-fu movie then by an Arnold fucking Schwarzenegger movie:: approximately a murder a mile for 7 hours & it drove me fucking crazy (it was better after the speaker unit fell out & hit me on the head, because I didn't have to listen to it anymore)... What I should have told him was porque me gusta el aire fresco, because several of the train windows were broken out, but it's probably fortunate that I wasn't clever enough at the time... I can't wait to hear some of your English adventures...

Tool is on the jukebox now:: I think they're from your neck of the woods:: their lyrics and music aren't very pretty, pretty hard core really, guitars like baseball bats & sharp knives, but their brutality seems to be out of a desperate attempt to feel something, anything:: which I think is the underlying theme of a great deal of late-20th-century fringe pop culture:: tattoos & body piercing, mosh pits & stage diving, fist-fucking (which is what one of their songs getting a lot of airplay seems to be about). But they have their soft spots, too: "And the walls come down/ There's a look in your eyes/ I remember all of the times/ I have died, I will die/ It's all right..." It's alright...

Well, Elizabeth, I'd be glad to e-mail you, but I'm still hopelessly stuck in the 20th century. I'm going to have to rely on crude media like pen & paper or paint-stick & boxcar (watch all those passing trains carefully) but I promise that every message you get from me will involve some sort of visual or tactile or olfactory experience that your computer can't do yet.

OK, sweetie:: I hope your life is good, tell Gina howdy if you talk to her:: I hope I hear from you soon & in the meantime

Hale-Bopp till you drop,
(love)
boog

21 July 1997, Darlene Altschul, Woodland Hills, CA

Howdy Darlene,

Yes, I'm still alive. My correspondence has gotten sporadic lately because my dad has been sick—he was diagnosed with lung cancer 6 weeks ago—and so I've been trying to spend as much time in Garnett (yes, the same town that Eric lives in) as I can. So I don't get much done on the weekends. Otherwise life is almost back to normal now... thank

God us humans are so adaptable...

This doesn't mean I get to see Eric any more, though: he tends to spend his weekends here in Lawrence. I passed him on the road coming and going last weekend. Lately he's been here at least one night a week, & he leaves me messages because I'm out doing something else.

Thanks for the chickens. There's something I like about chickens, but it may just be the sound of the word: chickens, chickens, chickens. Always good for a laugh.

So you've inspired me to think more about printing with body parts, although I haven't conceived a project yet. Here are some hands for you, anyway: one lifesize & made with the imprint of my very flesh, the others approximately 10% of original size & brought to you through the magic of xerography. I've thought about printing other body parts, too, but the inspiration has always faded before I've gotten around to it. Feel free to print any body part you like & send it in for the archives (be sure to let me know if it's not for publication).

I think I am going to start a new project soon, though, & don't have announcements ready yet, but: send me an image of yourself in a funny hat. Stampsheet to all participants. Ongoing. The stamps will look something like the one on the envelope.

OK, Darlene, a friend of mine is going to be over soon to wire up a new hard drive for me, so I can upgrade my software & get e-mail so he can contact me after he moves to Austin. OK, fine. If I have anything more to report I'll do it with 19th-century utensils.

love,
boog

1998–2002

death of my father • crumbling infrastructure & outrageous debt • gay in the former Soviet Union • is Kosovo Serbian for Vietnam? • dysfunctional cesspool • Joan Jett in Atchison • a whole other set of sadnesses • Sister Frisky • Julie shave me, why not? • Ubu Roi hunts again • duct tape • counterfeiting postage stamps • Diane's xérox «lâche la patate» • if it weren't for all the drugs • googlewhacking • Butthole Surfers riot

17 February 1998, Donna Eades, San Francisco, CA

Dear Donna,

Thanks for your sweet & insightful letter. Everything you wrote was right on target. I've been realizing lately that my life probably isn't as back to normal as it seems on the surface. I've always had a tendency to push big emotions under the surface & I probably am doing so again. I haven't been really depressed, just a little lacking in ambition (the letters & e-mail have piled up, & [I have been] kind of absent-minded). The latter isn't as bad as it used to be, though: one day after Dad had taken a turn for the worse I showed up at work in Topeka without my suit jacket—I noticed I was a little colder than I should have been as I was walking up to the building, but it wasn't until I got up to the office & took my coat off that I noticed something was missing. Too bad it wasn't my pants that were missing instead—perhaps I would have noticed that before I made it to work.

Yes, you're right, there is an emptiness, but I am convinced that it does get better. My mother has handled it all very well. I think she is making an effort to keep busy, but it also seems like she is letting herself do things that she didn't get to do while Dad was around and that she is really enjoying herself a lot of the time.

Yes, I loved & respected my father very much & I do miss him. But he had a good life, right to the end, & I'm thankful that I made the choice to stay around here so I could see him fairly often. I can think of dozens of little things that we ran out of time to do, but I don't think he died leaving anything important unresolved between us. I feel very lucky.

One thing that I find very reassuring is that this experience hasn't shaken my faith in life. I still embrace this incarnate existence—all the suffering still seems like a small price to pay for the joy. It seems to me that if that faith has survived this far, it will endure for quite a bit longer.

And, faith or no faith, the wheels keep turning, children are conceived, babies are born, kids learn and grow, people get married, love blooms. I seem to be embarking on a new relationship. [...]

Brian is back in town. Hopefully I will get to see him tonight, at the Bottleneck, where Tim's band is playing. Brian is here on business—somebody flew him up here & is paying him big bucks to do computer work for social service agencies. My job just got upgraded, too—if freaks like Brian & me are making real money, it's a sure sign that the economists are right when they say the labor market is dangerously tight & that the Fed is going to have to clamp down on this soon. But in the meantime, let's party, dude... [...]

all my love,
boog

12 November 1998, Guy Clark, Columbia, MO

Howdy Guy::

Your letter arrived at precisely the right time. Whatever is right in front of me when I have a free minute or two is what gets paid attention to. Today, you're it.

Yes, it's good to be connected again. I figured it would happen again eventually... these things seem to run in cycles. Given our past history I figure that we now have perpetually intersecting orbits...

I'm hardwired now, too, although I still prefer paper & ink & glue & smells & all that non-electronic moist messy materiality... [...] & to add fuel to this techno-happy fire I'm listening to Ani DiFranco even as we speak on my very first CD player... which also happens to be my computer. O Brave New World to have such gizmos in it! I *love* this country...

Life here at the Country Folks house is good. Brenda just had her second baby, sweet Estrella Marie, & her firstborn, Cypress, just turned 7. We bought the farm a few years ago, & so all this crumbling infrastructure & outrageous debt is all ours... It makes me feel like the GOVERNMENT...

I've been hanging out with a beautiful sweet smart compassionate artist named Jane & her 5-year-old son Ezekiel. Maybe we'll get married, maybe not. In the meantime it feels pretty domestic. I spend a lot more time with Ezekiel than the *New York Times* says an average single mother does with her children (9 hours/week). I'm working ½ time as an attorney for the state Department of Health & Environment, & in the rest of my time I'm doing private attorney work, being on the board of the local food co-op (we beat our chain store competition and will do $3.5 million worth of business this year), writing (etc.) for a new community paper, trying to oversee my father's business & handle some of my mother's financial affairs, hanging out with Jane & Ezekiel, trying to be a good co-op housemate, doing as much mail art as I can manage, breathing occasionally. Something has to give eventually, but in the meantime this is why my correspondence has been erratic.

Yes, I'm glad to see you're doing the good work. I would imagine it feels very fulfilling to work with your hands & play with dirt & make things grow. I will think of you tomorrow as I cruise to Topeka on the fast highway in my lawyer clothes to work in a tall building. Jane & I have talked about making a trip to St. Louis & Columbia sometime soon. I'll keep you posted. In the meantime,

namasté yourself,
boog

28 November 1998, T., former Soviet Union

Howdy T.,

Thanks for your last letter with bookplates, postcards, and stickers. I'm glad to hear that the ruble crisis has not seriously affected your country yet. I was disappointed to hear that you didn't get to go to St. Petersburg, but your trip to the Czech Republic sounds like it was great. I haven't been able to do much traveling lately, but Jane and her 5-year-old son Ezekiel and I did get to go to St. Louis for a couple of days. There are some great museums there, especially for kids. The place I liked best was called the City Museum. It is located in an old warehouse near downtown, and the artist who runs it has been [able] to create a fantasy world inside full of mosaics, giant animal sculptures (of real and imagined animals), salvaged stonework from old buildings, reused industrial parts, and big trees. There is a small aquarium and lots of tunnels for kids to crawl in and a little train for kids to ride on. A couple of Jane's sculptures are installed upstairs. If you are ever in the middle of the United States, I recommend checking it out. (After you visit us, of course.)

No, my friend T., it doesn't matter to me one way or the other that you are gay. I have quite a few good friends here who are gay. In the United States, most people now are fairly tolerant, I think, although there are still sometimes incidents like the recent one in Wyoming where a gay man was killed. The town that I live in has long been known as a safe place for gay people and there is a fairly active and open gay community here. I have enclosed an article I wrote recently for a local magazine that talks about this. What are attitudes like in your city? Can you be open about being gay without having to worry about discrimination or violence? I look forward to the day when we can all live together in joy without judging each other because of how we show our love.

boog

4 February 1999, Magda Lagerwerf, Sellingen, Netherlands

Beste Magda,

Thank you for your last letter with your beautiful eraser carvings. I like them very much and I can see why you won the contest. I am impressed that you are trying new things—I seem to keep doing the same things over and over. Here are some more lips, this time from Dimitrij Z. in Latvia. [...]

I also liked your map-envelope... I love seeing maps with names in languages other than English. It makes the places seem even more exotic to me: Tsjaad, Marokko, Bovenvolta. Yes, there are so many places of sorrow in the world. But so many places where our governments, who say they are trying to make things better, only inflict more suffering, as in Irak. The proper course of action is not always clear. NATO troops to Kosovo? I will wait to see whether they can bring peace or whether Kosovo is Serbian for Vietnam.

Have fun on your art museum trips. I look forward to your next letter.

boog

23 June 1999, Brian Schwegmann, Austin, TX

Brian Schwegmann
Grand Wazoo
Austin, Texas, wherever you are

Re: Y2K compliance

Dear Mr. Schwegmann,

It's a little bit slow here on the farm today. My immediate supervisor got canned a few days ago & the Secretary hasn't been paying much attention to me, & I finished the last administrative order that's due for over a month, so my plate is fairly clean today, as they say in the business. Or I have a happy plate, as we say at my house. Our house. Our very, very, very fine house. Etc.

Over the last few months I've been doing a little Internet research for a committee that is looking at ways to improve end-of-life care for Kansans. One of the things they're looking at is making it easier for doctors to prescribe narcotics to people dying of cancer without the doctor having to worry about getting busted. At a site maintained by the University of Wisconsin I just ran across an article titled "From Florianopolis (1994) to Santo Domingo (1996): A Progress Report on Opioid Availability." That reminded me of a certain journey we made together some time ago, & I imagined that an article about it could be entitled "From Lawrence to Guadalajara (1991?): A Progress Report on Cannibinoid Availability." We should go to Mexico again. I started to say "... before we get real jobs," but I guess it's too late. This job is almost real, even though it's only halftime, but I've got an application out for a full-time job (back at the Defender Project doing legal work for prisoners, wish me luck) but even if that doesn't pan out I think I'm ready to go full time. I hope your job isn't driving you crazy yet.

Full-time or not I'm ready to get out of this seamy hole. I'm finally sick of the politics. This place is a dysfunctional cesspool of back-stabbing & pettiness and anybody who tries to do anything about it gets thrown to the dogs. Environmental enforcement seems to already be at almost a standstill & the new Secretary received a congratulatory note from a certain state senator who was glad to see there was finally somebody here who could "wrestle this out-of-control agency to the ground." Well, there may be people around here who need to be wrestled to the ground, but my old supervisor wasn't one of them. I just got a notice of my merit pay increase for the next fiscal year. By my calculation my salary just went up by $666, and that pretty well sums it up right there.

Well, at least my relationship... never mind. At least the Free State is still open, & at least they haven't started building the building that's going to block the view of the sunset from the porch. And I can still ride there on my bicycle.

I'm sorry I've been such a crappy correspondent. I still haven't heard much about your flood—have you recovered? And thanks for the response you sent to my e-mail about energy & economics. I've thought about it a lot, but as you can tell I haven't managed to respond, even though I've really been needing that sort of intellectual interaction. Perhaps I'll do better as I careen through the summer.

Thank you for your attention to this matter.

Sincerely,
Dennis J. Highberger, Attorney
Office of the Secretary

1 July 1999, Brenna Hoffmann, Berkeley, CA

Brenna Hoffmann
PO Box X
Berkeley, CA 99999

Re: "If you see her, say hello—she might be in Tangier"
—Bobby Z.

Dear Ms. Hoffmann,

As you might have noticed, it's a slow day at the office. My supervisor was canned last week, and that has had a positive effect on my work load, not that it was all that stressful here before. A new general counsel was appointed today, but it's too early to tell how much this is going to impact my life. But I'm getting tired of the politics & I need to use more of my brain, so I'm starting to look for a way out of here. [...]

The big news from the dictionary at dinner last night was that "avocado" ultimately comes from a Nahuatl word meaning "testicle" [through the Spanish "aguacate"]. It sort of makes you wonder a little about those Aztecs. "Mole" (as in MO-lay) comes from a Nahuatl word meaning sauce, & so guacamole just means "avocado sauce" or... no, I won't go there. Jane and Ezekiel and I recently ate at a truck stop outside of Salina that had Rocky Mountain oysters on the menu. I didn't go there either.

Thanks for sending the *Funny Times*, because these are, indeed, funny times. It usually gets read by most of the people in the house. It is noticeably funnier than the *New York Times*.

Have you been to Morocco yet? Without thinking about it I picked up a book at the library called "Tangier," & only after reading a hundred pages did I think that you might be there. This book is mostly literary gossip, about people like Paul Bowles, Truman Capote, William

Burroughs, etc., but I was fascinated by the history of Tangier, which apparently was an "International Zone" governed by US & European consuls from most of the time from the Twenties (?) to the early Fifties. Lots of smuggling, hashish & young boys for sale, expatriates lounging in seedy bars, spies in the souk (oh, waiter!), anything goes. Now, apparently, Tangier has fallen on hard times, & even the king refuses to go there. I hope your Sufi expedition is fun and intriguing and I would love to see you & Frank dancing under the sheltering sky. I look forward to hearing your stories. [...]

Well, I could yammer on about a lot of things but my typing finger is starting to smoke. I should probably find some other way to pretend to be busy for a while & then get the hell out of here for a long weekend of independence. Sir Richard Burton claims that "Voyaging is victory!" is an old Arab saying. He may be full of beans, but either way I hope we both win big soon.

Sincerely,
Dennis J. Highberger
Attorney, Office of the Secretary

27 July 1999, Anne Tangeman, Seattle, WA

Hey Anne—

I ½way expected to see your smiling face here in Lawrence this weekend, but as you probably noticed, I didn't. ¡*Que lastima*! I hope that this deficiency can be corrected soon. [...]

Friday night I was sitting on the porch drinking a Tecate con limon & reading Thursday's *New York Times* when Honna drove up in her mother's beat-up Econoline van with her girlfriend's 4-year-old daughter & said "Joan Jett's playing at a lake in Atchison would you like to go? and we have to leave now..." How could I turn down an offer like that? And of course I thought of you. We got there just as she was starting... It was kind of a strange scene. As far as I could tell Honna was the only person in the audience with different-colored hair. It was kind of like a mutual freak show, but the crowd seemed to like the band. It was about 100 degrees and Joan was wearing rubber and leather clothes and I wondered how she was ever, ever going to get her pants off.

OK, Anne I should go pretend to be a professional. I hope I see you soon...

boog

14 January 2000, Jana Svoboda, Corvallis, OR

Day 14, Year Zero

Hey jana,

You look pretty good digitized. But then again, you look pretty good in real life. I still prefer the latter, & I'm sorry I didn't get to see you in non-virtual reality over Xmas—I got your postcard the day you said you were leaving. I'm glad you got some more time with your family—the story about eating your mother's frozen vegetable soup just about made me cry. I've already preconceived the saddest moment in my life—when sometime after she has died I eat the last of my mother's pickled beets—sweet, sweet, but so bittersweet—but of course life may have a whole other set of sadnesses planned for me.

As you can see, I've been doing some digitizing, too. The permutations of our friends' lips seem endless. You too can join this lipfest & probably get a smattering of strange mail out of the deal. Just send me a lip print—dark colors work best—most people have used lipstick, but ink and watercolors have been used, too. At a minimum you will get in return a stamp sheet with yours & 9 other lip images (send me 10 different lips and get a sheet of your very own). Just recently, about a dozen lucky participants got rubberstamp images of their lips. The possibilities, perhaps, are endless. [...]

Well, I was a little disappointed that civilization didn't collapse just a little bit for Y2K, but I still don't think the beast is as invincible as it seems. At least for a consolation prize we got the battle of Seattle—which may be the first anarchist action in the US or Europe since the Spanish civil war to actually accomplish anything. I wish I could have been there. We still have a long way to go, but now we've got their attention...

I don't know about you, but I've decided that 2000 is going to be a better year. I took a friend out to a swanky restaurant last week, during which we discussed the pros & cons of intimacy without diving into commitments (she has an eight-year-old, & I'm recently divorced, or at least it feels like it...). The next day I got a fortune cookie that said "Your nights will be filled with happiness and glee." Today at the new Chinese restaurant in Garnett I got one that said "Be careful how you wield your persuasive power." And Ani diFranco's on the jukebox now & she says "Let's not ask what's next or how or why, I'm leaving in the morning so let's not be shy..." I'll keep you posted.

Trust your midlife crisis, Jana—if something inside you tells you you're in danger of getting old & stodgy it may be right. Luckily, I believe this can all be corrected with enough attention & a little booty-shaking. I think in your case the required efforts should be minimal. As you said, fuck it let's just dance. Or as Jamie Mercury Future used to say, "Fuck dance, let's art." Indeed.

Current odds on my visiting Oregon & Washington this year are 50/50. Place your bets now. Until then, shine on you crazy diamond...

boog

3 February 2000, Brian Schwegmann, Austin, TX

Day 34 Year Zero

Hey Brian,

Pay toilets are illegal in Kansas, and enforcing this law is one of the many duties of the Department of Health and Environment. I'm proud to be a part of an agency that makes sure that Kansans pee for free. We should print bumper stickers:

(I suppose they could say "Free Pee We" but then people would get us confused with the Paul Reubens Defense Committee.) It's not quite as catchy as "Don't Mess with Texas" but it does have a certain *je ne sais qoui*, don't you think? But of course this wouldn't be as good for anagramming as our current "Don't Spoil It!" bumper stickers. Maybe you saw this when you were here last, but Mikey has started covering his van with cut-up versions of that one, like "STOP LINT, I DO!" and "DON'T SPIT OIL!" and (my favorite) "O, STILTON DIP!" (Mikey being a big stinky cheese fan). "Don't Mess With Texas" is harder to work with, but "DON'T TASTE SEX WHIMS" comes to mind. Or "SIX TONS METH WASTED." But I digress.

This was supposed to be a birthday card. So HAPPY BIRTHDAY. I hope you've been having a good millennium. I had a great time when I was down to see you & I hope I can make it down again this year. And maybe this time for a $65 viaje a Matehuala por autobús Méxicano. But maybe I should work on my Spanish first.

Day 35 Year Zero

HEY BRIAN I JUST DOWNLOADED SOME NEW FONTS [discussion omitted here because of Font Licensing Issues] **I HAVE FALLEN IN LOVE WITH ANOTHER FONT CALLED SISTER FRISKY BUT IT COSTS NINETY NINE BUCKS AND SOME CHANGE FOR THAT PRICE SHE WOULD HAVE TO BE REALLY FRISKY... WELL, I'M SURE THEY'LL COME IN HANDY FOR SOMETHING SOMEDAY, AND IN THE MEANTIME AT LEAST THEY'RE CLOGGING UP MY HARD DRIVE.** this one is called "samarkan" for some reason. it is supposed to look like sanskrit, as far as i can tell. sanskrit is not the first language that comes to mind when i think of samarkand (which is now in uzbekistan). arabic or russian, maybe, but not sanskrit... although around 300 to 200 bc it was a mixing ground for greek and buddhist cultures... so maybe there were some hindi speakers there... it's wacky world and getting wackier all the time...

Enough of this nonsense... did you hear about the low-power FM rules just issued by the FCC? The pirates got almost everything they asked for... There are a few big problems with the decision, but it's still the most anti-corporate government action in recent memory. I'm curious to see how Free Radio Austin responds... Recklessly, no doubt...

Alright Brian, this is just getting gibberisher and gibberisher... I hope you are having fun, I hope you still have broccoli, I hope your rec room is not moist, I hope I see you soon...

Please give my hellos (or is it *helloes*? Shit, now I'll never be **PRESIDENT**...) to Melissa and to Tim and Jenny...

besos y pesos,
boog

29 May 2000, Julie Green, Norman, OK

Day 150 Year Zero

Hey julie,

It was great to see you & Clay in Okrahoma, & I look forward to seeing you in Oregon. I am very happy to have one of your paintings in my house, & Brenda & Mikey like the painting a lot too. I should tell you a little story: Years ago, we used to go the Panda Garden when anybody in the house had a birthday. If you go to Panda Garden on your birthday, they give you ice cream and sing you Happy Birthday in Chinese. "Happy Birthday" in Chinese sounds remarkably like "Julie shave me, why not?" & that is still what we often sing to each other on birthdays. So now, it's hard to look at your painting [titled "She Shaves"] without that popping into my head. But it's OK. [...]

Until soon,
boog

22 February 2001, Eric "Slim" Jeffreys, New York, NY

Hey Slim,

[...] So have you been enjoying the new Bush era? On Jan. 20 there was a big headline on the Topeka paper—"BUSH INAUGURATION"—that just begged to be anagrammed. The best I could do, though, was UBU ROI HUNTS AGAIN, or maybe BUSH II U ORANGUTAN. I sent these off to a correspondent in Québec, and she wrote back saying that in French (or in Québecois at least), "bush" is "bois épais," with épais (thick) having the same extended meanings as in English. Ah well, it can't be as bad as the Reagan years, and at least there are conservatives of different colors in this administration.

I just got another batch of rubber lips—I'm up to about 30 now. If you see Stacy, please tell her that hers are on the way.

OK, Slim, my head seems to be full of jello today, so I'll write more when I achieve higher consciousness. If Veronica is there, please give her my abrazos & amitiés, & if not please pass along an e-howdy from me.

Hasta la vista baby...
boog

11 March 2001, Etta Cetera, Pittsburgh, PA

Hey Etta—

What do you mean mediocre? You remain one of my favorite contributors to

@RtH*Le

I loved the pieces you sent this time & I have doled them out carefully to other people who sent me curious handmade things.

This special hardbound @RtH*Le is in honor of your duct tape project and the 200th issue of @RtH*Le. So you can consider this a contribution to the duct tape project, but I've got another conception that hopefully I can execute & send before July. I think you're onto something here, Etta—duct tape is BIG, huge... it's iconic, it somehow sums up all of western civilization in its grey plasticky sticky indestructibility and deadening practicality. Long after genetic engineering, the internal combustion engine, and the Game Boy have faded into myth, duct tape will endure as one of the few monuments to what was western civilization, along with the fork, Spandex, and Elvis.

I hope I catch up with you soon—tell tENT howdy.

Cheerio,
boog

19 March 2001, John Held, Jr., San Francisco, CA

Howdy John, wherever you are,

I really liked your "Mail Art ABC" in *Kairan 2*. I appreciate your inclusiveness and vision of mail art as something that brings people together, and it's refreshing to see it in print. I thought your story about Ken Friedman and buZ blurr was very instructive. It reminds me of your patience with me back when you were perforating for me, & I still appreciate your attitude of encouragement.

So I've tried to keep a similar attitude with @RtH*Le, although occasionally I get some junk that obviously doesn't have much thought or time or inspiration in it. I've been very pleased overall with the works that have come in... It has been another great refutation of the Tragedy of the Commons theory... even if somebody sends in something sloppy the first time, they almost invariably send something that they've put more of themselves into if they participate again... I just cranked out issue 203, for Giovanni Strada... There are a lot of regulars now, like Jürgen Olbrich, Jörg Seifert, Magda Lagerwerf, Diane Bertrand, Pascal Lenoir, John M. Bennett, J. Ricart, and Antonio Gomez, but also enough new blood to keep it interesting.

I haven't heard anything about you being apprehended by the postal inspectors, so I assume that hasn't happened yet. Let me know if it does. I represented somebody accused of counterfeiting postage stamps once, & the US attorney seemed more interested in getting information and destroying any existing counterfeit stamps than in getting a criminal conviction. You probably know this, but each color copier has its own unique identifying number that it supposedly imprints on the back of every sheet it prints. I haven't actually observed one of these numbers, so I can't guarantee that it's true, but it's probably prudent to act as if it's true. But all that doesn't matter, of course, if you're trying to get busted.

And you probably also know that David Zack is dead. I hadn't heard anything reliable until I got an e-mail message out of the blue last month from Judith Conaway, Zack's former girlfriend. I asked about Zack and Judith said that in March 1995 someone at the halfway house he was at confirmed that he was dead, although the last trace of him she found was a record of his admission to an intensive care unit, but that she couldn't get access to any death records. So in the off chance you haven't heard all of this, let me know & I will forward the relevant parts of Judith's message. I liked it better when his fate was just a mystery. Like everything else.

I look forward to your next. Happy trails.

boog

3 décembre 2001, Diane Bertrand, St.-Léonard, Québec, Canada

Allô postale,

et merci pour tes nouvelles feuilles pour

Merci aussi pour les informations des projets d'arte postale. Tu dit que tu espères que ton xérox <<ne lâche pas la patate.>> Quelle veux dire <<lâcher la patate>>? En anglais si on dit qu'une personne a "dropped the potato", il veut dire que cette personne a manquée a faire quelque chose. Si une machine bientôt aura une panne, on dise qu'il va "break down," "shoot craps," "throw a rod," "give up the ghost," "kick the bucket," ou que "it's time to put it out on the back 40."

I hope your xérox n'est pas mort and I look forward to your next mail.

Linguistically yrs.,
boog

[Postal greetings,

Thank you for the information about the mail art projects. You say that you hope your xerox "hasn't dropped the potato." What does "drop the potato" mean? In English if one says of a person that they have "dropped the potato" it means that person has failed to do something. If a machine is about to malfunction, one says that it is going to "break down," "shoot craps," "throw a rod," "give up the ghost," "kick the bucket," or that "it's time to put it out on the back 40."

I hope your xérox has not died and I look forward to your next mail.

2 February 2002, Oakdale College, Oakdale, NY (fake reference letter for Sean Santoro)

Oakdale College
Idle Hour Blvd.
Oakdale, NY 11769

Re: Reference for Sean Santoro

To Whom It Should Concern,

It is my understanding that you are considering hiring Sean Santoro to teach a class in business, society, and ethics as part of your MBA program. Even though I have known Sean for a long time, I can unqualifiedly recommend him for this position.

If it weren't for all the drugs, Sean Santoro would be a highly competent and motivated attorney. Sean's professional life stands as a shining example of Oliver Wendell Holmes' famous dictum, "The life of the law has not been logic, but experience." Sean can be a very entertaining speaker, especially if you get him a little liquored up beforehand. I would love to see him in front of a classroom full of your uptight MBA students. For someone of his mental competence and emotional stability, Sean will be a great asset to your program.

Sean was very inspirational to me during my time as a law student. Every day I said to myself, "If Santoro can do this, anybody can." With Sean as a role model I learned how little I really had to do to get through law school.

Please don't believe any of those rumors you might have heard from some crazy judge or some other so-called attorney. If Sean were as corrupt as they say he is, he wouldn't have offered me 50 bucks to write this reference letter for him. An attorney of Sean's caliber could easily have just forged the letter himself and billed the time to one of his drug-addled clients.

Please give Sean a job. He probably won't pay up if he doesn't get hired, and I need the money.

Sincerely,
Dennis "Boog" Highberger

12 April 2002, Peter Lamborn Wilson, New Paltz, NY

Howdy Peter,

Thanks for the postcard. I haven't spent any time up in your neck of the woods—the closest I've been is probably Poughkeepsie or western Mass.—but I don't doubt that it's beautiful. This place has its beauty, too, but it's harder to capture on a postcard. So you get a letter instead.

Tad asked me to forward the enclosed article to you. I think he's going stir crazy (literally this time) & he has really appreciated hearing from you. I've been bad at writing, but because I'm nominally his attorney I can go out to see him whenever I need to or want to. Our new county jail is a real monstrosity. It's got a lot of control features that you used to see only in federal maximum security prisons, but this seems to be the wave of the future. Their medical treatment (or lack of it) also seems to be really poor. They probably need to be sued, but unfortunately I'm not quite in the position to do that right now. [...]

For a while early this year I became inordinately fond of "googlewhacking," which if you're not familiar with the concept involves running a search for two words on the Google search engine to try to get a single result—meaning there's only one page in all of the three billion plus pages indexed by Google that both words appear. It's quite a bit easier than it sounds, & not surprisingly your name comes up from time to time. For instance, if you run a search on "shamanic phalansteries" (or was it "zombie phalansteries"?) you will find exactly one page that has both of those words, and that page is composed of some selections from TAZ. Another page I pulled up recently was a long, fairly interesting article about Burning Man which included a quote from you about temporary autonomous zones. I don't have the URL, but if you're interested in seeing it you can just run a Google search on "digerati mundanity" (or "Lamarckian supplicants" or "truculent rebar") and go to the single page that comes up. I realize of course that you may have zero interest in such techno-happy foofaraw but I thought you might like to know that I've been seeing you in cyberspace (although I would prefer to see you in meatspace (I just learned this word—it's the complement of cyberspace, "where the meat lives.")) Plus it gives me an opportunity to say things like pettifoggery jubilation, unpalatably clabbered, labial bacchanals, and unsullied jodhpurs.

boog

17 August 2002, GL, Whiney Museum, La Habra, CA

Howdy GL,

Thanks for the nice letter. Flattery will get you everywhere, or at least into

@RtH*Le

[…] Boy, I feel silly that I sent your @RtH*Le to the Whitney Museum. So much of the time we look without seeing, & just scan the surface & fill in the blanks with our preconceived notions. It was a good reminder to me to PAY ATTENTION.

La Habra, eh? If I'm not mistaken my long lost buddy Ron lived in La Habra, where I visited him once. I met him at the anarchist gathering in Toronto in 1987(?). He stopped through here on his way back to LA, & my pal Mikey & I decided to ride back with him. He was in a hurry to get back for a Butthole Surfers show at the Palladium(?, in Hollywood?), so we drove nonstop except for a brief sleep in Tucumcari. We got in just before midnight, drove straight to [the] theater, & as soon as we got in they announced that they sold too many seats & the fire marshal had canceled the show. People started ripping the doors and seats up, & on our way out we saw a phalanx of riot cops marching down the street toward us so we ducked down into the basement. Ron apparently knew the producers & somehow he got us our money back. We met some of his friends in La Habra, & the only thing I remember about them is that one of them had just gotten back from Australia, & the thing that blew him away most about Australia was that there was space between the cities. I lost touch with Ron years ago & have no idea where he is today. So it goes.

Thanks for letter. I'll see you in the mail.

boog

2003–2011

sirocco gleet • frivolity is a harsh taskmaster • Mexican shoe sizes • the best rollercoaster ride of your whole life • "He is good dog" • Hoo Hoo monument • mankind is noodlekind • the naming of Burroughs Creek • borscht in Tepotzlán • Portland is more fun than a barrel full of porcupines

21 December 2003, John M. Bennett, Columbus, OH

OK, John–

I was googlewhacking last night, and "sirocco gleet" brought me to a page that contained this:

L'ENVOI

It is pilly-po-doddle and aligobung
  When the lollypop covers the ground,
Yet the poldiddle perishes punketty-pung
  When the heart jimmy-coggles around.
If the soul cannot snoop at the giggle-some cart,
  Seeking surcease in gluggety-glug,
It is useless to say to the pulsating heart,
  "Panky-doodle ker-chuggetty-chug!"

John Bennett

I just thought you should know. Or maybe it's some other John Bennett...

And a few days ago your face appeared on a letter from buZ blurr. Somewhere wheels are turning...

cheerio,
boog

10 January 2004, buZ blurr, Gurdon, AR

Howdy buZ,
Thanks for the stampsheets for

@RtH*Le

& for the dandy package of cheap graphic stuff. I wish I could have made it to your opening, especially with the blackout thrown in. Next time...

It was also great to see the article about the Arts Center of the Ozarks show (although I noticed they left the "Absence" out of the title of the "Art et Absence d'Habits" piece... The absence of absence = what?). Did you get a good response to the show? I think the great thing about a show like yours in a place like that (or like I'm imagining it to be, like places around here) is that it could be the spark, even if just for one person, that could change their whole way of looking at the world or blow wide open their perception of their own possibilities...

I would love to be a guest of the White Trash Bed & Breakfast again, but I'm not sure when I can pull it off. I'm supposed to be in Fayetteville a couple of weekends from now, but somebody else will be driving & it will be nonstop meetings... The next gig is in May, I believe, & it's possible that I could scam an extra day to swing down to Gurdon... I'll keep you posted...

Congratulations on your retirement, although I'm sure it's a double-edged sword. Art demands freedom, but it thrives on limits... & sure, I suppose mail art is frivolous, like all the best things in life... Like Zippy the Pinhead says, "Frivolity is a harsh taskmaster."

Until next time, I remain frivolously yrs.,

boog

5 February 2004, John M. Bennett, Columbus, OH

Howdy John,

Thanks for your latest contribution... Intriguing collaborations... & for the copy of *Lost & Found Times*. Could you send me a copy of your hiStOrietas alFabéticaS? In payment I have enclosed 3 Yankee dollars and a 3 REAL dollar William Burroughs bill, which you can still spend in a few places in Lawrence, including the Free State Brewery, where it will buy you one of the best oatmeal stouts in the country & still leave enough for a tip.

Today is Constitution Day in Mexico & that brings back a story from when I visited David Zack in Tepoztlán in 1988. My friends & I had been traveling around in a Volkswagen bus, & for about a month I had a hole in one of my shoes. I figured out a sure-fire way to make Mexican shoe store clerks laugh—just walk in and ask for the Mexican equivalent of a size 13. "Trente-tres?" "Ha ha ha ha..." Sometimes I asked people where the basketball players got their shoes, & the answer was invariably "los Estados Unidos." While we were staying at Zack's we took the bus into Mexico City for a couple of days. One night I asked the desk clerk my basketball shoe question, & he told me about a place a couple of blocks away near the zócalo. I went there first thing next morning—and it was closed. For Constitution Day. We left very early the next morning on the bus back to Tepoztlán, & I traveled all the way back to Kansas with a hole in my shoe.

¡Viva la Constitución!
until next time,
boog

4 May 2006, Julie Green, Corvallis, OR

Howdy Julie,

Thanks for sending the Last Supper announcement. It's great to hear that it will be at KU. I look forward to seeing you & Clay when you are in town.

The city commissioner/mayor thing has been an interesting cross between being broken on the rack and the best rollercoaster ride you ever had in your life. However, we have managed to liven it up a little bit [proclaiming International Dadaism Month]. This is about as close as I get to being an artist these days, but I have been reading Daniel Spoerri's *An Anecdoted Topography of Chance*, & it makes me think of you. If I were to do an anecdoted topography of my own desk right now, it would include a Julie Green business card, with a very nice lip print & a note that says HI BOOG + ALL

I hope you & Clay are well...

cheerio,
boog

12 October 2007, Margaret Robinson, Sabanilla, Montes de Oca, Costa Rica

Howdy Margaret—

It was great to hear from you. I should have known that you would retire in style. Of course, now everyone you ever knew will pester you & come visit, & I certainly hope I can too someday.

That was a great story about the dog on the bus. I took the blurry photo at left [omitted, of a dog looking out the window of a train compartment] a couple of weeks ago on the train from Brno to Prague in the Czech Republic. His human friend was a young dreadlocked Czech woman. She understood enough of my gestures & bad phrasebook Czech to confirm that she had to buy him a ticket. She looked at me with her big wide-set blue Slavic eyes & said in a voice that was soft like honey, "He is good dog." Yes, he was a good dog.

I love the description of your back yard, with all the clotheslines & surrounded by beautiful trees. It reminds me of a couple of pensiones I have stayed at in Mexico. I say right on to clotheslines. One of the things I have wanted to do as city commissioner, but haven't gotten around to, is banning homeowner's covenants that prohibit clotheslines—I think that is pretty much standard out in the new subdivisions out west. Now might be a good time to move on this—maybe people will be too embarrassed to let their bourgeois sense of esthetics stand in the way of the environmentally correct thing to do.

I envy your e-mail inaccessibility. E-mail is a curse and a burden, and of course I do it every day. I think e-mail is a perfect example of what I have taken to calling Boog's Law:

> *Any increase in speed or convenience of any form of communication or transportation increases the time we spend engaging in that activity and decreases the quality of the experience.*

Just like more roads and faster cars mean that people spend more time driving & more time stuck in traffic. I hope the Costa Ricans (and the Indians and the Chinese, and...) can avoid making some of the mistakes we have made, but I don't have much hope. Voluntary simplicity seems to be a lot more appealing to people who have had too much than to those who have never had enough. But at least maybe they can figure it out faster than we have...

I have enclosed the contact info you asked about—I hope it is what you needed. Thanks again for your letter, and I look forward to hearing from you again.

boog

7 June 2008, Gianni Simone (a/k/a johnnyboy), Tokyo, Japan

Howdy Gianni—

Thanks for your overly generous e-mail message. I agree that it's good to connect again. The last 5+ years of public service have wreaked havoc on the rest of my life, including my correspondence, but I have less than a year left & I already have more time and feel relaxed. So I've got @RtH*Le jumpstarted again, I've been having fun with the show at the Percolator that I told you about, and I've been sending things to a few mail art projects.

So the enclosed things are for your Xerography project, and they are all made with actual photocopiers. The Hoo Hoo sheet is plain old black & white photocopier on sheets from an old road atlas. The image is from the Hoo Hoo Monument in Gurdon, Arkansas, from one of my trips to visit buZ blurr. The (partial) Vigo/Padín sheet was made with two passes through a single-color photocopier that also had red and blue toner cartridges. The sheet with the letters was made on a color laser printer, which uses a separate scan for each color, by moving the letters around after each scan. I really like the concept of copies without originals, and I've been making a lot of things for @RtH*Le on a home color scanner/photocopier/inkjet printer by piling things on the glass. I suppose it's just another form of collage, except that the pieces aren't glued down.

I'll try to send the Percolator show documentation soon, and I've to see/hear more about what you've been up to.

Cheerio,
boog

25 August 2008, Jill Innes, Madison, WI

"Say yes to beautiful without paying the price."

"Mankind is noodlekind."

Jill dear—

I'm not sure what either of these mean, but they seem to cry out to be quoted. The latter is a quote from Momofuku Ando, inventor of ramen noodles, as quoted in a recent NPR story about the 50th anniversary of ramen noodles. I suspect that the inventor of Kraft's mac & cheese won't get the same treatment (although I vaguely remember a story about the passing of the inventor of the corn dog a few years ago...). The first quote is from a shampoo bottle that has been in our bathroom for a long time, in a place where I see it every day. I have said "OK—Yes!" and so far no bill has arrived.

Thanks for your sweet letter. I'm glad you liked the chocolate, and I'm glad Max & Nancy had a good time. Your family is way too nice to me, but I won't complain. I think that they are all great, smart, funny people & it is a real honor to be sort of a part of the family. I am up for attending future gatherings, as long as I get to see you there too. It was especially nice to spend some quality time with Max—it was so much fun to interact with him as the bright, adventurous adult he has become. I realize that part of that was probably there waiting to happen when he was born, but it is also due to lots of love & good work on your part, too. [...]

Max left just a couple of days too early to meet the latest addition to the family (see picture below). Her name is Zoorafa—It was love it first sight when I saw her in the window gallery at the Percolator, and now she has come to live with us. I think we could probably be very happy together, but I'm sure she's not as good a kisser as you. (Thank you for sharing your secrets, by the way. My secret: I saw the mayor naked every day for a whole year!)

Jill—It was great to see you, I miss you, I hope we can figure out some way to spend some time together again, & in the meantime you are in my head and my heart.

boog

Zoorafa

29 August 2008, John M. Bennett, Columbus, OH

Howdy John—

I'm having the computer randomly cycle through my stash of African music tonight—it started with some electronica from Burkina Faso, reflexively recalling Samuel Johnson's aphorism about a dog walking on its hind legs... yes, one is surprised to find it done at all. And from there it jumped straight to I Want a Break Thru' by the Hykkers, an obscure Nigerian band from the 70s, but this tune is one of the wildest electric blues funk free-your-ass-and-your-mind-will-follow ditties I've ever heard.

I saw James Grauerholz at a city commission meeting last week, where he was encouraging us to stay committed to funding for the Burroughs Creek rail trail. I'm not sure what old Bill would think about having a creek (at least parts of which were formerly known as "the Atchison Topeka and Santa Fe Ditch") and a bike trail named after him, but we've gone and done it anyway, despite one county commissioner's grumblings about the appropriateness of naming something after a junkie and a wife-killer—I suppose we should have stuck with slave-owners, war criminals, alcoholics, and adulterers like usual, but it's too late now... I gave James your regards & he sends his.

Thanks for your latest, & I look forward to your next...

boog

2 April 2010, Crackerjack Kid (a/k/a Chuck Welch), Eton, NH

OK, Crackerjack, here it is—

"Rainbow House" in all its glory.

Here's the story: I had been corresponding with Zack for a while before some friends of mine & I headed off to Mexico in a Volkswagen bus in December of 1987. The photo to the left [omitted] is a shot of the "image wall" at Zack's place in Tepoztlán, which he sent me before we left—the big thing in the center is an imaginary map of our expedition that I had sent him earlier.

We got to his place in early February, and stayed about a week. Tepotzlán, despite having a big expatriate colony, was a great & beautiful place, and Zack's house was a magnet for intriguing characters like Viviana la Cosmica and Hector, who wanted me to send him information that would help him in his project of constructing platillos voladores...

The first night we were there we found everything we needed in the market to make a big vat of borscht... another night we drank way too much nasty cane liquor & chanted Aire Aire Aire Fuego Fuego Fuego Fuego Agua Agua Agua Tierra Tierra Tierra while Zack played the bass...

We could tell that something was up, but we weren't sure what it was until we got back to the States & heard that he had been busted... the story I heard was that he was arrested while he was in his bathhouse, shown in the photo at right [omitted] with Maija Woof shiny beast paintings. As we were leaving he handed me an envelope with the Rainbow House manuscript in it, which he wanted me to take & try to find a publisher for. I tried to refuse but I eventually gave in. I have made some halfhearted efforts over the years to find someone interested in publishing it, but without any success. I have made one other copy of the manuscript (which is a copy itself—I have no idea where the original might be), which I think I sent to Vittore Baroni but I wouldn't swear to it.

So I'm interested to hear what you think. It's way different than any other Zack material I've ever seen. If you can think of somebody who might be interested in publishing it, that would be great, or if you are interested in working on a publishing project, I have a (limited) amount of time & cash I could contribute to such a project.

Thanks for calling—it was great to talk to you. You were responsible for getting me plugged back into the mail art network, and it has been a very important & satisfying part of my life. I hope things are well with you & I look forward to talking to you again soon.

boog

19 January 2011, Simran Sethi, Lawrence, KS (from Portland, OR)

Howdy Sim:

Portland is more fun than a barrel full of porcupines—A Google search shows 10,400,000 results for the phrase "and yet it was not enough." I saw a great poet named Mindy Nettifee at the Café Magnolia and again at the backspace... you should check her out... I hope you are well and I look forward to seeing you soon—XO,

boog

the Walter letters

I adopted my cat Walter from the Lawrence Humane Society in November of 2010. He was named after Walt Whitman at the suggestion of my girlfriend at the time. This turned out to be highly appropriate, because they both (Whitman and the cat, not the girlfriend) had long grey hair and sang the song of themselves on a regular basis.

Like many Americans, Walter was mostly uninterested in politics except as it impacted his food bowl. On a couple of occasions it did so to such an extent that he felt compelled to contact leaders in the Kansas House of Representatives to share his concerns. The first time was in 2016, after a day when the House overrode its own "midnight rule" (as it always does when leadership wants it to) and worked until 2:00 in the morning, and the second time was in 2017, when the House was called into session on a Sunday, after a long legislative session where enormous amounts of time were wasted.

Sadly, Walter died in the summer of 2019. He will be missed very much, and I am concerned about who will keep the House leadership in line.

2 May 2016, House Majority Leader Jene Vickrey, Topeka, KS

Majority Leader Jene Vickrey
State Capitol, Room 372-W
Topeka, KS 66612

Dear Majority Leader Vickrey,

Thank you for your service to the State of Kansas.

However, I must write to you about the rule of the House of Representatives called the "midnight rule." It is a good rule and you should stick to it!! Representative Highberger did not get home until 2:30 last night!!! I was very hungry and I was worried about him, but mostly I was hungry.

Also, it is not a good idea to make laws when people are tired and grumpy and they just want to go home. Also, it is not nice to the people who work for you because some of them probably have cats who were hungry too.

Please don't let this happen again.

Sincerely,

Walter

4 June 2017, Speaker of the House Ron Ryckman, Jr., Topeka, KS

Speaker Ron Ryckman, Jr.
State Capitol, Room 370-W
Topeka, KS 66612

Dear Speaker Ryckman,

Here we go again. Once again I must write to you or somebody about the shenanigans of the Kansas House of Representatives.

Representative Highberger came home all mad today because you are going to make him go to work on Sunday. He doesn't get mad very often, but when he does—whoo boy! Fortunately he is not one of those people who carries guns around all the time, but he does have that big stick.

He already missed the Pinckney neighborhood picnic!! he says. He is going to miss his uncle's 90th birthday party in Westphalia, Kansas! he says. He is not going to get to see his 96-year-old mother in the nursing home in Garnett, Kansas, and his sister on Sunday!!! he says. I got tired of listening to him, so I went outside to chase squirrels.

He was still going at it when I came back in. Personally, I think he should just calm down but also I think he is not the only person in this situation. Even Representative Blaine Finch Republican of Ottawa has a cat that probably wants to see him on Sunday!! Even Representative John Carmichael Democrat of Wichita has a cat that might like to see him! I don't know if Representative Ron Ellis Republican of Meriden has a cat but I am sure that he has barnyard animals that would like to see him at least on the weekends.

I don't want to go through this again, so please let's get down to business and get this session over with soon. Thank you in advance for your assistance.

At least you don't make him work in the middle of the night like that other guy.

Sincerely,

Walter

e-mails, texts, and Facebook posts

(Just kidding.)

notes

Full citations to all the books and articles referenced below can be found in the bibliography.

epigraph

fruits as quoted in *Goethe: Life as a Work of Art*, Rüdiger Safranski.

the Costume Party

An insurrection of clowns and gurus quote from *Unfinished Animal* by Theodore Roszak ("the clowns and gurus" in the original).

Milton Friedman quote from his book *Capitalism and Freedom*.

the gentle anarchist

I don't know what money is as quoted in *The Money Bazaars* by Martin Mayer.

Men have agreed as quoted in S. Herbert Frankel, *Money and Liberty*.

Georg Simmel quotes are from his book *The Philosophy of Money*.

S. Herbert Frankel quote is from his book *Money and Liberty*.

Trade is the reduction from Murray Bookchin, *Toward an Ecological Society*.

What we call the primitive from "The Politics of Ethnopoetics," in *The Old Ways*.

feces of hell ... feces of the gods from Ernest Bornemann, *The Psychoanalysis of Money*.

money is like muck from Francis Bacon, "Of Seditions and Troubles," *Essays*, 15.

money doesn't smell from Ernest Bornemann, *The Psychoanalysis of Money*.

a new dependence as quoted in S. Herbert Frankel, *Money and Liberty*.

Today we have more freedom from S. Herbert Frankel, *Money and Liberty*.

ABOLISH PAPER MONEY from *The Velvet Monkey Wrench*, John Muir.

We should think of the machine Georg Simmel, *The Philosophy of Money*.

Knowledge – Zzzzzp! from the Tennessee Williams play *The Glass Menagerie*.

Raoul Vaneigem from his book *The Revolution of Everyday Life*.

Isle of Man this may be in error—see *Isle of Man* note for Disorientation later in this section.

Go out and fight from the Clifford Odets play *Awake and Sing!*

Disorientation

Strategic Shopping Initiative At the time, President Reagan was proposing a space-based anti-ballistic-missile program known as the "Strategic Defense Initiative" (SDI), and local activists were battling a proposal to demolish a large part of downtown Lawrence for the construction of an enclosed shopping mall.

Jerry Toebone Gary Toebben, president of the Lawrence Chamber of Commerce.

mossbacks and lardbutts this was a phrase used by local newspaper editor Dolph Simons, Jr., to describe downtown mall opponents, who adopted it as a badge of honor.

Mike Walnut Michael Almon, mall opponent.

Barney Kominsky Barry Shalinsky, mall opponent.

Bob Buildings Bob Billings, a local developer responsible for Alvamar, among other things.

Ten years later the quotes in this paragraph are from "Another Bottle Sold," a 1906 essay by William Allen White in which he retracted most of what he wrote in "What's the Matter with Kansas?" Both essays are reproduced at http://courses.missouristate.edu/bobmiller/Populism/texts/documents/What%20-%20Kansas.htm.

One historian has argued see Henry Littlefield, "The Wizard of Oz: Parable on Populism."

Isle of Man I have not been able to locate the book that inspired the REAL Dollar program, and it may in fact have been a book about a currency scheme implemented on the island of Guernsey between 1815 and 1837, the most likely culprit being *An Example of Communal Currency* by Joseph Theodore Harris.

Lies and Libels According to Ms. Stephens, "If his 'fame' carries Frank the False-hearted to posterity, he will be remembered as a harpy man who defiled whatever he touched in one of the filthiest and lyingest books that has ever burdened the earth[.]"

Don Johnson an actor probably best known for starring in the TV show *Miami Vice* in the 1980s, he is claimed as an alumnus by KU on the basis of the couple of semesters he spent in the theater department there.

Kaw Valley Independent

Bob Marley at Hoch Auditorium (now Budig Hall) on the KU campus, on December 6, 1979.

the bar where the mayor worked while she was mayor, now-Senator Marci Francisco worked Friday afternoons at the Catfish Bar and Grill, later known as the Crossing, at the north end of campus where the Oread hotel is today.

funky basement kitchen at 1614 Kentucky, now the Olive House.

first woman dentist Lucy Hobbs Taylor, who lived and had her dental office at 809 Vermont, most recently the location of Bzar hair salon.

cat food at the Dillons grocery store at 1740 Massachusetts.

Off the Wall Hall a music venue at 737 New Hampshire, where the Bottleneck is now.

the Forgotten Empire in the 1970s and 1980s, KU physics professor Daniel Ling owned a large number of houses in the Oread neighborhood. Most received little maintenance and were in poor condition, but the low rents he charged enabled many people to afford to stay enrolled at the University. Most have also since been demolished, the above-mentioned Olive House being one of the rare exceptions.

Droppers see "Bernofsky of America" in the Disorientation chapter of this book.

old Theta Chi house was located on top of the hill at the southwest corner of Ninth Street and Emery Road, on the site of Lawrence's windmill, which had burned in 1905. It was constructed in 1958 and abandoned in the late 1960s. In my undergraduate days it was a three-story graffiti-covered concrete shell and what my law school education would later teach me to identify as an "attractive nuisance."

crane "ostrich" in the original. Thanks to Barbara Watkins for the correction.

Love Thy Neighbor the sign is still on the garage at 1301 Vermont.

Diane di Prima from "Song for Baby-O, Unborn," in *Pieces of a Song*.

speeches

Try to be good to each other the quote from the Spider Grandmother is from William Least Heat Moon, *Blue Highways*.

said NO to ... discrimination In April 2005, 70% of Kansas voters approved an amendment to the Kansas Constitution prohibiting the state from recognizing or performing same-sex marriages or civil unions.

Douglas County was the only county where the amendment failed.

the window we're shooting for we were apparently successful.

"Ich bin ein Eutiner." "I am from (or of) Eutin." This is also a direct quote from Carl Maria von Weber, a well-known early 19th-century German composer who was born in Eutin.

mannequin this is a reference to another well-known Lawrence resident also named Dennis.

Paul Paul Davis, former Kansas House minority leader and 2014 Democratic candidate for Kansas governor.

Abbie Abbie Hodgson, the other candidate for the 46th District nomination.

flotsam & jetsam

Bedtime for Bonzo a 1951 movie staring Ronald Reagan and a chimpanzee. Reagan's character conducts a secret experiment with the chimpanzee, with the goal of proving, in IMDb's words, "that environment trumps heredity in behavioral development."

Ed Meese served as Attorney General under Reagan. He was famous for opposing giving constitutional protections to criminal suspects, because, in his words, "If a person is innocent of a crime, then he is not a suspect."

James Watt Reagan's anti-environmentalist Secretary of the Interior, who once divided the citizens of the US into "liberals and Americans."

Cap Weinberger Caspar Weinberger, Secretary of State under Reagan. He was charged with lying to an independent counsel investigating the Iran-Contra arms for hostages deal, but was pardoned by President Bush I.

Strategic Defense Initiative a proposed space-based missile defense shield based on not-yet-existing technology. See *Strategic Shopping Initiative* note for Disorientation, earlier in this section.

Ollie North Oliver North, a lieutenant colonel in the Marines and a member of the National Security Council staff during the Reagan administration. He helped organize the Iran-Contra operation and was convicted of lying to Congress about it, although his convictions were later vacated.

constructive engagement a term used by the Reagan administration to describe its policy toward South Africa, which was essentially the opposite of what the divestment movement was advocating.

ketchup in order to allow schools to meet nutritional requirements despite funding cuts to the federal school lunch program, the Reagan administration proposed allowing condiments like pickle relish (and ketchup) to count as a serving of vegetables.

William Casey CIA director under Reagan, was suspected of participation in the Iran-Contra scheme. The day before he was scheduled to testify before Congress, he suffered two seizures, was hospitalized, and died not long thereafter. Some suspected foul play.

Admiral Poindexter National Security Adviser under Reagan. He was convicted of five counts of lying to Congress about the Iran-Contra affair, but the convictions were overturned on appeal.

urine specimen In 1986, Reagan issued Executive Order 12564, which mandated drug testing of over a million federal employees, despite recent federal court rulings finding mass random drug screenings to be unconstitutional.

I want to be everything as quoted in Katrina vanden Huevel, "Yevgeny Yevtushenko—His Poetry Engaged and Enraged Readers at Home and Abroad," *The Progressive*, April 1, 1987.

the idea of planets copulating Bookchin quote from *The Ecology of Freedom.*

Eric Jantsch quote from *The Self-Organizing Universe.*

The principle of collage as quoted in "Donald Barthelme Is Dead at 58; A Short-Story Writer and Novelist," Herbert Mitgang, *New York Times*, July 24, 1989.

The essence of Zen This quote may be garbled or spurious. Despite the assistance of KU Professor of Religious Studies Tim Miller, I was unable to verify it or find a source for it. After a survey of some former colleagues of Mr. Gaskin at the Farm, one of them said that "[n]obody recalls the quote but would not discount it either."

Laughter is a form of angst relief I have not located the source of this quote.

Sometimes the truth from chapter 78 of the *Tao Te Ching*. The translation cited in the bibliography gives the line as "The truth often sounds paradoxical."

there is only jello as you might have noticed, this quote doesn't actually appear in *a juxtapositionist manifesto*.

Every membrane I suspect that this quote is from *Semi-Permeable Membranes: Twenty Songs of the Revolution.*

licentiousness the Marquis de Sade, quoted in Georges Bataille, *Erotism.*

James Gleick quote from his book *Chaos.*

György Doczi from his book *The Power of Limits.*

Nothing defines perception from *The Time Falling Bodies Take to Light* (I think), by William Irwin Thompson.

Zero and infinity I have not located the source of this quote.

Georges Bataille from his book *Erotism.*

Fakir Musafar as quoted in V. Vale, ed., *Modern Primitives.*

letters 1985–1988

ellipses see letter dated 10 October 1994.

Law Day USA May 1 is "Law Day" in the United States for the same reason that it is Labor Day in almost every other country in the world. On May 1, 1886, a number of striking workers at the McCormick plant in Chicago were shot and one killed by Pinkerton guards. At a workers' rally a few days later, someone threw a bomb that killed at least 11 workers and policemen. Eight local labor leaders, mostly identifying as anarchists, were rounded up, put on trial, and quickly convicted, without any evidence that they had anything to do with the bomb. Four were hung, but the others were later pardoned and released. Around the world, outrage at these events led May 1 to be declared Labor Day in honor of the striking workers, while in the US "Law Day" honors one of the biggest travesties of justice in American history.

the Village Inn an all-night pancake house, located on Iowa Street in Lawrence where the Red Pepper is today.

Pleasant Farm a place I used to live on top of the hill on Highway 59 south of Pleasant Grove (about 6 miles south of Lawrence). It was bulldozed in 2011 when the highway was rerouted.

Houndogs the Lonesome Houndogs, Lawrence's premier psycowdelic band.

Rock Chalk otherwise known as the Catfish or the Crossing, located at the north end of campus, where the Oread hotel is today.

Rainbow House a cooperative house on the 1100 block of Tennessee.

once the flames from the Peter Gabriel song "Biko."

I'll copy an article "Technology," in *the gentle anarchist*, No. 11 (reproduced in the "gentle anarchist" chapter of this book).

Magical Pig from "Sy Borg," *Joe's Garage: Acts II & III*, Frank Zappa.

milpa a milpa is a field periodically cleared from the jungle and then left fallow for a number of years. In his previous letter Zack had suggested that we help someone clear a milpa, but I don't recall that it came up while were in Teptozlán.

Headquarters Headquarters is a crisis counseling center in Lawrence that teaches reflective listening skills to its volunteers. One of the long list of words that we were given to reflect how our callers were feeling was "well-equipped," which was the source of some jocularity among the volunteers during my time there.

perfect taco Before I left for Mexico I asked my friend Meredith what I could bring her from Mexico, and she said "the perfect taco." We found the perfect taco in a town called Polotitlán, at the "Tacomovil," which clearly hadn't moved in many years. The taco was the perfect taco to bring back to Meredith because it was so gristly as to be inedible. We put it in a jar, and it was so decomposed by the time we got to the border that the border guard refused to open the jar, making us realize that, if we had wanted to smuggle something in, that would have been the way to do it.

biting the meat from an old blurb for David Crowbar's magazine *Popular Reality*.

furthur spelling by Ken Kesey.

crummy downtown apartment 824½ Massachusetts Street, over what was then Gunther's Jewelry and the Downtown Barbershop.

old Theta Chi house see *old Theta Chi House* note for Kaw Valley Independent, earlier in this section.

Oh that motorway livin' "Motorway," from the Kinks, *Everybody's in Show-Biz*, 1972.

video "Rub Out the Word," https://www.youtube.com/watch?v=vlD0YU-PHfQ.

reading Jung *Memories, Dreams, Reflections*.

the Sanctuary a bar and private club formerly located at 7th and Michigan. It was demolished not long before the letter was written.

making love with bodies from Lawrence Ferlinghetti, *Her*.

goal of love quote from Alan Watts, *Behold the Spirit*.

letters 1989–1990

SORT Save Our Recycling from Trash, a community group that advocated for curbside recycling in Lawrence and achieved the appointment of the city's first part-time recycling coordinator.

cut-rate shopping mall the Riverfront Outlet Mall at 6th & New Hampshire, now completely devoid of shopping opportunities. The eagles came back.

Corso poem "Marriage," from *The Happy Birthday of Death*.

learning to walk on sharp knives a line from a Josh Mars song.

Locke's theory of money see George Caffentzis, *Clipped Coins, Abused Words, Civil Government*.

why can't I go into a grocery store quote from "America," in *Collected Poems, 1947–1980*; in the original Ginsberg says "When can I go into the supermarket and buy what I need with my good looks?"

letters 1991–1992

Factsheet Five to quote from the bibliography of my 1992 Helen F. Snyder Book Collecting Contest entry, "The magazine *Factsheet Five* was one of the major forces that helped galvanize the anarchist/ marginal scene in the late '80s. Mike Gunderloy, the editor, reviewed every marginal 'zine (as they came to be called) that he received, and in the process put thousands of politicos and wackos all over the world in touch with each other... I watched *Factsheet Five* grow from a few typed, xeroxed sheets that arrived on an irregular schedule to a hundred-page, bimonthly, typeset, saddle-stitched, professional looking magazine that sold for $3.50 a crack."

Dali Max Gérard, *Dali... Dali... Dali...*

sammiches the following was a footnote in the original: "this is a Pogo word usually seen as in 'peeny bunker sammiches' which Albert the Alligator was quite fond of."

Ooblecks members of the Chicago artistic collective Theater Oobleck.

Art's & Mary's an excellent brand of potato chips made in Wichita, Kansas.

utopian colony the Spencer Research Library at KU has an interesting manuscript on this subject, titled *Cat's-Paw Utopia.*

Apache 7 a hotel in Los Mochis, Sinaloa, Mexico, that rented rooms by the hour. A comment by Mike Mont on a December 15, 2016, post by Koko Lizarraga on the Facebook page for Bar El Mahone suggests that it's not there any more.

letters 1993–1994

The horror! from Joseph Conrad, *Heart of Darkness.*

Ray Bradbury story from "The Long Rain," in *The Illustrated Man.*

I left my pants quote from "Some Introductory Remarks, or, How to Have Fun," in Bill Griffith's *Yow Comics No. 1.*

Dreamtime Village a "hypermedia permaculture village" founded by mIEKAL aND and Liz Was of Xexoxial Endarchy in the Driftless Zone in southwest Wisconsin.

Bless us oh the postcard referred to was from the Dickeyville Grotto in southwestern Wisconsin. The image was of a four-sided sort of gazebo with a sentence that started out "Bless us oh Lord..." written around the top in white letters, but all you could see on the postcard was "Bless us oh."

Subgummers members of the great Chicago band Maestro Subgum and the Whole.

The Nine Billion Names a short story by Arthur C. Clarke, in a collection of the same name.

The "rivets" in Ecclesiastes quote from Richard Brautigan, *A Confederate General from Big Sur.*

I can show you baby from "Song for Baby-O, Unborn," in *Pieces of a Song*, by Diane di Prima.

Time is an ocean from "Oh Sister" on Bob Dylan's *Desire*.

the rails you ride are ... rusted from "Hobo Chang Ba," *Trout Mask Replica*, Captain Beefheart and the Magic Band.

1 Liner notes, *Freak Out!*, Verve, 1966 (this and the following numbered notes below were all footnotes in the original letter).

2 The Central Scrutinizer, Side 4, *Joe's Garage, Acts II & III*, Zappa, 1979.

3 "Evelyn, A Modified Dog," *One Size Fits All*, Discreet, 1975.

4 "Cheepnis," *Roxy & Elsewhere*, Discreet, 1974.

5,6 "Outside Now," *Joe's Garage, Acts II & III.*

7 "Eddie Are You Kidding?", *Just Another Band From LA*, Reprise, 1972.

8 "No Not Now," *Ship Arriving Too Late to Save a Drowning Witch*, Barking Pumpkin, 1982.

Kurt Vonnegut from *Slapstick*.

four pounds of muscatel from Richard Brautigan, *A Confederate General from Big Sur*.

mayonnaise from Richard Brautigan, *Trout Fishing in America*.

enclosed article "An Authentik and Historikal Discourse on the Phenomenon of Mail Art," David Zack, *Art in America*.

Alfalfa a great vegetarian-friendly restaurant in Lexington, Kentucky.

Camille Paglia quotes from her book *Sexual Personae*.

Deer Run Court an aptly named street in the aptly named Fox Chase Addition referenced in the next letter, because at that point the deer had run and the foxes had been chased away.

a subdivision where his house is now the "Fox Chase Addition" to the city of Lawrence.

Renaldo Columbus "The Rediscovery of the Clitoris," Katharine Park, in Carla Mazzio and David Hillman, eds., *The Body in Parts*.

letters 1995–1997

Full Moon in the back of the Casbah, 803 Massachusetts, where the lower level of the Burger Stand is now.

can there be joy from Céline, *Castle to Castle*.

до свидания (do svidaniya) goodbye.

Brain Cell an ongoing project of Japanese mail artist Ryosuke Cohen. Participants send an original rubberstamp image or 150 stickers and receive a multicolored A3 (approximately 11" x 17") size sheet, printed on a Gocco printer, with images from 30 or so other artists from around the world, along with an address list of all the participants in that issue. The first *Brain Cell* was produced in 1985 and it has appeared every 10 days or so ever since—the 1000th issue came out in December 2017.

Night on Earth a 1991 film by director Jim Jarmusch

burning of the Böögg also known as Sechseläuten, is actually a traditional spring holiday in Zürich, usually celebrated on the third Monday of April.

"Mister Boogie" the book referenced is *Boogie 3*: "*El Aceitoso*," by the Argentinian cartoonist Fontanarrosa.

that other French impressionist the painting I was trying to think of was actually Seurat's "A Sunday on la Grande Jatte"; I believe that the other artist I was trying to think of was Paul Signac.

Лучще... Better later than never!

el inodoro Pereyra Inodoro Pereyra (also known as "El Renegáu ("The Renegade") is a comic strip character in a series by the same name, created by Argentinian cartoonist Fontanarrosa, about the life of a lonely gaucho on the pampa. "Inodoro" is a Spanish word for "toilet."

Dear friend Edgardo This translation by Pat Wittry intentionally intends to convey the flavor of my bad Spanish

porque no me gusta la television because I don't like television.

porque me gusta el aire fresco because I like fresh air.

"*And the walls come down...*" "H.," from *Ænima*.

Hale-Bopp an unusually bright comet that appeared in 1997.

letters 1998–2002

Tsjaad, Marokko, Bovenvolta Chad, Morocco, Upper Volta.

"*If you see her, say hello...*" "If You See Her, Say Hello," from Bob Dylan's *Blood on the Tracks*.

"*Tangier*" Iain Finlayson, *Tangier: City of the Dream*.

"*Voyaging is victory*!" from Sir Richard Burton, *Personal Narrative of a Pilgrimage to Al Madinah and Meccah (Volume 1)*.

a whole other set of sadnesses As it turned out, there were other sadnesses in store, and as I should have expected, they were worse than I expected. My mother came down with dementia and was in a nursing home for nine years. The last things that she canned sat on shelves in her garage while she was there, and when we cleaned her house out they were so old that we had to throw them away.

battle of Seattle a series of protests surrounding the World Trade Organization Ministerial Conference of 1999.

"*Let's not ask...*" from Ani diFranco's "Shy" on *Not a Pretty Girl*.

Pay toilets are illegal see K.S.A. 65-1,110.

Paul Reubens otherwise known as Pee-wee Herman, he was arrested in July 1991 for indecent exposure in an adult theater in Sarasota, Florida.

sanskrit more accurately, Devanagari, a script used for writing Sanskrit.

arabic or russian not to mention Uzbek.

helloes in 1992 Vice-President Dan Quayle was given an unreasonable amount of grief for spelling "potato" as "potatoe" at a New Jersey elementary school spelling bee.

Kairan was a mail art magazine published by Gianni Simone (a/k/a johnnyboy) in Yokohama, Japan.

TAZ a book by Hakim Bey, subtitled *The Temporary Autonomous Zone, Ontological Anarchy, Poetic Terrorism*.

letters 2003–2011

another John Bennett in fact, it was another John Bennett, the one quoted apparently being a late 19th-century writer of children's books. This verse appears in *A Nonsense Anthology*, edited by Carolyn Wells.

"*Art et Absence d'Habits*" "Art and the Absence of Clothing," a series of performance art events organized by a French artist known as Le Peintre Nato.

frivolity the actual quote appears to be "Frivolity is a stern taskmaster," but I haven't located the exact source.

REAL dollar a local currency that circulated in Lawrence, Kansas, in the early 2000s (see "The REAL Dollar," in the Disorientation chapter, for details).

Last Supper is a project of Oregon State University professor (and former Lawrence resident) Julie Green, in which she documents the last meal requests of death row inmates with paintings on ceramic plates. She has completed over 500 of them and plans to continue until the death penalty is abolished. See https://greenjulie.com/last-supper/.

liven it up a little bit this refers to the proclamation of "International Dadaism Month" on 27 December 2005 (for details see International Dadaism Month Proclamation in the flotsam & jetsam chapter of this book).

Rainbow House a manuscript novel by David Zack about living in a communal house in San Francisco in the mid-1960s.

platillos voladores flying saucers.

Aire Fuego Agua Tierra air fire water earth.

the Walter letters

that big stick a forearm crutch.

bibliography

Ackerman, Diane, *A Natural History of the Senses*, Random House, NewYork, 1990

Amado, Jorge, *Tent of Miracles*, Avon Books, New York, 1971

aND, mIEKAL, *Samsara Congeries*, BlazeVOX [books], Buffalo, NY, 2016

Bacon, Francis, *The Essays of Francis Bacon*, Houghton, Mifflin and Co., Boston, 1936

Bataille, Georges, *The Accursed Share*, Zone Books, New York, 1988

Bataille, Georges, *Erotism: Death and Sensuality*, City Lights Books, San Francisco,1986

Bataille, Georges, *Story of the Eye*, City Lights Books, San Francisco, 1987

Bateson, Gregory, *Steps to an Ecology of Mind*, Ballantine Books, New York, 1972

Baum, L. Frank, *The Wonderful Wizard of Oz*, HarperCollins, New York, 2000

Beck, Julian, *The Life of the Theatre: The Relation of the Artist to the Struggle of the People*, City Lights Books, San Francisco, 1972

Beck, Julian, *Semi-Permeable Membranes: Twenty Songs of the Revolution*, Bliss Press, San Francisco, 1984

Bennett, John M., *hiStOrietas alFabéticaS*, Luna Bisonte Prods., Columbus, OH, 2003

Bey, Hakim, *TAZ: The Temporary Autonomous Zone, Ontological Anarchy, Poetic Terrorism*, Autonomedia, Brooklyn, NY, 1991

Bloom, Murray Teigh, *The Brotherhood of Money: The Secret World of Bank Note Printers*, BNR Press, Port Clinton, OH, 1983

Bookchin, Murray, *The Ecology of Freedom*, Cheshire Books, Palo Alto, CA, 1982

Bookchin, Murray, *Toward an Ecological Society*, Black Rose Books, Montréal, Québec, 1980

Bornemann, Ernest, *The Psychoanalysis of Money*, Urizen Books, New York, 1976

Bradbury, Ray, *The Illustrated Man*, Doubleday & Company, Inc., Garden City, NY, 1951

Brautigan, Richard, *A Confederate General from Big Sur*, Grove Press, New York, 1964

Brautigan, Richard, *The Pill versus the Spring Hill Mine Disaster*, Dell Publishing Co., New York, 1968

Brautigan, Richard, *The Tokyo-Montana Express*, Dell Publishing Co., New York, 1980

Brautigan, Richard, *Trout Fishing in America*, Dell Publishing Co., New York, 1967

Brevda, William, *Harry Kemp: The Last Bohemian*, Bucknell University Press, London, 1986

Brillat-Savarin, Jean-Anthelme, *The Philosopher in the Kitchen*, Penguin Books, New York, 1981

Burroughs, William, *The Soft Machine, Nova Express, The Wild Boys*, Grove Press, New York, 1980

Burton, Sir Richard, *Personal Narrative of a Pilgrimage to Al Madinah and Meccah (Volume 1)*, Dover Publications, New York, 1964

Caffentzis, Constantine George, *Clipped Coins, Abused Words, Civil Government: John Locke's Philosophy of Money*, Autonomedia, Brooklyn, NY, 1989

Calvino, Italo, *If on a winter's night a traveler*, Harcourt Brace Jovanovich, New York, 1981

Céline, Louis-Ferdinand, *Castle to Castle*, Carroll & Graf Publishers, Inc., New York, 1987

Clanton, O. Gene, *Kansas Populism*, University Press of Kansas, Lawrence, KS, 1969

Clarke, Arthur C., *The Nine Billion Names of God*, Harbrace Paperbound Library, New York, 1967

Conrad, Joseph, *Heart of Darkness*, Penguin Books, New York, 1981

Corso, Gregory, *The Happy Birthday of Death*, New Directions Publishing Co., New York, 1960

Crump, Thomas, *The Phenomenon of Money*, Routledge & Kegan Paul, London, 1982

de Sade, Marquis, *Selected Letters*, October House, New York, 1965

Díaz del Castillo, Bernal, *The Discovery and Conquest of Mexico*, Farrar, Straus and Cudahy, New York, 1956

di Prima, Diane, *Pieces of a Song: Selected Poems*, City Lights Books, San Francisco,1990

di Prima, Diane, *Revolutionary Letters*, City Lights Books, San Francisco, 1974

Dillard, Annie, *An American Childhood*, Harper & Row, New York, 1988

Doczi, György, *The Power of Limits: Proportional Harmonies in Nature, Art, and Architecture*, Shambhala Publications, Boulder, CO, 1981

Duras, Marguerite, *The Lover*, Harper Perennial, New York, 1992

Eco, Umberto, *The Name of the Rose*, Vintage Books, London, 1998

Ferlinghetti, Lawrence, *Her*, New Directions Publishing Co., New York, 1960

Ferlinghetti, Lawrence, *Tyrannus Nix?*, New Directions Publishing Co., New York, 1969

Finlayson, Iain, *Tangier: City of the Dream*, Flamingo, London, 1993

Flanagan, Thomas, *Louis "David" Riel: Prophet of the New World*, Goodreads, Toronto, 1983

Fontanarrosa, *Boogie 3: "El Aceitoso*," Editorial Patria, Mexico City, 1989

Forbes, Jack D., *Columbus and Other Cannibals: The Wétiko Disease of Exploitation, Imperialism and Terrorism*, Autonomedia, Brooklyn, NY, 1992

Fourier, Charles, (ed. Beecher, Jonathan and Bienvenu, Richard), *The Utopian Vision of Charles Fourier: Selected Texts on Work, Love, and Passionate Attraction*, Beacon Press, Boston, MA, 1971

Frank, Thomas, *What's the Matter with Kansas?*, Henry Holt and Co., New York, 2004

Frankel, S. Herbert, *Money and Liberty*, American Enterprise Institute, Washington, DC, 1980

Frater, Alexander, *Chasing the Monsoon: A Modern Pilgrimage Through India*, Holt, New York, 1992

Friedman, Milton, *Capitalism and Freedom*, The University of Chicago Press, Chicago, 1962

Gardella, Peter, *Innocent Ecstasy: How Christianity Gave America an Ethic of Sexual Pleasure*, Oxford University Press, New York, 1985

Gérard, Max, *Dali... Dali... Dali...*, Harry N. Abrams, Inc., New York, 1974

Ginsberg, Allen, *Collected Poems, 1947–1980*, Harper Perennial, New York, 1988

Ginsberg, Allen, *Kaddish*, City Lights Books, San Francisco, 1961

Gleick, James, *Chaos: The Making of a New Science*, Penguin Books, New York, 1988

Goodwyn, Lawrence, *The Populist Moment: A Short History of the Agrarian Revolt in America*, Oxford University Press, New York, 1978

Griffith, Bill, *Yow Comics No. 1*, "Some Introductory Remarks, or, How to Have Fun," Last Gasp, Berkeley, CA, 1978

Grogan, Emmett, *Ringolevio: A Life Played for Keeps*, Little, Brown and Company, Boston, MA, 1972

Halifax, Joan, *Shamanic Voices: A Survey of Visionary Narratives*, E.P. Dutton, New York, 1979

Harris, Frank, *My Life and Loves*, Obelisk Press, Paris, 1945

Harris, J. Theodore, *An Example of Communal Currency*, P. S. King & Son, London, 1911

Hašek, Jaroslav, *The Good Soldier Švejk and His Fortunes in the World War*, Penguin Books, London, 1988

Hofstadter, Douglas, *Anti-Intellectualism in American Life*, Vintage Books, New York, 1963

Hyde, Lewis, *The Gift: Imagination and the Erotic Life of Property*, Vintage Books, New York, 1983

Ivo, Lêdo, *Snake's Nest, or A Tale Badly Told*, New Directions Books, New York, 1981

Jantsch, Eric, *The Self-Organizing Universe*, Pergamon Press, Oxford, UK, 1983

Jung, C.G., *Memories, Dreams, Reflections*, Vintage Books, New York, 1975

Kerr, John Leeds, *Destination Topolobampo: The Kansas City, Mexico and Orient Railway*, Golden West, San Marino, CA, 1968

Kindscher, Kelly, *Edible Wild Plants of the Prairie: An Ethnobotanical Guide*, University Press of Kansas, Lawrence, KS, 1987

Koehnline, James, and Sakolsky, Ron, eds., *Gone to Croatan: Origins of North American Dropout Culture*, Autonomedia, Brooklyn, NY, 1993

Kohn, Howard, *The Last Farmer*, Harper & Row, New York, 1988

Krafft-Ebing, Richard, *Psychopathia Sexualis*, Rebman Company, New York, 1906

Kundera, Milan, *The Joke*, Penguin Books, New York, 1983

Lao Tzu, *Tao Te Ching*, translation by Feng, Gia-Fu and English, Jane, Vintage Books, New York, 1972

Least Heat Moon, William, *Blue Highways*, Ballantine Books, New York, 1984

Least Heat Moon, William, *PrairyErth*, Houghton Mifflin, Boston, MA, 1991

Littlefield, Henry, "The Wizard of Oz: Parable on Populism," *American Quarterly*, Vol. 16, No. 1 (Spring, 1964)

Martínez Estrada, Ezequiel, *X-Ray of the Pampa*, University of Texas Press, Austin, TX, 1971

Marx, Groucho, *The Groucho Letters: Letters to and from Groucho Marx*, Simon & Schuster, New York, 1987

Mayer, Martin, *The Money Bazaars*, E.P. Dutton, Inc., New York, 1984

Mazzio, Carla, and Hillman, David, eds., *The Body in Parts: Fantasies of Corporeality in Early Modern Europe*, Routledge, New York, 1997

McNall, Scott, *The Road to Rebellion*, University of Chicago Press, Chicago, 1988

Melville, Herman, *Moby-Dick, or the White Whale*, Penguin Classics, London, 1972

Middleton, Kenneth A., *Manufacturing in Lawrence, Kansas, 1854–1900*, master's thesis, University of Kansas, 1940

Miller, Henry, *Money and How It Gets That Way*, Bern Porter, Berkeley, CA, 1946

Millman, Lawrence, *Last Places: A Journey in the North*, Houghton Mifflin, Boston, MA, 1990

Muir, John, *The Velvet Monkey Wrench*, John Muir Publications, Santa Fe, NM, 1973

Nin, Anaïs, *The Diary of Anaïs Nin, Vol. 2*, Harcourt, Brace, World, New York, 1967

Nin, Anaïs, *Spy in the House of Love*, Swallow Press, Chicago, 1984

Nugent, Walter, T. K., *The Tolerant Populists*, University of Chicago Press, Chicago, 1963

Paglia, Camille, *Sexual Personae: Art and Decadence from Nefertiti to Emily Dickinson*, Vintage Books, New York, 1991

Rabbit, Peter, *Drop City*, Olympia Press, New York, 1971

Roszak, Theodore, *Unfinished Animal: The Aquarian Frontier and the Evolution of Consciousness*, Harper & Row, New York, 1977

Safranski, Rüdiger, *Goethe: Life as a Work of Art*, Liveright Publishing Co., New York, 2017

Salaman, Redcliffe, *The History and Social Influence of the Potato*, Cambridge University Press, Cambridge, UK, 1985

Shaw, Bernard, and Harris, Frank, *The Playwright and the Pirate*, The Pennsylvania State University Press, University Park, PA, 1982

Simmel, Georg, *The Philosophy of Money*, Routledge & Kegan Paul, London, 1978

Snyder, Gary, *The Old Ways: Six Essays*, City Lights Books, San Francisco, 1977

Spoerri, Daniel, *An Anecdoted Topography of Chance*, Atlas Press, London, 1995

Stein, Gertrude, *The Autobiography of Alice B. Toklas*, Modern Library, New York, 1993

Stephens, Kate, *Lies and Libels of Frank Harris*, Antigone Press, New York, 1929

Thomas, Lewis, *The Lives of a Cell: Notes of a Biology Watcher*, Penguin Books, Middlesex, England, 1978

Thompson, Hunter, *Fear and Loathing in Las Vegas*, Granada Publishing, New York, 1972

Thompson, William Irwin, *The Time Falling Bodies Take to Light*, St. Martin's Press, New York, 1981

Vale, V., ed., *Modern Primitives: An Investigation of Contemporary Adornment and Ritual*, Re/Search Publications, San Francisco, 1989

Vaneigem, Raoul, *The Revolution of Everyday Life*, Left Hand, Oxford, UK, 1983

von Sacher-Masoch, Leopold, *Venus in Furs*, Blast Books, New York, 1989

Vonnegut, Kurt, *Breakfast of Champions*, Dell Publishing Co., New York, 1973

Vonnegut, Kurt, *Cat's Cradle*, Dell Publishing Co., New York, 1963

Vonnegut, Kurt, *Mother Night*, Dell Publishing Co., New York, 1966

Vonnegut, Kurt, *Slapstick*, Dell Publishing Co., New York, 1976

Vonnegut, Kurt, *Slaughterhouse 5 or The Children's Crusade*, Dell Publishing Co., New York, 1969

Watts, Alan, *Behold the Spirit*, Vintage Books, New York, 1972

Wells, Carolyn, *A Nonsense Anthology*, C. Scribner's Sons, New York, 1903

Williams, Tennessee, *The Glass Menagerie*, Dell Publishing Co., New York, 1950

Wilson, Peter Lamborn, *Scandal: Essays in Islamic Heresy*, Autonomedia, Brooklyn, NY, 1988

Zack, David, "An Authentik and Historikal Discourse on the Phenomenon of Mail Art," *Art in America*, Jan./Feb. 1973

In Memoriam

In memory of all my family, friends, & acquaintances mentioned herein who aren't with us any more: BC, Gene Budig, Robin Crozier, Norm Forer, Jamie Mercury Future, Julie Green, Marissa Hattemer, Bill Hatke, Clarence & Norma Highberger, Tad Kepley, William Kunstler, Jacob Neuhaus, Reggie Robinson, Meredith Rothrock, Greg Walstrom, Liz Was, Ezekiel Heter Wegscheider, Peter Lamborn Wilson, and David Zack, not to mention Charlotte, Jagger, Jezebel, Lawrence, Lemon, Oedapuss, Samurai, Slim (a/k/a Simon), and Walter.

www.ingramcontent.com/pod-product-compliance
Lightning Source LLC
Chambersburg PA
CBHW031106260626
47172CB00001B/247

* 9 7 8 1 7 3 4 6 3 8 1 0 3 *